THE
STORM
IS UPON US

THE
STORM
IS UPON US

HOW **QANON** BECAME A MOVEMENT, CULT, AND CONSPIRACY THEORY OF EVERYTHING

MIKE ROTHSCHILD

monoray

First published in the USA in 2021 by Melville House

First published in Great Britain in 2021 by Monoray,
an imprint of Octopus Publishing Group Ltd,
Carmelite House,
50 Victoria Embankment,
London EC4Y 0DZ
www.octopusbooks.co.uk

An Hachette UK Company
www.hachette.co.uk

ISBN 978-1-80096-038-1

A CIP catalogue record for this book is available from the
British Library.

Printed and bound in the UK.

10 9 8 7 6 5 4 3 2 1

This FSC® label means that materials used for
the product have been responsibly sourced

This book is dedicated to John C. Garner,
the smartest guy in every room.

Contents

"I still vividly remember the first time he asked me to watch one of the QAnon videos. He mocked it and laughed at the idea that anyone would fall for it. Then, over the next couple of months, something changed."

—Anonymous, via email

The Plan to Save the World

On January 6, 2021, an armed mob of Donald Trump supporters accomplished what no Confederate soldier, Nazi storm trooper, or Al Qaeda jihadist had ever managed to do: they sacked the United States Capitol Building.

That day was the final act of a two-month stretch that saw Trump lose his reelection bid only to repeatedly tell his millions of supporters that he had not only not lost, but he had won in a landslide. According to him, it was a win that the liberal deep state, its media minions, and its globalist backers were desperate to keep from the masses. So Trump devotees gathered in the cold to protest as Congress voted to certify Joe Biden's election as president.

In a thunderous speech before the crowd, the lame-duck president declared, "I know that everyone here will soon be marching over to the Capitol building to peacefully and patriotically make your voices heard." He told his flock to "fight like hell" or else they wouldn't "have a country anymore." He even claimed he'd join them.[1]

He didn't, and they did not march peacefully. Many in the crowd were fueled by false information that Vice President Mike Pence had the authority to throw out the electoral votes of states with voting anomalies. And a significant contingent held Trump to be a god emperor and golden-haired champion. They were ready to fight for their leader and shed blood. And they did.

Thousands of ride-or-die MAGA believers pounced on the Capitol, intending to cross the American Rubicon. And once they crossed, they didn't stop. They breached the building's ramparts in an armed attack that appeared to have at least some assistance from insiders, killed one of its defenders, looted sensitive material, beat Capitol police with flagpoles, and occupied the immediate area for hours. In the process of their insurrectionist attack, they were seconds from forcing their way into the Senate chamber while the body was still in session, chanting "hang Mike Pence."[2]

But while the insurrectionists looked to be nothing more than a sea of rage only differentiated from each other by their level of military costuming, the attackers had a variety of end goals that day. Some believed that Pence was a traitor who deserved death for his failure to throw out the certified votes of the Electoral College. Some were prepared and out for blood, strapped with guns, bombs, and plastic flexible handcuffs for hostages. Others were happy to wander around the halls of Congress, take selfies, and maybe grab a letter off Speaker Nancy Pelosi's desk. There were Trump acolytes who claimed they merely got caught up in the moment, neo-Nazis looking to recruit new members, clout chasers finding content for their monetized livestreams, wannabe special-operator types finally living out their covert-ops dreams, actual ex-military and police types flexing their familiarity with arms and tactical skills, and trolls just out to have a good time overthrowing democracy. Most were arrested within days of the insurrection, aided in no small part by the fact that many left their phones' GPS on, refused to wear face masks, wore identifiable militia patches, and used their full names during their livestreams.

But across this chaotic range of motivations, levels of competence, and genuine commitment to the cause was another commonality. Many were believers in the cultish conspiracy theory called

QAnon. Everywhere you looked during the frenzy of January 6, you could find symbols of QAnon iconography: a man in a Q T-shirt was one of the first rioters to bust through Capitol defenses and brawl with an officer. Images of the "Q Shaman," clad in furs, face paint, and a horned helmet, were reproduced everywhere in the flood of media that covered the events. There were Q flags flying and signs with Q slogans on them. Insurrectionists screamed the text of one of QAnon's cryptic 8chan "drops" as they destroyed the camera equipment of one news outlet, and several of the day's mortalities were avowed QAnon believers with social media feeds that expressed full-throated belief in QAnon and a willingness to die for Trump—right until the moment they did.[3]

These insurrectionists didn't just believe that voting machines had been hacked, China was partially responsible, Trump had really won the election, and efforts to decertify the vote had legal merit that would eventually pay off. They also believed that if legal measures were unsuccessful, the military would step in, Trump would be installed as president for life, liberals and traitors would be hanged, and freedom would reign. And that's not the only fantastical reality these people had immersed themselves in—many of the rioters believed they'd be given secret cures for deadly diseases, the path to economic stability and prosperity, access to powerful new technology, and possibly even the truth about aliens.

All of this is part of QAnon—a cult, a popular movement, a puzzle, a community, a way to fight back against evil, a new religion, a wedge between countless loved ones, a domestic terrorism threat, and more than anything, a conspiracy theory of everything.

In fact, no conspiracy theory more encapsulates the full-throated madness of the Donald Trump era than QAnon. From its beginnings as a few posts on the message board and trolling haven 4chan in October 2017, QAnon and its complex mythology grew to overwhelm conservative thought and media. It is virtually impossible to discern how many people believe in QAnon, but there are likely hundreds of thousands who buy into at least some part of the complex mythology—not just in the United States, but all over the world. Many don't even know that what they believe is associated with QAnon. Some will publicly distance themselves from those "crazy people." Others wear their allegiance on T-shirts, bumper stickers, and flags on their boats. They hold rallies and conferences. They write books and become QAnon social media influencers.

Before the insurrection at the Capitol made QAnon an international news curiosity, the movement had already saturated Republican politics. Former National Security Advisor Michael Flynn has embraced his status as a hero among QAnon followers for supposedly faking an admission of guilt to go under deep cover in the deep state. Roger Stone extolled Q's virtues and urged Trump to declare martial law—a go-to fantasy of QAnon mythology—in the run-up to the 2020 election. Conservative stalwarts, including Donald Trump's sons Donald Jr. and Eric, and many other popular right-wing pundits, have begun pandering to the movement. Between 2018 and 2020, nearly one hundred Republican candidates declared themselves to be Q believers, with several actually winning their elections. And before his Twitter account was shut down, Trump himself retweeted hundreds of Q followers, putting their violent fantasies and bizarre memes into tens of millions of feeds. When asked by a White House press corps member to denounce Q, Trump evasively replied "I don't know much about the movement other than I understand they like me very much, which I appreciate."[4]

As Trump's presidency came to an end, QAnon was covered by every major media outlet in the country, getting air time on virtually every cable news channel including the president's beloved Fox News. Everyone from *The New York Times* to NPR to TV stations around the world have tried to figure out what the hell Q is, what it's about, and what to do with the people who think it's real. And yet, many of these same people were shocked when a mob, drunk on conspiracy theories and misplaced rage, sacked the Capitol building.

They shouldn't have been shocked. QAnon has centered around violent ideation since its very inception, and before the brutal attack on the Capitol, several killings, numerous incidents of domestic terrorism, multiple child-kidnapping schemes, police chases, and even a botched attempt to kill Joe Biden and destroy a coronavirus hospital ship were committed in the name of QAnon. It is a movement premised on the idea that a "storm" of mass arrests and executions will sweep corruption, child molesters, and liberals out of government forever, so it should not have been so jarring a surprise when Q's believers decided to carry out that long-promised purge themselves.

Still, the question remains as to how something that started on the anarchic message board 4chan could go on to power right-wing thought to the point where QAnon believers were erecting a gallows on the lawn of the Capitol.[5] To answer it, we need to look closely not just at what QAnon is, but where it comes from and how it lodges itself so stubbornly into the mind of its adherents.

Featuring a mythology that's virtually impenetrable to outsiders, the QAnon conspiracy theory revolves around an anonymous group of military intelligence insiders who collectively refer to themselves as Q. These patriots are supposedly under orders from Trump to leak clues and prompts that reveal secret knowledge of an upcoming and world-changing event called "the storm." While anyone can read these "drops" online, only the special and highly attuned believers in Q can understand them. These believers see themselves at the center of a secret war between good and evil—a war that will end with the slaughter of the enemies of freedom.

And it's getting more popular by the day. QAnon has sucked in an amorphous, but certainly massive, number of people through its unchecked growth on social media—probably including someone you know.

If a great massacre for peace carried out by patriots on a mandate that supersedes the Constitution sounds troubling to you, it should. The problem is that for all the people who dismiss Q as a fascist fantasy, there are others who are drawn to it specifically because it is one.

But there is also a "conspiracy theory of everything" aspect to QAnon, which makes it a big tent welcoming to all those who question authority, distrust the media, and do their own research. They fight not primarily with guns or bombs but by making memes and decoding deep-state "comms." They refuse vaccines and COVID-19 masks, and do their part by waking up "normie" friends to "what's really going on." They fight in Twitter mentions and text messages and in tiny interactions with nonbelievers.

As the war consumes its "digital soldiers," people outside of the conspiracy are left behind.[6] Q believers embrace their online community, and push away friends and loved ones as their "secret knowledge" curdles into violence and madness. It's especially bad for older social media users who lack the digital literacy to realize they're being lied to, but enjoy the community of like-minded patriots they've found. Studies have found that baby boomers are far more likely to share fake-news stories on Facebook, and it's this same cohort with which QAnon has found pay dirt and a devoted audience.[7]

Clearly, the danger posed by QAnon is real. But why do people believe it? Are QAnon followers true believers who really think they have been tipped off by military intelligence about a secret war? Are they dupes of Russian intelligence? Cynical trolls who enjoy riling people up? Marks in a giant grift that's drained them dry? Should we mock them or pity them? Scorn them or help them? And is there any way to get believers to leave behind their fantasies and rejoin the rest of us?

This book is my attempt to answer these questions. Because the people who keep asking me how to save their loved ones deserve an answer.

I've been writing about QAnon since January 2018—long before the costume-clad Q Shaman even existed, let alone rose to prominence as an iconic image of the Capitol siege. The first time it caught my eye was when there was a hubbub in conspiracy theory circles about pictures of John McCain and Hillary Clinton wearing orthopedic walking boots on both feet, along with hashtags like #WWG-1WGA and #FollowTheWhiteRabbit.

"Why was this a big deal?" I asked over Twitter. Q followers immediately filled me in: McCain and Hillary were wearing orthopedic boots not because of ankle injuries, but because they had already been arrested and released. The walking boots covered up the ankle monitors they wore to prevent them from fleeing the country.

My interest was piqued, and I began writing regularly about it. As I wrote more about QAnon, I started hearing more and more from family members of QAnon believers—and they had no idea what the hell had overtaken their loved ones. Over email, Twitter DMs, and blog comments, distraught loved ones have asked me, over and over, what they should do about QAnon. They'd lost parents and relationships to it, and had no idea what to do or how to help. Or if they even could.

"I've followed you for several years after my sister and mother became followers of QAnon," Nicole (a pseudonym) wrote to me. "This past week my husband's employer was targeted by [QAnon followers] and employees are receiving death threats. I may never get my mother and sister back as I knew them, but you remind me I'm not alone in missing them and that my own kids are sane and okay."

Another woman, Olive (a pseudonym) emailed me about her husband, who was becoming increasingly withdrawn and depressed as he sank deeper into the QAnon ecosystem—to the point where they'd briefly broken up over it. "My husband has been a zealous QAnon believer since December 2017," she wrote to me. "I think there is the tiniest part of him that may slightly doubt, as he came to the realization that he may regret losing me. He is unable to discuss any issue without bringing up QAnon or the 'evil' Democrats and leftists."

And a man named Curtis (a pseudonym) got this text from his conspiracy-obsessed mother, from whom he'd been disconnected for years after she became convinced that Barack Obama and his cronies were about to go to prison: "Hold on to your seats, HRC is about to go down. It will be announced very soon, the first of many to come. All is good. You are not obligated to believe me. I still love you. It's already starting . . ."

Curtis's mom had gone fully down the rabbit hole of QAnon, and as he told me, he wasn't going down with her. "I will no longer visit her for any occasion," he said to me. "I don't even think that I will be talking to her again."

Even with Q's explosion into the mainstream, many gaps still remain. We're still trying to put all the pieces together of how it jumped so quickly from typical conspiracy circles to Bernie Sanders-voting yoga moms, why so many people believe a story that proves itself false over and over, how to help QAnon believers walk away from the movement, and what exactly President Trump and his staff know about it.

What is it about Q that repels most people but strongly attracts a few? And what hole does it fills in the lives of those attracted to it? Because it does fill a hole—one that family, hobbies, work, church, or even spouses and children struggle to patch.

This is the story of Q—what it is, what it means, and where it goes. And be warned—none of it is pretty.

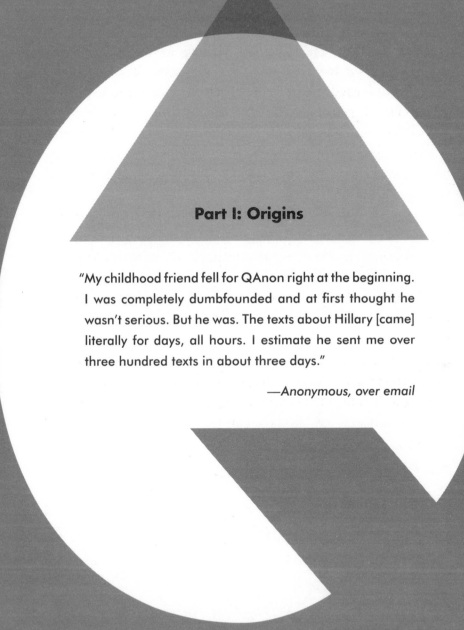

Part I: Origins

"My childhood friend fell for QAnon right at the beginning. I was completely dumbfounded and at first thought he wasn't serious. But he was. The texts about Hillary [came] literally for days, all hours. I estimate he sent me over three hundred texts in about three days."

—Anonymous, over email

CHAPTER 1

Learn to Read the Map: The Basics of QAnon

WHAT IS QANON?

Before we can address what QAnon means in today's political and social landscape, we have to start with the basics of what Q is.

At its very basic definition, "Q" is an unknown figure claiming to be a military intelligence officer who posts purposefully vague and cryptic messages on imageboards about an upcoming great purge of the deep state—with anonymous users called "anons" encouraged to research and interpret those messages, taking them in whatever direction they choose.

But of course, it's much more than that.

What has grown to be called "QAnon" is a complex web of mythology, conspiracy theories, personal interpretations, and assumptions featuring a vast range of characters, events, symbols, shibboleths, and jargon. It can be understood as a conspiracy theory, for sure, but it also touches on aspects of cultic movements, new religions, Internet scams, and political doctrine. It's impossible to fully explicate every aspect of QAnon because it is so diffuse and has so many different plot strands and meanings. But the most important thing to know is that all of it started with an anonymous poster on 4chan.

The poster, who called themselves Q Clearance Patriot, a name that references an actual US government clearance provided by the Department of Energy, claimed to be the collective avatar of a small military intelligence team.[1] Their task was to disseminate information about a secret war taking place right beneath our noses, unbeknownst to the vast slumbering masses. They were sending out these messages because this war between good and evil was soon to end, and with it would come the end of evil, the end of the child-trafficking rings, the end of the "deep state," and the beginning of true freedom.

If that sounds like standard end-times preaching, it more or less is. But there's a distinctly modern twist: Q talks directly to the people, and the people talk back to Q. It's not monologuing, it's dialogue. Q drops encourage collaboration, and Q rewards anons who go above and beyond in their theorizing and interpretation.

So anyone can read the original Q drops from the very beginning and they are encouraged to construct their own mythology. If you want magic to be real, millions of dollars to be coming your way, or even time travel to be possible, then you can find all the confirmation you need in Q's posts – called "drops" by the Q poster.

Our only shot at clarity in attempting to make sense of a phenomenon that is not itself coherent is to start at the beginning and keep the major questions in mind. We have to define how Q works, and why; who the players are; how Q followers communicate with each other; and how they gather and discern information. We have to know what we're talking about before we can understand it. As Q says, we have to "learn our comms."

TWO TRUTHS AND A BUNCH OF LIES

It should already be clear that getting to the bottom of what QAnon is depends almost entirely on who you ask.

If you were to ask a believer in QAnon what it is, they would tell you that they are witnessing a military intelligence information-sharing operation in real time over the Internet. Central to this myth is the belief that Q is a team of "less than ten people" and that "three are military." That is, Q is a hybrid military-civilian task force giving cryptic pieces of intelligence to the general public via online message boards. The intelligence is free for anyone to read, but only a select few people—the "anons"—are able to understand what the coded bits of text actually mean.

Before you chime in to ask how anyone could believe that military intelligence would share their secret operations on 4chan (and later, the even more disreputable 8chan), keep in mind that there is some precedent for the belief that coded messages were being transmitted via modern communication channels. For decades during the Cold War, shortwave radio enthusiasts could tune their dial to frequencies known as "numbers stations," semisecret channels that broadcast long strings of number blocks bracketed by cryptic phrases or bits of music. Only message recipients with a special primer could decode the secrets locked within those numbers. To anyone else, they were nonsense. What's a Q drop, then, if not a twenty-first-century number station?

So what military intelligence, exactly, is being revealed? Drops first centered on a set of indictments that would lay out all the crimes committed by a cabal of evildoers at the heart of our government and media. The drops promised that a quick series of secret military tribunals would follow, and finally result in the imprisonment or execution of everyone found guilty of treason or sex trafficking.

If you don't understand anything else about Q, you should at least understand this one dimension. It's not just a conspiracy theory or game to these people. It's a ringside ticket to the final match between good and evil—and when the hammer finally falls, the supporters of evil will need to be put down with brutal swiftness. This mix of biblical retribution and participatory justice has drawn in fans around the world.[2]

And its vague, predictive premise makes it more resilient and flexible than you might expect. Republican failure in the 2018 midterms didn't kill it; the coronavirus pandemic didn't kill it; bans by Facebook, Twitter, and YouTube didn't kill it; even Donald Trump losing the 2020 election didn't kill it—each loss is merely folded into "the plan." This makes sense in light of the fact that Q has always held itself to be telling the truth, despite how things might appear.

On the other side, if you were to ask journalists and debunkers who have covered QAnon with a skeptical eye since it emerged in 2017 what it is, they would tell you Q is a prosperity scam that managed to get a bunch of baby boomers on the hook with a mythology that blames everything wrong with society on Barack Obama and George Soros. To them, it all fits in to a tradition of past scams that went on for years and separated millions of dollars from their marks. Those scams, like Q, also promised a great world-changing event that's always just about to happen.[3]

But lumping QAnon in with these previous scams implies some level of intentionality and a concrete goal on the part of the people promoting the conspiracy. If you were to ask even more skeptical observers what QAnon is, they would tell you it is the product of trolls toying with gullible marks and milking it for as much as they possibly could.

Wherever you fall on the spectrum between true believer, long-con debunker, and witness to an out-of-control prank, one thing is certain: its followers are very real and their numbers just keep growing.

DO WE REALLY HAVE TO CALL THEM "DROPS?"

In his 1951 study of mass movements, *The True Believer*, the scholar Eric Hoffer writes that if the doctrine of such a movement "is not unintelligible, it has to be vague; and if neither unintelligible nor vague, it has to be unverifiable."[4]

If QAnon is a mass movement—and it is—then the Q drops are its doctrine. And the drops meet all three of Hoffer's criteria: they are unintelligible, they are vague, and they are unverifiable. Often all at once.

Q drops are bits of text that ask rhetorical questions, give the reader a riddle to ponder, toss out bits of information to decode, or function as public affirmations to those who are in the club.

A Q drop can be hundreds of words, or as short as a link to a tweet. It can be a meme, or a picture, or a screen capture. Sometimes Q repeats drops. Sometimes they make typos and later correct them, using the excuse of being "on the move" to explain the errors. Some are mishmashes of military-sounding jargon, others are number puzzles. Q has posted links to ambient music, cribbed photos from old news stories, made lists of "Rothschild central banks," and bombarded fans with pictures of the American flag. Q has been fooled by obvious hoaxes and fake stories, and, at least a few times, has had their inner workings penetrated by hackers.

You might ask, if they're anonymous, can't anyone post as Q at any time? The answer is found in the inner workings of Q's eventual message boards of choice, 4chan 8chan, and later 8kun. On these boards users do not register accounts using email addresses. Instead, users are identifiable and differentiated by "tripcodes," which are scrambled versions of the password they use to log in. So each user only has a username and a password, and that password is visible on their public posts in a scrambled or "hashed" form. Thus, theoretically, whoever posts as Q has a consistent tripcode that identifies them as the one and only Q.

While tripcodes have the veneer of cryptographic certainty and they are somewhat difficult to unscramble, they are fundamentally insecure and easy to hack. And there have indeed been several moments of mass confusion when Q's tripcode was hacked. In each case, Q would suddenly have a new tripcode, with Q announcing that their account had been "compromised" by their enemies.

The vast majority of drops are full of conspiracies, riddles, rhetorical questions, and uncut delusion. Here's a typical Q drop, Drop #2559:

RUSSIA = THE REAL CONSPIRACY.
Define 'PROJECTION'.
What happens when they lose control and the TRUTH is
exposed?
What happens when PEOPLE no longer believe or listen to
the FAKE NEWS CONTROLLED MEDIA, CONTROLLED
HOLLYWOOD, CONTROLLED BLUE CHECKMARK
TWIT SHILLS, ETC ETC???
THE GREAT AWAKENING.
SHEEP NO MORE.
WE, THE PEOPLE.
FOR GOD & COUNTRY - WE FIGHT!
Q[5]

And those little bits of text at the end? Yes, Q has catchphrases, like Steve Urkel or Iron Man. Q fans will repeat them to each other—things like "Where we go one, we go all" (supposedly etched on the bell of JFK's yacht) or "They never thought she would lose," referring to Hillary Clinton in 2016—to tip the virtual hat to other believers.

Sometimes Q posts frantically: fifteen or twenty drops in a day. Other times, they vanish for weeks at a time – or even longer. Some drops provide nothing whatsoever of use, others are gold mines of cryptic information and "secrets." Some drops merely serve as "proof" that Q is who they claim to be. Over the 4,953 drops made during the Trump years, Q laid out a frustrating, elliptical, fascinating story that leaves even the most devoted followers scratching their heads at times and wondering just when the hell the deep state is going to get mulched.

Q's response? Usually something along the lines of "[SOON]" or "NEXT WEEK." Which, of course, never arrives.

THE NEXT LAYER

Q followers read the drops like holy texts—and a structure remin-
iscent of early Christianity has formed around Q's gospel. A set of
gurus or "decoders" have become microcelebrities in the Q world.
They operate by reposting drops on Twitter or reading and inter-
preting them on YouTube videos or on blogs. They tease out the
meaning, make the connections the dreaded "they" don't want you
to know about, provide context with the day's news, and loop new
drops back to old ones.

The gurus are almost as important to Q as Q himself. It's not
uncommon for certain major names in the Q universe, people with
usernames like Praying Medic and InTheMatrixxx, to rack up hundreds of thousands of social media followers on their videos and
Twitter threads. And those gurus are rewarded with a kind of viral
fame. They speak at rallies, pose for pictures, and usually have thriving Patreon pages and online merch stores. Yes, Q is a "Plan to Save
the World," to use the title of a multimillion-view video by Q guru
Joe M.[6] But it can also be a lucrative grift if you do it right.

I GOT SOUL BUT I'M NOT A DIGITAL SOLDIER

To fight in Q's war requires no military or intelligence training.
There's no endurance test, no kitchen duty, and no uniforms to wear.
All you have to do is have Internet access, read the Q drops, and participate. That participatory element is what makes Q different from
every other run-of-the-mill conspiracy theory out there. Other conspiracy theories make you a passive observer—you can only sit there
and wait for the Catholics or Jews or Masons or Illuminati or New
World Order or Muslim Brotherhood or Tyrannical Government
or Jews to kick down your front door. Maybe you grab your gun,
maybe you go willingly. But overall, there's not a lot you can do.

But if you're a "digital soldier" (a Q catchphrase copped from a

Michael Flynn speech praising Trump's ad hoc troll army shortly after the 2016 election), you can fight back.[7] Some Q believers even film themselves taking the US military oath of enlistment, pretending that being a digital soldier is like being an actual soldier. That concept would become a huge part of Q's identity as former military and intelligence figures flocked to QAnon, either because they believed it was real, or in some cases because they saw a big money-making opportunity in exploiting those who did. Flynn even filmed himself taking the "digital soldier oath" over Fourth of July weekend 2020, part of what would become a total enmeshment between Flynn's inner circle and QAnon.[8]

But the real "digital soldiers" didn't care about base things like money. They wanted to get into the fight and take down the bad guys. And Q makes it remarkably easy to do nothing while believing you're doing a lot. You can make a meme of Trump with angel wings or Trump riding a tank or Trump with Rocky Balboa muscles. Or you can make memes of Attorney General William Barr's head on a Teutonic Knight, or ones that "prove" Barack Obama is a secretly gay Muslim usurper, or graphics of alt-right mascot Pepe the Frog crying happy tears over the latest "boom" provided by Q. You can make cool Q logos or merchandise. You can make YouTube videos or Twitter threads decoding Q drops, and share other videos and threads—or at least you could until those platforms banned Q content.

You can wear your Q swag when you go outside, donate to the Patreon pages or GoFundMe accounts of Q acolytes to get exclusive material, tell other people about Q to the point where they no longer want to talk to you, or put a Q bumper sticker on your car. You can even just tweet "Q sent me!" at some random person whose tweet is shared by Q. Believing in Q isn't hard, you just have to do it actively. And most of these things can be done by anyone with enough time on their hands. Having a little cash to spend on merch or a book helps.

Q lets people feel like they're part of something bigger than their small lives. It gives believers a higher and noble purpose.

It offers explanations for terrible things. After all, it's easier to believe that a dark cabal is orchestrating negative events than it is to believe that powerful people, including our leaders, are simply greedy or incompetent.

In a digital world where we are increasingly physically isolated and alone, particularly in the time of COVID-19, this combination of a participatory game played alongside a digital community against an easy scapegoat is hugely compelling. It's one of the reasons why baby boomers have fallen in with Q to such a surprising degree—many are empty nesters, on their own, or retired. One day they looked around, realized they didn't get everything they were promised out of life, and wanted someone to blame.

And then they found Q. And Q gave them enemies to hate, and a way to get back at them. And legions of new friends who want to get back at them, too.

THE DEEPEST STATE

If Q, the decoders, and the flock are fighting on the side of good, then who are they fighting? We know the good guys—who are the baddies?

To put it simply—Democrats, Hollywood elite, business tycoons, wealthy liberals, the medical establishment, celebrities, and the mass media are the bad guys. They're controlled by Barack Obama, who is secretly a Muslim sleeper agent; Hillary Clinton, a blood-drinking ghoul who murders everyone in her way; and Washington power broker, John Podesta, and they're funded by George Soros and the Rothschild banking family (no relation to the author).

They employ scores of traitors and pawns, all of whom infest the government, intelligence community, and Justice Department. This is the so-called "deep state"—anti-Trump career intelligence personnel, the heads of worldwide banks, Hollywood stars and sports heroes, "activist judges," almost anyone who stands against

Trump and freedom. They are the enemies of democracy who own the major media companies and distribute daily talking points to be doled out on CNN and MSNBC. They "expend ammo" on false-flag terrorist attacks, or on complex hoaxes like COVID-19. They infuse Hollywood movies, music, and TV with Satanic symbols meant to weaken our resolve and stop us from asking questions. They force vaccines, cheap sugary food, and antibiotics on us to ensure we never break the chains of our mental and physical slavery. They've attempted to assassinate Donald Trump dozens of times, tried to scuttle his achievements as president, and done everything they could to undermine the public's faith in Trump's righteous justice. And most of us have no idea they exist, nor do we care about finding out. That's the greatest trick the enemies of QAnon ever pulled.

But Q knows who they are. And Q will stop them—with the help of God, a few chosen leaders, and countless patriots around the world fighting in the trenches of a digital war that most of us have no idea is taking place.

Q WHO?

It's hard to tell how big QAnon actually is, but it's nowhere near as big as the conspiracy's devoted fans think. Believers will tell you the number runs into the hundreds of millions, though there's no evidence for this lofty number, and no real way to measure it. Skeptics surmise that the number is probably closer to the amount of people who publicly believe in Scientology—less than one hundred thousand. But again, this is very hard to measure.

It also doesn't really matter. Q's base of acolytes is small, but intensely devoted—and there are many more people who believe in the mythology of Q without identifying as "QAnon believers." Many profess to spending their every waking hour entirely ensconced in "research"—rereading Q drops, watching Q videos, listening to Q podcasts and livestreams, and "digging" to find the connections at which Q only hints. And they confess that they have trouble sleeping when they're not researching. They profess their lack of enjoyment at things they used to love. And they discard anything that doesn't confirm the conspiracy theory. This is the devotion you find only at the most observant levels of religion, or the most obsessive reaches of fandom.

Isn't this the behavior of a cult? If it is, who exactly is the leader?

The identity of the person or people making the Q posts has probably changed hands several times, to and from unknown people. There are theories, some better than others, and a few likely suspects. But as of now, not a single person has ever admitted to writing a Q drop and provided the evidence to support their claim. And the reality is that anons think Q is real because they want to believe that Q is exposing hard, vital truths. If the name of the person doing the posts were revealed, it wouldn't sap the devotion of Q's followers. Even if they are proven without a doubt to have no connection to Trump or military intelligence, no believer's mind would be changed. They would either create a special pleading answer for it (i.e., claim whoever this person is serves merely as a vehicle for the drops) or just call the reveal fake news. All of this is to say: disconfirmation only makes believers believe more and harder. And Q being unmasked as a fake would be the ultimate disconfirmation—a vessel for skeptics to mock believers, and for believers to loudly and proudly declare that it doesn't matter to them.

DOWN THE RABBIT HOLE WE GO

Q's identity and the original drops are a big part of the mythology, but each is just that—a part. To really understand QAnon, one must delve into a bizarre, hopelessly complex world of conspiracy theories, decades-old Internet chuff, cryptography, cultic thought, centuries-old anti-Semitic tropes, wellness and medical pseudoscience, and moral panic over child trafficking and white slavery. The elements of QAnon run so deep and are already so deeply ingrained in western thought that you can find some aspects as far back as the blood libel trope of the twelfth century, or even before that, to a sixth-century Byzantine tome called *The Secret History* that makes some suspiciously Q-like claims about the sexual escapades of the Empress Theodora.[9]

In fact, some aspects of the Q movement have little or nothing to do with the Q poster. Huge parts of the widely accepted Q mythology, such as John F. Kennedy Jr. still being alive (yes, many of them think that) or prominent politicians being secretly executed and replaced by clones (yes, many of them also think that), have never been mentioned by Q. Very little of Q's explosion into the mainstream as the COVID-19 pandemic gripped the world was based around Q drops. Many of the people taking their first steps into this world of conspiracy theories amid the pandemic hadn't even heard of Q, even as they repeated its slogans and regurgitated its iconography. That is to say, if you asked a major contingent of QAnon about QAnon, they'd say they weren't crazy like those people. They just would rather die than wear a face covering to buy groceries.

Ultimately, Q tells a story—and it's one that its followers want to believe. Understanding the nuances of that story, and what about it is so appealing to believers, is the first key to unlocking the puzzle that is Q.

And all of it started with a fantastical, bizarre technothriller laid out in public—stating not only that Hillary Clinton was going to be arrested (after all, Donald Trump had been chanting that for years already), but that she *already* had been arrested, pinched on a desperate flight to escape the clutches of Trump's Justice Department. And the revelation of her arrest, and the crimes she committed to justify it, would shatter American life as we knew it.

The storm was gathering.

CHAPTER 2

The Calm Before the Storm: How QAnon Started

"YOU'LL FIND OUT"

Like so many recent lurches into the bizarre and inscrutable, the QAnon conspiracy theory began with a cryptic comment made by America's first conspiracy theorist president: Donald Trump. And like so many of Trump's other conspiracy adventures, it was a comment that was understood by nobody around him.

On the night of Thursday, October 5, 2017, Trump called the White House press corps, who had been dismissed for the day, back to the State Dining Room. The president was holding court with top-ranking military officers and their families, enjoying the pageantry and adoration of the office. Military salutes, pomp and circumstance, a motorcade at your beck and call, and a briefcase full of nuclear codes that could destroy the world.

In that magnificent room, with cameras clicking away, Trump stood in the middle of a line of uniformed and evening-gowned military staffers and spouses, looking around, enjoying what he saw.[1] And in that muddled, speaking-to-nobody-in-particular tone into which Trump so often dropped when speaking off the cuff, he casually launched a conspiracy theory that would shatter America's brain.

"You guys know what this represents?" Trump asked the room full of press. They did not.

"Tell us, sir," said one reporter, as cameras clicked and generals duly smiled.

"Maybe it's the calm before the storm," the president quietly intoned, as if he were the holder of a great secret that he could no longer contain.

When one of the reporters reasonably asked what "storm" he was referring to, Trump continued his cryptic riddle: "Could be. The calm before the storm." Then there was silence as Trump and the best and brightest of the military continued to grin and cameras continued to snap. Finally, he spoke again. "We have the world's great military people in this room, I will tell you that," he continued, pumping his fist and moving his hand around in a circular motion. "And uh, we're gonna have a great evening," he concluded.

Then he thanked everyone for coming and began ushering out the reporters he had just ushered in.

But the media wasn't done, and the questions kept coming. "What storm, Mr. President?"

"You'll find out," Trump said, to nervous titters among staffers as White House aides desperately tried to wrap things up before the president said anything else so potentially war-starting. The whole exchange lasted less than forty seconds, and was just one comment in a presidency full of strange utterances, empty boasts, misspelled threats, and unhinged ramblings about things that may or may not exist.

Naturally, it was also the only thing the media wanted to discuss the next day. After all, when you've got a room full of high-ranking military officers surrounding the head of the National Command Authority as he makes ominous proclamations, questions need to be asked. Was Trump hinting at a new offensive against ISIS? A pre-emptive strike on North Korea or Iran? Something even worse that wasn't on anyone's radar?

Follow-up questions the next day didn't help matters, as Trump merely smirked, winked, and repeated, "You'll find out," when asked about "the storm" as he took questions before a cabinet meeting.[2] The rest of the Trump administration scrambled to make it clear that whatever Trump was talking about, they had nothing to do with it. Vice President Mike Pence told reporters to take it up with his boss.[3] And then–press secretary Sarah Huckabee Sanders offered up this word salad: "As we've said many times before, I know the president has, as I have from this podium on quite a few occasions, we're never going to say in advance what the president's going to do."[4]

Trump's "enemies of the people"—as he was fond of calling them—in the mainstream media were clueless as well. *Vox* called the remark "odd and ominous," while NBC News labeled it simply "cryptic"; *The Washington Post* lamented that the "stridently stupid" remark had "put the world on edge," and *The New York Times* rhetorically asked "What Did President Trump Mean?" by the remark.[5] It was clear that nobody knew.

But while the mainstream media was trying to figure out exactly what Trump meant, if indeed he meant anything at all, a few anonymous Trump admirers decided that they knew exactly what it meant. And they liked it.

Not only was it indeed related to a military operation, it was the first public stirrings of a secret and enormous one, involving people at the very top of the food chain being brought to justice in the bloodiest way possible. Once revealed in full to the American public (most of whom were far too asleep to recognize it), it would change the face of American life for good. And so, in a few posts on 4chan, a movement that would soon be called QAnon was born.

"EXTRADITION ALREADY IN MOTION"

The anonymous avatar that would lead to madness and murder started as another in a long line of 4chan posters who claimed to be a whistleblower letting their readers in on closely held secrets. Rather confusingly, these accounts are also known as "anons"—not to be confused with the term for people who read and interpret Q's drops.

4chan is an imageboard that was launched in 2003 by a fifteen-year-old New Yorker as an English-language counterpart to the hugely popular Japanese imageboard 2chan. It offers total anonymity, virtually no moderation, and lightning-speed information flow in a way that is so chaotic that it makes the board almost illegible to outsiders. In turn, these qualities were embraced by some of the worst people on the Internet. Its owner stepped away and sold the board in 2015 due to the constant legal trouble 4chan users were getting into, and by the time QAnon emerged, 4chan had become a haven for right-wing trolling and Trump worship.[6] Most "normies" know of 4chan as the home of popular memes and cutting-edge Internet trends, but extremism researchers and journalists know it to be a preeminent safe space for neo-Nazi babble, shock porn, unrelenting harassment of women in the media, violent threats, and conspiracy theories.

If you wanted to pretend to be a government operative neck-deep in a secret operation to take down the bad guys, 4chan's anarchic / pol/ forum would be the perfect place to do it. Users knew exactly what the board was about, and loved to play along. There was FBI Anon, who claimed to have "intimate knowledge of the inner workings of the Clinton case." Another anon, HighwayPatrolman, made over a thousand posts alleging that high-level child-trafficking rings drained the blood of infants for a supposedly super-powerful drug called adrenochrome. Another anon, called Anon5 or Frank, created a crude map of "deep-state trafficking networks"—a concept that would resurface again and again in Q.[7] High Level Insider Anon used 4chan to host long question-and-answer sessions, dispensing nuggets of cryptic wisdom like "JFK challenged the secret societies and usury so he was killed for it."[8] And CIA Anon, CIA Intern, and WH Insider Anon could also all be found in the dankest corners of the Internet, supposedly airing the dirty secrets of the elite under the cover of anonymity.

The majority of these anon accounts used the same style of posting that QAnon would come to embrace. One, a 4chan anon who went by Victory of the Light, had spent the summer of 2017 describing "the Event"—a great upheaval where the deep state would be brought down by mass arrests, followed by the "liberation of Planet Earth from dark forces."[9]

But most "anonymous insider" accounts quickly got tired of whatever it was they were trying to do and gave up on the gag. Or maybe the deep state got them. Whatever the case, High Level Insider Anon posted only from June 2016 to March 2017, while HighwayPatrolman spent eight months in character and vanished, and FBI Anon dropped all of their content in one furious session on July 2, 2016, never to be heard from again.

All of this is to say, it should come as no surprise that the first official post by the insider who would come to be known as QAnon was a reply to another anonymous claim on 4chan's /pol/ board. The comment was made on October 28, 2017, a few weeks after Trump's comments in the State Dining Room, on a /pol/ thread with the subject line "Mueller investigation," and read:

Hillary Clinton will be arrested between 7:45 AM–8:30 AM EST on Monday—the morning on Oct 30, 2017.

That "proto-Q" comment is sometimes referred to as Drop #0 by Q watchers and aggregators. Its poster, going only by the tripcode "gb953qGI," had also made references on the same thread to a "plan" and underacted [sic] files. Naturally, nobody in the media would believe their shocking revelation. At first glance, it was no different than the claims made by FBI Anon or Victory of the Light. No proof was offered or asked for. It was just another bit of trolling on a board full of trolling.

Except someone ran with this one, quoting the claim of Hillary's impending arrest and playing telephone with it. Someone took proto-Q's leak, and added depth and detail to it—starting a world-wide phenomenon in the process. What's now known as Drop #1, posted as a reply to that earlier comment, reads in its entirety:

> HRC extradition already in motion effective yesterday with several countries in case of cross border run. Passport approved to be flagged effective 10/30 @ 12:01 am. Expect massive riots organized in defiance and others fleeing the US to occur. US M's will conduct the operation while NG activated. Proof check: Locate a NG member and ask if activated for duty 10/30 across most major cities.

As the opening paragraph of a techno-thriller, this was as good as anything Robert Ludlum could come up with. In just a few sentences, you had Hillary Clinton making a run for her life, getting flagged at the border of an unknown country, followed by her secret arrest, the instant and spontaneous crumbling of the social fabric, and the National Guard ("NG") and Marines ("M's") being activated in response. If bystanders wanted to see the theory proven, they just had to locate one of the uniformed military members making their way into their city to restore order. And all of it was going to happen within days.

The second drop, which went up half an hour later in the same thread, took the story even further and explicitly referenced Trump's "calm before the storm" remarks, rhetorically asking:

> Why does Potus [sic] surround himself w/ generals?
> What is military intelligence?
> Why go around the 3 letter agencies?

And in the first example of the rampant anti-Semitism and paranoia that would undergird QAnon, the second drop twice mentions the wealthy Hungarian Jewish financier, George Soros. It cryptically asks: "Why did Soros donate all his money recently?"—an event that did not actually take place.

Drops continued at a frantic pace after those first few. There were eleven the next day, nine two days after that (Q took a day off from "the storm" in between), and posts each of the next fifteen days.

Early posts told of a "mind blowing" [sic] truth that "cannot fully be exposed," involving Nancy Pelosi, George Soros, Obama holdovers in the intelligence community, the NSA, Jeff Sessions, the antifa movement, and the deep state. Q told us that Trump was secretly meeting with generals and the Department of Justice in hidden rooms with no phones (so that there would be no leaks). Q's posts (or "comms") were the only thing letting patriots in on the hell about to be unleashed.

According to Q, nothing was what it seemed. Early posts claimed Robert Mueller's investigation into potential coordination between the Trump campaign and Russia was actually a front for Mueller to investigate the real bad guys, John McCain's cancer surgery was fake, the military had enlisted Trump to run for president because he was too rich to be corrupted by the Washington swamp, Barack Obama was travelling to foreign locations ahead of Trump to undermine him, and Trump was in total control of everything—even if the optics of a leaking, bumbling administration said differently.

It was a lot—a fully formed, massively detailed plan to bring down the biggest foes of the MAGA movement. All it would lack was any kind of fruition.

SEEING THE FULL PICTURE

Over the first 120-plus posts, a timeline of immediate future events was handed down for patriots to decode and prepare for. Hillary would be arrested on October 30, Podesta on November 3, and Hillary's chief aide, Huma Abedin, three days after that. You might ask why they wouldn't all be arrested at the same time. It's a good question, but don't expect an answer. Whatever the case, the National Guard was being prepared, with citizens alerted to potential "uprising[s] or other domestic violence," (likely a reference to right wing conspiracy theories about an "antifa uprising" supposedly taking place on November 4) and aircraft carriers were being moved into position to prevent another country from taking advantage of the upheaval. POTUS and his top aides had their protection redoubled, and formerly untouchable targets were being acquired for swift removal. When it was time to bring the hammer down, Trump himself would post on Twitter that "the storm is upon us." Then the arrests would begin.

In those first few days, the poster still had no name, and was referred to as Info Dump Anon or LARPer Guy.[10] With Q's thirty-fourth and thirty-fifth drops, though, the central character formally introduced themselves as Q Clearance Patriot. The actual term "QAnon" was introduced, ironically, by a Canadian 4chan poster the next day.[11] As the mythology solidified, Q declared in Drop #34 that "over the course of the next several days you will undoubtedly realize that we are taking back our great country (the land of the free) from the evil tyrants that wish to do us harm and destroy the last remaining refuge of shining light." The taking back of the country would involve temporary martial law, the leaking of false information to the media, and activation of the Emergency Alert System, which was misstated by Q as "Emergency Broadcast System (EMS)," despite the Emergency Broadcast System having been shut down in 1997. Q also promised the lifting of "certain laws" designed to prevent the military from operating as civilian law enforcement, along with troops in the streets, extrajudicial arrests and trials, dissenters hauled away, and a president who crushed all opposition to his plans. And all of it would unfold in a few short days.

Believers in the nascent conspiracy benefited from being the first to know about the imminent upheaval. They would have the tools they needed to understand what was about to happen and to help participate in any necessary quelling that would take place. And that special status was emphasized in Drop #60, which noted that the only people who had the "full picture" of what was happening comprised "(less than 10 people) [and] only three are non-military." Believers joined this hyperselect and elevated group, thinking they were seeing the first rays of a new rising sun.

To anyone who might have been looking at it from the outside, what Q was proposing looked something you might see in the chaotic politics of a dystopian thriller. It wasn't the American way, for sure. Due process is guaranteed by the Constitution, after all. But it looked a lot like truth and justice to conservatives watching Donald Trump continuously beset by a deep state of leakers and wreckers. Q painted an incredibly compelling story, where the Obama cronies were running like hell, the noose was tightening, and Drop #75 claimed Trump was preparing to return from his latest trip to a world made "a different place." And unlike so many other conspiracy theories of the past, the people watching it also had a part to play in it—sharing the news with fellow patriots and preparing them for what was to come.

It wasn't quite a game. It wasn't quite a puzzle. And it wasn't quite a conspiracy theory. It was, as Drop #38 claimed, "the calm before the storm." Just like Trump said.

And "the storm" was a hit.

"IS IT HAPPENING???"

As Q spun out their first few dozen posts, a community already primed to accept conspiracy theories that they already agreed with decided they agreed with this one too. There had already been plenty of talk on /pol/, the 4chan board where Q first posted, about corrupt deep staters going to Guantanamo, who "really" killed DNC staffer

Seth Rich,* and who amongst the wealthy and powerful was a pedo-phile. It was all pretty standard conspiracy theory stuff. So this was a crowd ready for handcuffs to be slapped on Hillary Clinton.

And she was the key. The far right had already been conditioned by three decades of conspiracy theories about Hillary Clinton to see her as a cold-hearted killer, a corrupt vacuum cleaner sucking up foreign cash, and the mastermind of a political operation that was essentially above the law. Other anons knew what 4chan wanted—Hillary dragged away to the gallows—but Q laid out how it was going to happen.

"Lock. Her. Up." replied one anon to the first drop, with another adding "She's is [sic] going to Gitamo [sic]. PERIOD." Other Q posts drew similar reactions—anons asking how they could get access to the evidence to corroborate the plot and telling the poster to screencap their work for safety. There was also the usual 4chan deluge of anti-Semitism and racism. Even just in those first days, it was clear that the poster found an audience that desperately wanted to believe them.

Or as one anon wrote on /pol/ after an early post, Q's drops con-stituted "sustenance for cranial function":

thank you for the heads up
you're a great American and we got your back.[12]

---

* Rich was a DNC staffer in voter outreach who was shot dead in DC in what police say was a botched robbery on July 10, 2016. His unsolved murder has for years driven conspiracy theories that he was really behind the hack of the DNC server and the leaking of its contents to WikiLeaks. Rich wasn't a hacker, had no access to this data, and supported the Democratic Party to the point that he had announced to his parents before his death that he was leaving the DNC to directly work for the Clinton campaign. Beyond that, Special Counsel Robert Mueller indicted over a dozen Russian intelligence officers for actually carrying out the DNC hack. Rich's death has led to a number of lawsuits by his family against the conservative news outlets who continued to push the theory that his death was a revenge hit by the Clintons and the DNC.

Q's thirty-fourth drop got several dozen responses in the form of Trump memes, well wishes, thanks for their service, and compliments. One anon summed up the fervor perfectly, declaring "this is gonna be so fuckin badass."[13] Other anons had found success on 4chan, but not this much—and not this fast.

Meanwhile, more high-profile names in the conspiracy continuum were noticing the growing popularity of the Q phenomenon. And they wanted in.

Conspiracy world figures immediately jumped on the growing popularity of the Q story, including prolific Q promoter Jordan Sather, who posted his first video referencing John Podesta's potential arrest on October 29, and first referenced "The Storm" itself several days later. The first major figure to find online success analyzing Q drops outside of 4chan was a freelance conspiracy theory journalist named Tracy Diaz—better known in the conspiracy theory community as Tracy Beanz.[14] Diaz had a small following on YouTube, where she commented on WikiLeaks drops and Pizzagate ephemera. Less than a week after Q's first drops, Diaz posted her first video analyzing the posts of Q Clearance Anon.

It shouldn't be surprising that a believer in the Pizzagate conspiracy theory was the first right-wing fringe media figure to get behind Q. While Q has a number of precursor conspiracy theories and scams, which we'll dive into later, no conspiracy theory feeds more immediately into Q than Pizzagate. Or, as the NBC News reporter on disinformation Ben Collins put it, Q is "Pizzagate on bath salts," referencing the powerful psychotropic drug.[15]

What became known as Pizzagate began with anonymous fake-news stories back when "fake news" actually meant a fraudulent story posted on a website designed to look like a legitimate news platform. It dropped just days before the 2016 election, using out-of-context snippets and words from Clinton campaign manager John Podesta's hacked and dumped emails to allege that Clinton and Podesta were involved in a child sex-trafficking ring operated out of

Comet Ping Pong pizzeria, a popular Washington, DC, restaurant.

Going beyond the supposed codes and phrases in the hacked emails, Pizzagate believers pointed to the "creepy" works of art hanging on the walls at Comet Ping Pong, referred to in a Reddit post of "Pizzagate proof" as "semi-overt, semi-tongue-in-cheek, and semi-sarcastic inferences towards sex with minors."[16] There were also rumors about tunnels leading in and out of Comet Ping Pong's basement, occult rituals, a laptop owned by Anthony Weiner said to be so full of sex abuse images so horrible that the NYPD members who saw them immediately killed themselves, and "coded references" to trafficking in John Podesta's emails, which had been leaked on WikiLeaks by this time. These references were based on a supposed "pedo code" that referred to young girls as "pizza" and young boys as "hot dogs."

In reality, Comet Ping Pong has no basement, not one child ever claimed to have been a victim of the Clinton-Podesta trafficking ring, law enforcement debunked the theory several times, and the references in the Podesta emails are either taken out of context or inside jokes with no nefarious meaning.[17] The "pedo code" was just another troll created by 4chan users—the same ones who ginned up the initial rumors that Podesta was a pedophile, and the many mentions of "pizza" in Podesta emails are almost all from ads or campaign emails Podesta was copied on—emails that, it should be noted, were stolen by Russian intelligence, not leaked by Seth Rich.[18] And no sexually explicit images were ever found on Weiner's laptop, which was examined by the FBI, not the NYPD.

Anti-Clinton media figures and foreign troll farms relentlessly pushed Pizzagate in the days before and after the election, leading to a torrent of threats against the restaurant from people who believed that children were being moved through it on their way to horrible sacrificial rituals. One such believer, North Carolina resident Edgar Maddison Welch, walked into Comet Ping Pong with an AR-15 in early December 2016, looking for children to rescue. After firing several shots into the ground, Welch was arrested and sent to prison for four years.[19]

While the sordid aspects of Pizzagate, like the abuse of children and the centrality of the Clintons and their inner circle, are only a small part of Q's mythology, they are an important one. And the Q poster would come back to Pizzagate concepts many times. Q never uses the term "Pizzagate," but one easily follows from the other. And it should be no surprise that the right-wing media figures who pumped out videos and memes about Pizzagate would shift to Q less than a year later.

One of these was Tracy Diaz. In her first video, Diaz claimed that Q's posts were "very specific and kind of eerie" about their claims, and that the poster "kinda seems legit." The title of her video said it all, rhetorically asking "Is it happening???" It racked up well over a quarter of a million views within weeks before eventually being pulled down and lost to history—a fate that would befall so many original tweets and videos about QAnon even before the big social media crackdown after the 2021 siege of the Capitol.

According to her blog, Diaz claimed she was approached by two /pol/ moderators, Pamphlet Anon (aka Coleman Rogers) and BaruchTheScribe (a South African web designer named Paul Furber) after they saw the success of her Q videos. They wanted to take the conspiracy theory to a bigger audience—one that would never ordinarily spend their time in a place like 4chan.[20] Diaz wrote that they approached her to launch a forum on Reddit, and on November 17, 2017, they launched the first subreddit devoted to QAnon, called r/CBTS_stream, with "CBTS" standing for "calm before the storm." It would eventually have nearly twenty-three thousand subscribers and almost seven hundred thousand posts—and it wouldn't even be Reddit's largest Q forum.[21]

It was the migration from the racist anarchy of 4chan to the relatively square (though still at times anarchic) Reddit that cemented Q's explosive takeoff. 4chan was hard to navigate, but Reddit was simple and welcoming to newcomers. And Reddit already had a robust conspiracy theory community, concentrated in the r/conspiracy subreddit, which had well over half a million subscribers at the time. So Reddit and Q were a natural fit, and r/CBTS_stream grew fast.

However, by November, it was clear that the initial story being spun by Q Clearance Patriot was going to need to be rebooted if it was going to justify the kind of attention it was already starting to get. After all, the first few arrests should have already taken place according to the timeline outlined in the first few posts.

On November 14, 2017 (more than a week after the initial target date for Hillary to be arrested), Q posted Drop #155—and with it a sense of finality. It was a blob of military-sounding jargon that seemed to signal that orders were being authenticated and indictments unsealed:

_Conf_D-TT_^_v891_0600_yes
_green1_0600
Bunker Apple Yellow Sky [... + 1]
Yes
Godspeed.
Q

And then? Nothing. Q went silent for three days, and there was no arrest of Hillary Clinton. No riots in the streets. No temporary martial law. No Emergency Alert System activation. Trump never announced "the storm" on Twitter, and nobody got perp-walked anywhere. It was a total bust. And the earliest QAnon believers came face to face with something else they'd have to accept in order to subscribe to Q's mythology: disconfirmation.

"DISINFORMATION IS NECESSARY"

As once recounted in Leon Festinger, Henry Riecken, and Stanley Schachter's classic 1956 study of UFO cults, *When Prophecy Fails*, the total and instant collapse of a UFO cult's proposed apocalyptic timeline spelled neither the end of the cult nor of the belief that the end-times were coming. So it's not a surprise that Q didn't fall apart after the big day came and went. Believers liked what they heard and wanted more—even though they hadn't gotten what they wanted in the first place.

But it did signal a change in how Q posted. Out went the specific dates and exact sequences predicting what would unfold. These were replaced by drops full of clipped mystery phrases, seemingly random pop culture references, and pat questions like "Why is this relevant?" Q quickly became better known for folksy encouragement than for explicit predictions—and Q fans ate it up.

Even before the anticlimax of Drop #155, Q would claim in Drop #128 that "disinformation is necessary." Essentially, they were telling their followers that sometimes Q would lie to them—and it would be for their own good.

When Q came back a few days after the adumbrated events failed to materialize, they unleashed a flood of posts that claimed that the real action was not the arrest of Hillary Clinton, but a purge in Saudi Arabia, where Crown Prince Mohammed bin Salman had orchestrated a mass arrest and detention of government ministers, minor royalty, and business luminaries who threatened his ascent.[22]

Never mind that Q had quite specifically referred to American figures in the original posts. Also never mind that nobody of consequence in the Q community thought this is what Q was talking about in the first place. It didn't matter. After all, disinformation is necessary. Q soon claimed in Drop #134 that one side of a mysterious "triangle" had been taken out, and that the rest of the cabal's days were numbered. At the same time, Q figured out that while you can keep predicting that the sky will fall, if you keep giving the exact date and time that the sky is supposed to fall, and it doesn't, people will stop thinking you know anything about the sky.

So the posts that followed contained lists of rhetorical questions, memes, links to Fox News stories, Bible verses, random bits of ephemera, and shout-outs to Q followers on Twitter—a favorite way of Q to acknowledge and keep faith with believers. Nothing concrete to plan for, but a great deal of anticipation—and more conspiracy theories to chew on.

Q hinted that the Steele dossier had been a Clinton forgery, and that numerous deep-state luminaries had *already been* arrested and were wearing walking boots to cover their ankle monitors. Q heaped praise on Trump and made insinuations about retiring Republicans being forced out due to their horrible crimes. Q claimed several times that the CIA had been overthrown in North Korea ("strings cut"), the Titanic was deliberately sunk to ensure the Federal Reserve would be founded, Hillary Clinton had been trying to make deals with the Q team (Drop #278: "we said NO"), and in Drop #533 started using a completely transparent codename for Trump, "4, 10, 20," for the ordinal number of the letters of his initials, DJT, in the alphabet. Q even insinuated in Drop #928 that German chancellor Angela Merkel was actually the daughter of Adolf Hitler, and claimed the truth of her parentage "will shock the WORLD"—an idea stolen from a 2007 post from fake-news blog WhatDoesItMean.[23]

Many of the most often-cited QAnon tropes were introduced in these weeks after the initial predictions fizzled. Drop #151 made what would be the first of many references to a clutch of "sealed indictments" being prepared by the Department of Justice—a list that would eventually bloat up to a quarter of a million. Drop #168, a few days later, introduced the concept of "the map" that connected all of the various players in the great Q conspiracy. Around that time, Q also started hammering the major social media companies, hinting that Facebook was a "spying tool" in Drop #214. And Drop #244 would be the first of innumerable times Q would point out "coincidences" between their postings and Trump's tweets to "prove" that it was "mathematically impossible" for Q not to be linked to Trump.

To add one more weapon to their arsenal of vaguedom, Q started posting pictures. There were blurry photos of the locations where

Trump's Singapore Summit with Kim Jong Un was to take place, extreme closeups of the president's signature and one of the pens Trump is known to use, and snaps of unnamed islands that Q bakers (the term they use for anons who compile decodings of Q drops into easily digested "breads") quickly "deduced" were taken from the inside of Air Force One. They were photos only someone with the deepest connection to the White House could possibly be able to take. Or, at least, only someone who had some kind of vague connections in Asia, and rudimentary Photoshop training.

More racism and anti-Semitism was also creeping into Q's posts. Q made four drops dredging up the anti-Semitic canard of the Rothschild family owning every central bank on the planet, then relentlessly hammered George Soros with the same language used by conspiracy theorists for years. Q began referring to Barack Obama by his middle name, Hussein, for no other apparent purpose than to win some points with birthers—advocates of the conspiracy that Donald Trump had been instrumental in promoting, which fixated on Barack Obama's middle name while asserting he was not born in the United States and thus not eligible for the office of the presidency.

Then, exactly a month after the first posts, Q dropped another tranche of posts full of gibberish, claimed in Drop #230 that 4chan had been "infiltrated," and left the site behind for its even more anarchic cousin board 8chan.

How could a secret military operation devoted to destroying the enemies of freedom and truth be infiltrated so completely and so quickly? How was it so wrong in the first place? And why did Q *really* leave 4chan?

Nobody who believed in Q at that point asked those questions, or cared what the answers would be. The phenomenon was so weird and off the grid that mainstream media outlets hadn't spotted it yet to any meaningful degree.

They should have. By the time Q jumped from 4chan to 8chan, it was a full-blown hit in the conspiracy sphere. QAnon quickly became a place where the puzzle-solving of Dan Brown, the special-forces cosplay of Tom Clancy, and the climactic *Turner Diaries*–like executions of liberals all stood shoulder to shoulder in an ever-expanding chronicle of the secret war between good and evil.

It was already on its way to spawning a massive number of disciples and a nascent QAnon merchandise industry, cranking out everything from T-shirts to handcrafted Q-shaped earrings. And it had set a pattern it would repeat time and time again: frenetic posts leading up to a disconfirmation, with the gurus pushing out Q's explanations to their flocks, who silently waited for Trump to bring deliverance.

But beyond the figures who made names for themselves through Q, the movement was also starting to make its way into the fringes of the mainstream right-wing media infotainment machine. It was crawling out of the swamp. The right-wing author and birtherism promoter Jerome Corsi had already jumped in with Q, heading to r/CBTS_stream to decode posts. And later that month, Q took its boldest step into the right-wing ecosystem yet: early 4chan acolytes Paul Furber and Coleman Rogers made an appearance on Alex Jones's Infowars.

CHAPTER 3

You Have More Than You Know: QAnon Hits the Big Time

AT THE PRESIDENT'S ELBOW

There's a school of thought that says Q is nothing more than an alternate reality game (ARG) that somehow went wrong—either through the malice of some of the people playing it or the machinations of a foreign intelligence service or domestic enemy who "hijacked" what had started as a puzzle-solving exercise.[1] And there is something to be said for the idea that it was merely an elaborate game or goof that got too big for its creators to handle. But however Q started off, whatever the intent was in those first posts, it quickly outgrew that.

It also outgrew its original promoters, including Paul Furber, the South African web designer who cofounded the first official subreddit, r/CBTS_stream. When Q jumped to 8chan (for reasons that remain unknown), they began posting on Furber's personal 8chan board, confusingly also called CBTS, while authenticating themselves with a unique tripcode—the coded password that imageboard users employ to prove they are who they claim to be.[2] At this point, the link between Q and Furber was inconclusive. Furber has consistently denied making the posts. But what's clear is that Q, who claimed to serve at the pleasure of the president, really posted at the pleasure of Paul Furber—who could have banned Q, or closed down his 8chan board, at any time. But he didn't. And while Furber rarely consents to interviews, he did leave a trail of livestreams and emails that prove he was either a true believer, or really good at faking it.

Furber believed that Q was exactly who they said they were, and that he had "undeniable proof" of Q "standing at the president's elbow" and in possession of incredible intel—things that only a high-ranking operator would know about.[3] Purges in Saudi Arabia, a foiled kidnapping of Lord Jacob Rothschild, Trump's Twitter account being taken down by the deep state. Big stuff, massive world events that would shock the slumbering populace if any of it became public. Which meant making it public was all the more important.

Furber and fellow r/CBTS_stream cofounder Coleman Rogers (aka Pamphlet Anon) seemed to understand that a message as important as Q's would need to be spread way past the racism and pornography of 8chan. And it would have to be done by people beyond just the few die-hards who had already attached themselves to the movement.

So they pitched Q to baby boomers—and they did it on the biggest conspiracy theory media outlet around: Infowars.

"BOOMERS! ON YOUR IMAGEBOARD!"

In the firmament of conspiracy theorists, there was no brighter star in 2017 than Alex Jones. The Austin-based provocateur had spent two decades turning himself into a mainstream figurehead, taking fringe ideas into the public consciousness and making millions of dollars in the process. He very quickly went all in on Q.[4]

But at the time of Rogers's and Furber's appearance, Jones wasn't present. The two didn't even get to talk to the master himself, settling for an interview with Rob Dew, one of Jones's senior producers. But it was enough of an opening to get their foot in the door. Furber and Rogers talked to Dew about the vital, world-altering information Q was dropping on CBTS and stuff "the deep state" would kill to keep bottled up. And don't believe what you read about 8chan, they implored. Q is a patriot, not a pornographer or racist. He wants to stop the real bad guys. And he needs help.

"There're a lot of people out there who can't function on the chans but they're a massive untapped resource themselves," Rogers told Dew. "They have all sorts of connections, a lot of them could be retired intel or military, there's so many people out there from older generations that are not involved in this fight."

"We're going wider," Furber added. "We're talking to YouTubers, we're talking to Infowars, we're talking to everybody." Well, not everybody. Furber made it clear that the mainstream media wasn't to be trusted. Only patriots. Only Q.

And it worked. Furber and Rogers had already established their Reddit board as a safe place for Q discussion, and now they had convinced a whole new cohort to join it. This move to take QAnon from the dank pits of 8chan to the staid, plastic-covered furniture of "older generations" who had little Internet savvy was the key to Q's growth. And Furber and Rogers were right on the money with the cohort they targeted: a 2019 study by researchers at Princeton and New York University showed that Facebook users over the age of sixty-five were as much as seven times more likely to share fake-news stories.[5] So they were perfect fodder to join the Q movement. The influx of older users was so sudden and intense that even 8chan's Twitter account got in on the act, posting stock photos of two older people examining computer screens and announcing, "we joked about it for years, but #QAnon is making it a reality: Boomers! On your imageboard."[6]

By the end of 2017, the QAnon that would eventually spread around the world and upend American politics was fully in place. Q was posting drops on 8chan, Q decoders were busy dissecting those drops, and the movement was growing by the day. Those decoders would become celebrities in their own right, including the previously mentioned Jordan Sather, and Twitter accounts like QAnon76,

StormIsUponUs, and InTheMatrixxx. These names might sound like silly video-gamer handles, and all have been permanently banned from Twitter. But in the QAnon community, their interpretations of Q's riddles get massive traction. A share from one of them can bring thousands of likes and retweets—along with death threats and histrionic abuse for those who oppose the movement.

Another major name in Q land emerged around this time. On December 28, 2017, a self-published author and "divine healer" who went by the name Praying Medic (real name: David Hayes) uploaded the first of countless YouTube videos he would make analyzing Q's drops. Hayes had started his YouTube career making videos that linked Christianity to self-healing. They usually got about a thousand views. But his first Q video jumped up to fifteen thousand views. Within a few months, Hayes was one of the most prominent and prolific Q bakers on the Internet, amassing a YouTube following of over a quarter of a million subscribers, routinely getting hundreds of thousands of views, and spawning a legion of imitators and collaborators. Among the most popular early Q adopters were prolific YouTube channel X22 Report, gossip columnist turned "trafficking expert" Liz Crokin, news blogger Dustin Nemos, and "Neon Revolt"; a failed screenwriter turned conspiracy theorist who grew into one of the biggest names in the Q ecosystem.[7]

"NO OUTSIDE COMMS"

A few weeks later, another new character would enter the Q story—one so integral to the QAnon phenomenon that major media outlets would eventually speculate that he actually was Q.[8]

That person was Jim Watkins, a middle-aged businessman and former US Army helicopter repairman who had launched a successful Japanese pornography website called Asian Bikini Bar, which he parlayed into a variety of tech companies and business ventures.[9] By 2017, when Q launched on 4chan, Watkins had taken control of the hugely successful Japanese imageboard 2chan—the same board that had inspired the creation of 4chan. He was also now the owner and operator of 8chan, the imageboard to which Q had recently migrated. Watkins had taken control of 8chan from its founder, the programmer Fredrick Brennan, who created the site in 2013.[10] Brennan had promoted 8chan as a free-speech alternative to 4chan, which had had the audacity to ban discussion of the Gamergate scandal in an attempt to stem an avalanche of harassment, doxing, and threats toward women in gaming media.

8chan exploded in popularity once 4chan became ever so slightly less friendly to anarchic content, but Brennan couldn't keep the site running. This was when Jim Watkins got involved—offering to host it and employ Brennan to run it. Brennan would move to the Philippines to work for Watkins, but like so many relationships in the world of fringe media, theirs curdled quickly. Brennan stopped administering or posting on the site by 2016, although he would spend another two years working for Watkins on other sites.[11] It was during this interim period that QAnon took off on 4chan—and soon jumped to 8chan. It's still not entirely clear why the move took place, though Q claimed 4chan had been "infiltrated" and Furber had told NBC News that the board had become unusable for Q because of "attacks."[12]

According to Brennan, as Q began posting on Furber's 8chan board, Jim Watkins and his son, Ron, who worked as an admin for 8chan, quickly took notice of its popularity and wanted in on it. Jim Watkins had already tried and failed to launch a right-wing conspiracy video channel called "The Goldwater," and he was still interested in putting his stamp on the conservative infotainment complex—a lucrative sphere of media where the more outlandish a lie was, the more likely a small sect of people would believe it. Speaking to the podcast *Reply All* in 2020, Brennan said that Ron and Jim plotted over Slack chats to take control of Q—though it should be noted that the Watkinses have always denied it and Brennan could not produce records of these chat logs.[13] Whatever the case, on January 5, 2018, in Drop #468, Q publicly claimed Furber's 8chan board had been infiltrated, and asked CodeMonkey—Ron Watkins's handle—to "secure IDEN" and "provide a secure board to post under your control to prevent future issues." Soon after, Q left the CBTS board—and Paul Furber's control.

The premise that Q was tightening its security by moving to 8chan is laughable. 8chan wasn't (and its successor 8kun isn't) a "secure board" with information "secured at highest level." Both 4chan's FAQ and Brennan flatly state that the unsecured tripcodes used on the chan boards are notoriously easy to crack—indeed, after Q jumped from 4chan to 8chan, so many people actually were cracking Q's tripcode that Furber had to keep changing it. Cracking the tripcode and matching it to the password also allowed other people to post themselves as Q. The journalist Dale Beran, who chronicled the rise of 4chan in his book *It Came From Something Awful*, reports he himself posted on another 8chan board as Q after he easily cracked Q's password, which at that point was the word "Matlock."[14] It was after one these many hackings and fake posts from fake Q's that the real Q announced, "Board compromised," and left the CBTS board, first for several other 8chan boards, then for the Q Research board, newly created by Ron Watkins just for Q to post drops on. Before that, Q had simply been another chan user – now they were the center of their own board, a place where no dissent or contradictory information was allowed.

What seems like silly hacker drama is a major turning point in Q's story. Before this move, no matter who was actually making the Q posts, there was no evidence that they were affiliated with the board on which they were being posted. Despite their claims about serving at the pleasure of Donald Trump, Q was just another user 8chan user. But with the move to /qresearch/, a board created and directly administered by Ron Watkins, Q's posts were now at least somewhat under the control of 8chan's ownership. Ron had control over the tripcodes, and therefore, had control over Q's identity—

even if he wasn't posting as Q. And Q was emphatic that this was an exclusive relationship: Drop #475 makes it clear that there would be "NO comms outside of this platform."

As of the first week of January 2018, Q would only ever post on 8chan or its successor 8kun. Their identity would only be confirmable by tripcodes that Ron Watkins could access—which Ron formalized in August of that year by adding "secure" tripcodes to 8chan, where the password was known only to the owner of the server. That person was Jim Watkins. Naturally, Q immediately began using secure tripcodes, locking anyone else out of posting as Q. Whatever happened after that, Q and 8chan, and therefore Q and Jim Watkins, would forever be linked.

"FIVE DIFFERENT PENTAGON SOURCES"

Virtually nobody in the Q sphere outside of Furber and the Watkins family knew or understood what was going on at this point. To Furber, Q was now being run by "a small group of imposters who play their followers like a cult."[15] But to Q believers, Q had dodged a bullet—shaking off a compromised honey trap for a more secure posting location from which to continue dropping intelligence nuggets that the deep state would do anything to stop.

Q was growing, and more big names in conservative media were taking notice. Alex Jones had already assigned Jerome Corsi, his "chief Washington correspondent" and one of the big names who pushed birtherism to cover QAnon. Corsi dutifully did his job, breaking down all of Q's drops for Infowars and on Twitter, sussing out what he called a "TIMELINE of CONSPIRACY to use CROWD-STRIKE and FUSION GPS to IMPEACH PRESIDENT TRUMP."[16]

Jones also began touting how close he and Corsi were to the military intelligence team running Q, and how much influence they had in the operation. Then Jones dropped an even bigger bomb: "The White House directly asked Corsi to be on the 8chan beat a month ago. So, [I] mean that's directly from the White House." It wasn't, but it sounded good to the people who wanted to believe it.

"You know, I've been told by five different Pentagon sources, high level, that that whole 8chan thing is real, and that they're basically forecasting what they'd like to see happen, and giving you information," Jones croaked in January 2018 to his massive audience.[17] Jones and Corsi would eventually sour on Q, calling it a "controlled op" run by the enemy—with Jones even ranting and screaming in the wake of the Capitol attack that he had always opposed Q. But in those early days, their stamp of approval was a big deal for the nascent Q movement.[18]

Around this time, the mainstream media started to pick up on story as well. In November 2017, a *Newsweek* story by Jason Le Miere reported on the orthopedic walking boots conspiracy theory.[19] And in December 2017, the *New York Magazine* writer Paris Martineau was the first journalist to put all of the pieces together, casting "the storm" as a violent and pedophilia-obsessed conspiracy theory along the lines of Pizzagate, only bigger and weirder—if such a thing was possible.[20] Immediately seeing the danger in a movement devoted to compiling a list of the United States's biggest enemies, Martineau presciently wondered, "Is the next [Comet Ping Pong shooter] Edgar Welch already out there, scrolling through the Calm Before the Storm thread, and if so, is it even possible to stop him?"

"PIMPS ALL OVER THE WORLD"

Despite the handful of early media hits, for much of 2018 the QAnon conspiracy theory bubbled quietly, out of the glare of media scrutiny. Q's only real brush with the mainstream news cycle in this period was its embrace by Roseanne Barr. The conservative comedian had hopped on the Q train early; she had asked her Twitter audience to "put [her] in touch" with the conspiracy avatar just weeks after Q's first drops. So it was a big deal for Q followers when she wrote in June of 2018 that "President Trump has freed so many children held in bondage to pimps all over this world. Hundreds each month. He has broken up trafficking rings in high places everywhere. notice that."[21] It wasn't just some crank anon making claims about massive pedophilia rings; it was a legitimate TV star. Mainstream reporters mostly greeted Barr's tweet with befuddlement.[22] But the small and growing clutch of people who followed QAnon knew exactly what Roseanne was talking about.

In another crucial development around then, Q-drop aggregator sites started to pop up, places like QMap, a site that catalogued Q's drops and gave followers a place to find and research Q content without having to wade through the anarchy of 8chan. Drop aggregators would come to play a major role in keeping the Q community informed.

Q began to obsess over things that would later become relentless drivers of discourse in the conservative media ecosystem. Q hyped the Devin Nunes "memo" highlighting perceived abuses of the FISA surveillance system against the Trump campaign—the first of countless such investigations and memos and reports by various US attorneys and Trump-aligned members of Congress that would supposedly bring the deep state crashing down. Q insinuated that major Democrats and celebrities would kill themselves rather than be brought to justice, and launched the concept that the mainstream media were all emailed 4 a.m. talking points by the deep state.

In the story Q was spinning, huge things were happening behind the scenes—battles fought in a silent war between good and evil. The media was corrupt and the Democrats were Satanic but the Trump administration's bumbling and leaking were all just for show. There was a plan. All Q believers had to do was trust it, and do their part to bring it to fruition. And some weren't content to just fight "the silent war" digitally. They wanted to take up arms against their oppressors. And at least a few started doing just that.

#RELEASETHEOIGREPORT

It was June 15, 2018, and Matthew Wright was heavily armed, pissed off, and wanted results.

The unemployed ex-Marine from Henderson, Nevada, was tired of the deep state obscuring the truth. Tired of the attacks on Donald Trump. But he knew Trump had . . . well, a trump card. It was a bombshell blockbuster report by the FBI's inspector general that would be the first in a series of revelations—that the deep state's minions in the Obama Department of Justice had conspired to try to prevent Donald Trump from being elevated to the presidency. While a report had already been released by the FBI inspector general excoriating the conduct of former FBI director James Comey and his agency during the Hillary Clinton emails "scandal," according to Wright this report was a fake, a phony designed to placate the doped-up sheep who put their trust in the liberal media and politics. What Wright wanted was a second report—the real report. And Matthew Wright knew that that real report, once made public by the president, would crush the cabal underneath the boot of truth.

Matthew Wright knew this because Q had told him so. In Drop #1496, posted to 8chan's Q Research board on June 13, 2018, Q laid it all out. Not only was there one secret report, there were *two*.[23] Q had seen it all and knew everything. The drop read, in part:

POTUS IN POSSESSION OF (AND REVIEWING):

1. Original IG unredacted report
2. Modified IG unredacted report [RR version]
3. Modified IG redacted report [RR version]
4. IG summary notes re: obstruction(s) to obtain select info (classified)
[#3 released tomorrow]

"RR" was the former deputy attorney general Rod Rosenstein—a name who appears frequently in the Q mythology. Q would go on to say that if the original, unredacted report ever came to light, it would cause a wave of resignations and firings in the FBI and DOJ—cutting a swath through the deep-state saboteurs who were trying to derail Trump.

"Be loud. Be heard. Fight for TRUTH," the drop ended.

So that's what Matthew Wright did.[24] He grabbed an assault rifle, a handgun, a flashbang grenade, nine hundred rounds of ammunition, and a sign making a very particular request. He tossed them all into his coal-black homemade armored truck that he'd modified to serve as his living quarters, complete with a gun port built into the driver's side door, and headed for Hoover Dam. Wright would spend ninety minutes stopped on Route 93's Mike O'Callaghan–Pat Tillman Memorial Bridge, just south of the dam that held back the United States's largest reservoir of water. His siege shut the dam and highway down, and terrified tourists were ordered to shelter in place as Wright demanded "full disclosure" in a video he shot for POTUS's eyes only.

"We elected you to do a duty," Wright continued. "You said you were going to lock certain people up if you were elected. You have yet to do that. Uphold your oath." And up went his sign—demanding President Trump release the OIG report.[25] The real one. The one Q told him existed.

Wright drove off after an hour and a half and took police on a chase that ended when his homemade armored car rolled into a ditch in the Lake Mead Recreational Area, its tires blown out. Nobody was hurt, no shots were fired, and Wright was arrested without resistance. The next month, Wright wrote a prison letter to President Trump claiming he wasn't a seditionist who wanted to fight the government. He was a patriot who had merely baffled the normie media with his request.

"I understand that the evil and corruption is limited to a select few in power and that the greater good is doing its best to combat this," he wrote to the president. "I never meant harm to my brothers and sisters. I simply wanted the truth on behalf of all Americans, all of humanity for that matter." If Wright was expecting clemency from the president for whom he'd given up everything, he didn't get it. In early 2020, Wright pleaded guilty to a charge of non-dangerous domestic terrorism, but prosecutors rejected it as too lenient.[26]

Matthew Wright's blockade of the Hoover Dam was the first public violent act connected to the QAnon conspiracy theory. It wouldn't be the last. And in theory, it could have ended Q. After all, a conspiracy live-action roleplaying game (also called "LARPing" and usually meant as an insult) is all fun and games until someone commits domestic terrorism. But just like how the concepts surrounding Pizzagate didn't magically disappear after Edgar Maddison Welch shot up Comet Ping Pong in December 2016, Q didn't end with Matthew Wright's failed siege. Q believers writing in posts that were archived before 8chan went down didn't believe Wright's blockade was real—just another deep-state fake job to stop the truth from coming out. Q had already said that "attacks would intensify" as the cabal's media lackeys fought Q.

"[False flag] on Hoover Dam to make those wanting the IG report to be released in full unredacted made to look crazy?" asked one anon on 8chan the day of the standoff.[27]

And if it was real, they reasoned, Wright didn't represent them. The bulk of Q followers weren't violent nutcases, they were patriotic researchers, able to find the tiniest bits of truth in a vast sea of garbage and fakery. "Autists," they called themselves—proudly insinuating that they had a developmental disorder that let them see things others can't. These were people who believed they could see the messages Q and the deep state were "really" sending. They knew that when Trump misspelled "IMBEDDED INFORMANT," using "I" instead of an "E," that Trump was shouting out Drop #753's use of "[I]" as its own sentence. Q didn't tell them that, nor was there a need to be told it—the autists figured it out.[28] They knew that when James Comey tweeted about the death of his dog Benji in early November 2018, he was *really* signaling to the world that George H. W. Bush would be executed two weeks later—because autists know that pictures of dogs sent by prominent deep-state members are actually secret messages announcing an execution.[29]

This is what Q believers do—or at least what they believe they do. They decode the "comms" of the powerful to deduce what they "really" mean and unlock secrets that the sheep sleeping their lives away in the normal world will never understand. They are peaceful researchers, not terrorists or violent seditionists.

"WE are NOT about violence, subversion or control. WE are simply providing FACT based information FREE of charge to the WORLD," wrote one anon in an 8chan post that Q quoted and responded to in Drop #1771, writing "Excellent! You cannot fool a massive group of dedicated gold star researchers."[30]

It was on July 31, 2018, at Donald Trump's rally in Tampa, that the world found out how "massive" that group appeared to be.

"TAMPA RALLY LOOKING GREAT!"

The movement that had slowly and quietly grown while a baffled media gave meager witness burst into the national consciousness in a way that even the most skeptical mainstream "blue checkmark" journalists on Twitter couldn't ignore.

"Tampa Rally looking great!" Q announced a few hours before the rally, showing pictures of believers waiting to get into Trump's event, all of whom were wearing Q shirts and holding up signs with Q slogans. The next day, Q was proven right. The event was swamped by the adherents of this bizarre theory, hundreds, maybe more. And they weren't shy either—they wore shirts and made signs and gave interviews to reporters, calling Q a good thing and a "counterbalance to the fake news."[31]

"Military intelligence has been talking to us, letting us know what's going on behind the scenes," exclaimed a wide-eyed Q believer named Tyler, who proudly showed off a metallic Q coin to a local reporter.[32] Other tweets from rally attendees showed off their homemade signs, posed with pictures for other fans, and extolled the public emergence of what had once been a shadowy secret.[33] QAnon even trended on Twitter, with hundreds of thousands of tweets sent by supporters of the movement and detractors alike. Afterward, Q was ebullient, exclaiming "you are now the news" (a near-identical phrase to one shouted by Capitol rioters destroying camera equipment nearly three years later) in Drop #1789 and highlighting the dozens of mainstream media articles written about Tampa—hit piece after hit piece calling Q insane and fringe and a "deranged conspiracy cult" and bizarre and nasty and dangerous.[34]

As a reservoir of weaponized grievance for Q's growing following, it was solid gold. These were people who were used to being mocked for their conservatism, ridiculed for their beliefs that Barack Obama and Hillary Clinton weren't paragons of virtue, and considered rubes and rednecks and flyover country racists by the mainstream media. And these people, this silent and loathed and forgotten majority, had chosen as a champion someone just like them. Someone underestimated and mocked, written off as an amateur and a joke and a racist just for wanting to drain the swamp and return power to the people. His people. That champion was Donald Trump, and even if he wasn't perfect, he was godly and a patriot and stood against the rising tide of socialism and Satanism. So if Q claimed to be serving at Donald Trump's elbow, fighting the people who hated him and them, then they would fight alongside Q.

After Tampa, Q began to become inseparable from the mainstream Republican Party. They danced around it at first—then-press secretary Sarah Huckabee Sanders couldn't change the subject fast enough when a reporter asked her about Q shortly after the Tampa rally.[35] But they didn't turn away from it, either. They didn't denounce it. And the media hit pieces kept coming, and so did the overt attacks, as Reddit abruptly banned the seventy-thousand-member r/GreatAwakening board because members had started harassing other users and had doxed (released the personal information) of at least one person they incorrectly claimed to be a mass shooter.[36] Once again, Q followers found other forums to communicate on, and the movement continued growing—on Twitter, in closed Facebook groups with tens of thousands of members, and on the gaming and chat platform Discord.[37] Q was becoming a huge source of shares for mainstream conservative sites and Q gurus alike.[38] Just in 2018, Q believers shared Q YouTube videos over 1.4 million times, and drove hundreds of thousands of shares to Fox News, *Breitbart*, *The Gateway Pundit*, various Q-drop aggregators, and *The Goldwater*, Jim Watkins's now revived right-wing blog.

Q began to take on the persona less of a military intelligence insider and more of a GOP cheerleader. Q started relentlessly attacking Trump foe John McCain, DOJ and FBI figures that only the most hardcore Fox News watchers would know existed, and the loose coalition of anti-fascist activists known by the right-wing media as "antifa." Long before these MAGA shibboleths became a foreign language that only die-hard Trumpists could understand, Q was attacking them as traitors and saboteurs. Q spent weeks predicting a "red wave" would swamp the 2018 midterms, claiming that Brett Kavanaugh would be confirmed to the Supreme Court by a 53-47 vote, that a slew of indictments were coming thanks to the inspector general report, that US Attorney John Huber was going to give testimony about the Clinton Foundation so explosive that George H. W. Bush had to be killed so that his funeral would stop the hearing, and that Trump would fire Deputy Attorney General Rod Rosenstein as part of a massive push to "declass" all the hidden documents that proved the Obama administration had spied on Trump's campaign.

None of it happened, of course. Kavanaugh was confirmed, but by a 50-48 vote. And those midterms weren't a "red wave" in any capacity, as the GOP lost forty seats in the House and dozens of other state-level legislature seats. The inspector general report was a bust, and had been for months. George H. W. Bush was a ninety-year-old man who died of natural causes following the death of his wife. Huber's Clinton Foundation testimony was so meaningless that he didn't even show up to the hearing—which was merely moved to a week after Bush's funeral.[39] And Rod Rosenstein hung on as deputy attorney general until May 2019—resigning with two weeks' notice, and no great declassification of documents.[40]

But nobody involved in Q cared. As 2018 ended, Q was a little over a year old, and despite none of Q's predictions coming true in a concrete way, the movement had taken the Republican Party and the mass media by storm. Q believers thought they were truly on the verge of something incredible that would change the world— and Q fed them everything they needed to keep believing that was true, even when world events proved otherwise. In December, just before Christmas, Q summed up what they wanted their followers to believe in their hearts:

> The [D] party will cease to exist once it's all exposed.
> FAKE NEWS can no longer control [dampen] public
> awareness of the TRUTH.
> DARK TO LIGHT.
> Q

To a growing mass of believers, it was an irresistible message.

CHAPTER 4

Boom Week Coming: The Scams and Conspiracy Theories That Begat QAnon

To understand the Q movement's explosive early growth, we have to explore another critical element of QAnon: it is far from original. In fact, very little of Q's mythology originates with Q. A rich tapestry of conspiracy theories, ancient hatreds, currency scams, moral panics, and social media rumors were stitched together to make QAnon, but few of these ideas are entirely new, nor is their original provenance difficult to trace. After all, what's the secret and all-powerful "deep state" if not a different term for the New World Order that was so feared in the 1990s, which in turn was a new formulation for the fear of the Catholic Church or the Freemasons that drove conspiracy theories in the eighteenth and nineteenth centuries? Even some of Q's catchphrases are stolen from past fringe movements. Before Q co-opted the concept of the "Great Awakening," it denoted several brief but intense periods of end-times fervor that laid the groundwork for much of the religious revivals of the seventeenth and eighteenth centuries.

The elemental parts of Q didn't start with meme culture or chan boards or Trump or social media. They didn't start with the Internet, the CIA, the Russians, or the Illuminati. They're baked into the way humans demand explanations for things that seem to defy reason. And they start with the one group that humanity has always managed to pin the blame on: Jews.

THE LONGEST HATRED

While Q believers hold themselves up as a nonpartisan, race-blind movement of researchers who believe "patriotism has no skin color," the fact is that QAnon is a deeply anti-Semitic movement. Like other conspiracy theory icons, Q holds up wealthy Jews as a protected class, scheming among themselves in evil cliques to hoard the riches of the world and destroy those who oppose them. And just as the anti-Semite of the twentieth century had tracts like *The Protocols of the Elders of Zion* or *The International Jew* (both of which were either published or promoted by iconic automobile scion Henry Ford), modern anti-Semites can look at Q's drops and the vast universe of Jew-hating on the chans as their own canonical texts.

In the Q pantheon, almost nobody spends more money to hurt more people than two bad actors: the Hungarian liberal philanthropist George Soros and the Rothschild banking family. When Q's second-ever drop made a reference to Soros "giving away all his money" as part of whatever scheme Q was aiming to stop (which, again, he did not do), it was the first dip into what anti-Semitism scholar Robert S. Wistrich called "the longest hatred" in a 1992 book of the same name. Q was scoring points off the latent hatred of Jews already found on 4chan, and it worked.

Q accused Soros of funding domestic terror, arranging the invasion of free nations, money laundering, election rigging, and child trafficking. He also claimed Soros deployed false-flag attacks against his own side and was responsible for the takeover of America's streets by antifa and countless more horrors, real and imaginary. The Rothschilds were posited as financiers so flush with their hundreds of trillions of dollars in holdings that they funded both sides in every war of the last three centuries, and owned almost every central bank in the world. Both were the moneymen behind a cabal so dark and evil it controlled almost every aspect of the media, banking, and politics.

Like most of Q, there's nothing new in the obsession with wealthy Jewish bankers. Soros has been the subject of decades of lies about his childhood, his business dealings, and his philanthropy—all of which have been debunked again and again.[1] And conspiracy theories about the five international financier sons of Mayer Amschel Rothschild go back all the way to the Battle of Waterloo in 1812, and hold just as little weight then as they do now.[2] Even the list of "central banks" owned by the Rothschilds that Q included in an earlier series of drops was cribbed from a right-wing conspiracy site called HumansAreFree that had posted it in 2013. But the growing right-wing, anti-globalism movement found succor in Q's hysterical drops about George Soros's globalist machinations and the Rothschilds holding human-hunting parties at their lodge in the Black Forest. It was a language spoken fluently on the chans and the other cesspools where Q drops were interpreted.

In fact, 8chan has been rated as one of the most anti-Semitic places on the Internet by the Anti-Defamation League, full of targeted harassment against Jewish journalists, praise of anti-Semitic mass shooters, and an endless supply of anti-Jewish memes and "jokes."[3] How deep does it go? A search of the archives of 8chan and 8kun (found on the Q-drop aggregator site qresear.ch) for just the word "Jews" brings up well over one hundred thousand references. And the vast majority are not pleasant, full of the same "string puller" stereotypes found everywhere else anti-Semites congregate. There are over thirty-two thousand uses of the anti-Jewish slur "kike," thousands of references to the murder of 6 million Jews during World War II being a "holohoax," and thousands more derogatory mentions of Zionism. And naturally, posters on /qresearch/ are complimentary of those older texts that have inspired so much violence against Jews—one anon wrote, "*The Protocols of the Elders of Zion*, pretty accurate whether a forgery or not."[4]

Beyond the constant pounding on Soros and the Rothschilds, the anti-Semitism of the Q poster is rarely that overt—though in Drop

#998, Q did quote a horrifically anti-Semitic cartoon posted on /qre-search/. It was left to Q's followers to read between the lines and come up with their own answers to what anti-Semites have called "the Jewish Question." But that's not the only way Q aimlessly throws anti-Semitic tropes out for their followers to lap up. Far from it.

FROM WILLIAM OF NORWICH TO HUNTER S. THOMPSON

The Q movement has also worked hard to advance centuries-old traditions of blaming Jews for horrible crimes against innocent Christian boys and girls. This so-called blood libel—named after an accusation in 1144 that a group of Jews ritually murdered and consumed the blood of an English boy named William of Norwich—has driven countless crimes against Jews, from organized pogroms in the Middle Ages to social media harassment in the twenty-first century.[5] And a new version of it drives Q discourse now.

The modern blood libel takes the form of paranoia over "adrenochrome," a supposed superdrug extracted from the adrenal glands of live children to confer eternal life to its consumers. The term has never appeared in a Q drop, but adrenochrome is still referenced constantly in the discourse of Q promoters, to the point where a number of major news outlets wrote about it in the struggle to understand why so many people were getting sucked into Q. Adrenochrome and Q fit together easily.

Adrenochrome is indeed a chemical compound—oxidized adrenaline, an easily available substance used to aid blood clotting. However in 1952, while studying the causes of schizophrenia, the scientists John Smythies, Humphry Osmond, and Abram Hoffer theorized that heavy amounts of adrenochrome could trigger schizoid episodes—or could cause a more potent high than any known hallucinogenic of the time. Writing in 1954, the trio warned that "to those who are familiar with [mescaline] and lysergic acid, we would emphasize that judging from the little experience we have, it does seem that adrenochrome is more insidious than those two hallucinogens."[6] Aldous Huxley soon grabbed onto this idea in *The Doors of Perception*, referencing the "adrenochrome hypothesis" for schizophrenia, and claiming the compound can "produce many of the symptoms of mescalin intoxication."[7]

Thereafter, it has been a mainstay in sci-fi and drug fiction. It shows up as a superdrug in Anthony Burgess's *A Clockwork Orange* and a book by *Dune* author Frank Herbert. But probably the most well-known pop-culture reference to adrenochrome is in Hunter S. Thompson's *Fear and Loathing in Las Vegas*, describing it as a narcotic so powerful it made "pure mescaline seem like ginger beer."[8] Thompson also added to the mythology that it was harvested from "the adrenaline glands of a living human body. . . . It's no good if you get it out of a corpse."[9] All of this—the powerful properties of adrenochrome, the need to get it from a living person, its scarcity— would eventually show up in Q's iconography.

But not right away. The adrenochrome and frightened children concept got off to a rocky start in the Q community, thanks at least in part to a misstep from a pre-Q anon, HighwayPatrolman, who claimed to have been part of a "special forces" team that intercepted a gigantic shipment of adrenochrome worth $100 billion, and was promptly run off 4chan for being unable to provide any evidence.[10] But despite that early failure, it eventually caught on with Q believers already primed to accept that "wealthy elites" like George Soros and the Clintons were child-blood drinkers.[11] And presumably like taking adrenochrome itself, when it hit, it hit hard.

"Adrenochrome is a drug that the elites love," claimed prolific QAnon promoter and "researcher" Liz Crokin in a now-deleted YouTube video. "It comes from children. The drug is extracted from the pituitary glands of tortured children. It's sold on the black market. It's the drug of the elites. It is their favorite drug. It is beyond evil. It is demonic. It is so sick."[12] Q social media was also full of rumors of Jews drinking the blood of children including since-deleted videos with names like "Jew Ritual BLOOD LIBEL Sacrifice is #ADRENOCHROME Harvesting."[13] There were whispers of vast rings of Hollywood elites and political titans holding demonic sacrifices to harvest it, Hillary Clinton murdering a young girl on camera and wearing her face while gorging on it (a video said to be so sick that the NYPD officers who saw it immediately killed themselves), and even Silicon Valley startups developing products to extract it more efficiently.

This was blood libel on a grand scale—except instead of one cadre of Jews drinking the blood of one child, it was a transcontinental network of elite pedophiles doing it to hundreds of thousands of children, aided by a media that's probably doing it too.

Once Q began to merge with extant "save the children" crusades, which had been a mainstay of conspiracy circles since the Satanic ritual abuse panic of the 1980s, "adrenochrome" trended on Q social media again and again, usually with photoshopped pictures of celebrities looking haggard (allegedly because they hadn't gotten their dose) and claims about hundreds of thousands of kids going missing every year. Even Dr. Phil gave the claims airtime, devoting a September 2020 episode of his show to a woman who claimed that her daughter had been kidnapped and ritually murdered to get adrenochrome.[14]

Not a single person has ever credibly been found "drained" of adrenochrome, and its powdered form is easily available online—a fact that Q believers wave off by saying it has to be taken from a living person, like Hunter S. Thompson said. Thompson himself later made it clear that he had made up most of what he wrote about adrenochrome, and drug experimenters have borne this out.[15] Those who have tried taking the compound to get high only reported crippling headaches and anxiety attacks on drug-experimentation message boards.

But as a blood libel for the social media era, adrenochrome goes well with the "elite cabal" mythology of Q. Wealthy elites are already seen as a vast cesspool of perversion, so why *wouldn't* they be doing horrible things to children to keep their decrepit husks alive? How could they prove they *weren't*? So many elements of these anti-Jewish canards found their way into Q that it became common knowledge among Q believers, passed around like stock tips or the name of a hot new bar.

But Q wasn't only fashioned out of anti-Semitism and blood libel tropes—if it were, it would be easier to refute and less appealing to Q's ever-expanding audience. Some of what powers Q is the same thing that's driven intel-laden conspiracy theories for decades: old-school greed.

OMEGA SUPREME

Sometime soon, there will be a world-changing event that will raise up high the lowest, and bring down low the highest. And the elites will do anything to stop it—because it's your last hope for a better and wealthier life that's free from the mental and financial chains they've put you in. But a few enlightened warriors have broken the matrix. They know the truth, and they're fighting a secret war to get that truth out to you. Day after day, these enlightened mystics are getting precious intel about the event, dispensing cryptic secrets on hidden channels, and uncovering all the enemies that stand in the way of the great event. And it's an event that YOU can be part of. Just for a tiny investment, of course.

This is the world of "affinity fraud." And it's a path that leads directly to Q.

Belief in QAnon requires no monetary investment—if it did, it would be straightforward fraud. But fraud *does* play a major role in the lineage of QAnon. What we know as some of Q's most important parts—secret intel from a guru, a massive event just around the corner, a secret battle between forces of light and darkness—are all the core of several lucrative scams that preceded Q, scams that many Q believers have *also* fallen for.

Affinity fraud is built around complex jargon designed to fool investors into thinking a small amount of money will be transformed in a gigantic one, and often involves a trusted member of an insular group marketing a low-risk, high-return "investment" to other members of that group.

The fingerprints of one such scam, Omega Trust, can be found all over what we'd eventually come to know as QAnon, though there's no proof of a direct link between the two.[16] Omega was the creation of Clyde Hood, a sixtyish resident of downstate Mattoon, Illinois, whose friends started to get very rich very fast in the 1990s. As the millennium wound down, town luminaries were suddenly driving around in multiple antique cars, minimum-wage workers were building enormous homes, and stories abounded of sacks of cash so full they would burst when picked up. The source of it all was Hood, who started claiming in 1994 that he was a Fortune 500 investment banker who was one of the only people on the planet with access to a life-changing financial instrument delivered to him by God Himself. They were prime European banknotes, which could be bought for chump change and, after a period of about 250 days, would "roll over" to return fifty times their investment. You could then roll that over, and return millions of dollars in profit—all based on Hood's divine visions and status as a "Supreme Commander" in the Army of the Lord.[17]

"There are only seven or eight people in the world that can do all this," he would tell investors, in language that would eerily presage Q's mythology of "less than ten people."[18]

Hood offered the services of his Omega Trust and Trading company to fellow Christians first, fronting them massive amounts of money in "private party loan agreements" as an advance on their fabulous payoff.[19] "Keep the Lord's warehouse full!" Hood was prone to exclaiming in one of the many letters and recorded messages he left goading his marks into investing more money. And for a while, it was. Fueled by the promise of a $250,000 return on an

$100 investment, people from all over the country bought "Omega units," sending bricks of cash wrapped in tinfoil, in accordance with Hood's eccentric instructions. Omega took advantage not only of the trust native to evangelical populations in small towns, but of early Internet adopters, with numerous Yahoo! groups forming to read the "intel" that Hood used to promise that the payoff was nearly at hand.[20]

"The international bankers around the world are hopping mad and demanding this be finished. This is blocking many other major transaction [sic] and we are about ready to have a world-wide financial crisis if this does not deliver," goes one Omega "intel" message reprinted on the scam clearinghouse website Quatloos. "Please send this to everyone you know in the program and others to lift this up in prayer and bind David Rockefeller and George Bush and allow this program to finish."[21]

Ultimately, it wasn't those hopping mad international bankers that Hood had to contend with, but a slew of federal and state law enforcement agencies. Because Clyde Hood wasn't a divinely touched Fortune 500 investment banker, he was a retired pool-hall manager with a talent for grift. In 2000, Hood and eighteen other Mattoon cronies who had balanced his books and talked down jittery Omega investors were arrested after a three-year investigation. They'd fleeced over ten thousand people out of anywhere between $12 million and $20 million, and had blown nearly all of it. Not a penny was ever "rolled over" in a "prime European banknote," because those don't exist. Hood admitted in court that Omega was entirely a scam, and was found guilty of fraud. The classic cars were auctioned off to pay Hood's victims, and he died in prison in 2012—with residents still marveling at the dump truck of money that landed on their tiny town. It would take years for victims to receive restitution.[22]

Omega continued at a slow burn for a few years after Hood's arrest in 2000. But one of its disciples wanted more—more money, more power, a more operatic story. Her actions would spawn a conspiracy cult that's been going strong for two decades, pulling in some of the people who now fervently wait for Q to deliver on their promises.

NESARA NOW!

Until she got involved in Omega, the crowning achievement of Shaini Goodwin's life was probably being crowned the queen of the 1962 McCleary Bear Festival—a big deal in that rural Washington town of sixteen hundred people. By the mid-1990s, Goodwin (born Candace Darlene Goodwin in May 1947) was living in Yelm, a small town outside Seattle full of New Age practitioners who were as ripe for Omega's swindle as the "Lord's storehouse" of easy evangelical marks.

"For whatever reason, this Omega thing hit the New Age spiritual community," the journalist Sean Robinson told me, flashing back to a movement he covered extensively in the early 2000s for the Tacoma *News Tribune*. Robinson spoke to a number of Seattle-area residents who lost money on Omega, and learned of many more, including a tax attorney who spent $280,000 on Omega units.[23] And while Yelm residents were more into the spiritual teachings of the thirty-five-thousand-year-old Lemurian warrior Ramtha as opposed to those of Jesus, what they did share was a desire to get a lot of money very quickly. "All these people who were part of that group hooked on with Omega, and some of them were clearly people who should have known better," Robinson said.

One of the people who fell in with Omega was Shaini Goodwin, and while it's not clear how much money she lost (she claimed to never have sold Omega units), it's clear that she saw an opportunity when the leader of the movement was taken out. Posting on early message boards and Yahoo! groups under the username Dove of Oneness, Goodwin excelled at reassuring the frightened community of Omega investors. As Omega collapsed, she began to spin lurid tales of what she saw as heroic "White Knights" fighting what she called the "Dark Agenda" that was trying to stop the Omega roll-over. Dove began delivering "intel drops," asking for group prayers, and recounting stories of federal judges fighting to free Omega. She even claimed that Clyde Hood's arrest was faked and would go away soon—despite eighteen of the nineteen arrests resulting in convictions. And when restitution for Omega started to become available, Dove urged her followers not to take it—lest they jeopardize their promised massive payoffs with smaller, yet real, ones.

Once Hood was definitively out of the picture, Goodwin began touting another prosperity program, a seemingly miraculous economic transformation known as NESARA. Short for National Economic Security and Recovery Act, this was a sweeping proposal to transform America's economy first developed in the 1980s by the engineer Harvey Francis Barnard, who proposed a massive overhaul to the US financial system . . .[24] He printed one thousand copies of this plan, which he dubbed NESARA, and gave the self-published pamphlets to Congress, where the idea went absolutely nowhere. He eventually gave the proposal away for free online.

At some point in 2000, Goodwin discovered Barnard's proposal and used it to, as Robinson put it, add a "secret-law component" to the base mythology of Omega. That is, NESARA was presented as an immutable law of the universe that would usher in the same sort of prosperity that Hood had promised with Omega. What Goodwin did was claim that NESARA was not a long-shot proposal from an amateur economist, but was an actual law that had been signed in secret by Bill Clinton. Its contents were so volatile and guarded that if anyone in Congress admitted to its existence, they would be executed. But once it went into effect, the government would be reconstituted with what fringe author and fellow NESARA guru Sherry Shriner deemed a "NESARA president and vice president designate," a new banking system based on gold, and an international declaration of peace.

Not that Goodwin didn't make some amendments to Barnard's original tract. Notably, Goodwin changed the "R" in NESARA from "recovery" to "reformation." After all, she was promising a complete transformation of the world's monetary system that would deliver trillions of dollars in "prosperity packets" to a chosen few believers. And just as Clyde Hood claimed to be one of the only people with access to prime European banknotes, only the Dove of Oneness had access to the NESARA intel—intel that revealed a movement bordering on both a new religion and a "Great Awakening" for the world economy.

Goodwin kept pushing the idea that NESARA would deliver any day, if not for a Dark Agenda holding it back. Then came the September 11 attacks, and in a move that QAnon would repeat time and time again, Goodwin took an earth-shaking world event and molded it to fit with the conspiracy cult she was creating.

Hours after the attacks, Goodwin posted a truly revelatory message to her email list:

The three targets today were ALL connected to NESARA and the banking changes. I just learned that at 9:00 a.m. in New York this morning, there was an IMPORTANT banking activity set to be activated in the IMF international banking computer center in the World Trade Center! That's right, at exactly 9:00 a.m. EDT! This IMPORTANT activity involved the U.S. banking system changes implemented by NESARA. This activity was REQUIRED today before the official announcement of NESARA which had been planned for tonight by the White Knights.[25]

Goodwin's message, perhaps the first significant footprint of the 9/11 truther movement, goes on and on, finding a conspiratorial reason for every single aspect of what happened that day. The attack on the Pentagon, the crash of Flight 93, the timing, the date, all of it. And Goodwin knew, before the fires were even out, who was behind it: "U.S. citizens who are trying to stop our deliveries/funding and NESARA."

Just as twenty years later Americans would find Q while they groped in the dark for reasons why the economic inequality was increasing and the COVID-19 pandemic was flourishing, there was enormous solace in being a NESARA believer as these horrible events unfolded. It was a sign that, despite the chaotic appearances, followers were about to get everything they ever wanted.[26] NESARA became an international phenomenon—with the Dove of Oneness as its figurehead. She organized letter-writing campaigns to Congress and the Supreme Court, had volunteers pass out flyers and march outside the World Court in the Hague, claimed that House members Ron Paul and Dennis Kucinich supported NESARA in secret, and even used the donations of one elderly devotee to pay for rolling billboards to drive down the streets of Washington, DC, proclaiming NESARA NOW!

"They weren't as expensive as they looked," Robinson quipped about the billboards.

All the while, even as Goodwin touted uncountable wealth coming any day, she could barely pay her bills. To get by, she lived off donations from NESARA believers. The NESARA scam would go on for years, getting more bizarre and detailed in its claims and excuses for each deferral of the "Great Awakening." By 2006, though, even hardcore NESARA believers were growing weary of the delays.[27] Dove's email blasts became less frequent and more rambling, while veering into niche conspiracies. Eventually, Goodwin was left only with people who, in Sean Robinson's estimation, clung not to the specific belief that the prosperity packets were coming, but to the general anti-authority bent found in many New Age movements. Goodwin herself "passed from this Earthly plane" in May 2010 after writing one last "Dove Report," a rambling message about alien wars and parallel universes.[28] When her death became public, many NESA-

RAites didn't believe it, and one NESARA message board claimed it was all proof that the Dove of Oneness had been right all along:

> Investors can still go to goldfornesara@verizon.net for a chance to invest in the very special trades that Shaini Goodwin set up, delivering more than favorable returns. All contacts are still viable.[29]

Just like with QAnon almost a decade later, there was always another can to kick down another road. Soon, it went from prosperity raining from the sky to great wealth only being a trivial investment away.

DANCING FOR DINARS

By the time Dove of Oneness sacrificed her life in spiritual combat to deliver the prosperity packets, the affinity fraud world had moved on to another scam based on phony "intel updates" about a permanently deferred delivery of wealth. And like NESARA with 9/11, it tried to act as an alternate explanation for geopolitical chaos—in this case, the war in Iraq. It was the Iraqi dinar scam, and it combined all the illegality of Omega with all the fantastical wealth conjuring of NESARA to make one of the most potent scams of the new century—and a direct precursor to QAnon.

It's unknown who the first person was who decided that investing in dinars, the nearly worthless paper currency of Iraq, would get them rich quickly. But on the surface, it's not hard to see the logic. After gaining independence from the UK in 1932, Iraq introduced its own currency, the dinar, which by the 1970s was one of the rarest and most valuable currencies in the world. The dinar had inflated in value thanks to scarce printing, limitless oil money, and Saddam Hussein's iron will, and was trading at as much as one dinar to $3.22.

Then came the Iraqi invasion of Kuwait, and crushing interna-

tional sanctions. Saddam Hussein's government overprinted infe-
rior quality dinars, and with the country's economy in shambles,
their value plummeted to roughly three thousand to the dollar. But
once the United States launched Operation Iraqi Freedom in 2003,
it began to look like it might become the investment opportunity of
a lifetime. If America rebuilt the country and installed a functional
government, it would theoretically bump the dinar up in value to
its Gulf War days, and anyone who had invested in dinars would
reap enormous profits with virtually no risk. Something similar had
happened to the Kuwaiti dinar, which lost most of its value after
Iraq's invasion, and regained it immediately after the Gulf War. And
the West German deutsche mark had experienced the same kind of
"economic miracle" after World War II, even without a massive oil
reserve underpinning its value. Ultimately, what did anyone have
to lose by spending a hundred bucks to buy a few hundred thousand dinars? The worst that could happen was nothing. The best was
fabulous wealth.

By 2006, there were robust Internet forums devoted to detect-
ing any sign of growth in Iraq's economy. The International Monetary Fund was besieged with calls about when the dinar would go
up in value. And most crucially, websites had sprung up selling the
currency in bulk. An ABC story from those early days spotlighted
numerous early dinar buyers who had snapped up tens of millions of
dinars, and believed that the "re-pegging" to the dollar would happen within a year, making them all rich.[30]

It didn't. But "dinarians," as they dubbed themselves, were only
just getting started. By 2012, there was a fully functional dinar ecosystem—full of the familiar tropes of affinity fraud. On one side were
the dinar brokers—slick websites like Currency Liquidator, Sterling
Currency Group, Safe Dinar, Bet on Iraq, and Treasury Vault, which
sold dinars as collectibles under the auspices of being "money service businesses."[31] And on the other end, you had the dinar gurus—
websites and message boards that didn't sell dinars, but pumped out

endless rumors, conspiracy theories, and straight-up lies. Gurus with names like TNT Tony, Dinar Daddy, and Wolfyman claimed that Iraq pulled three quarters of its currency out of circulation, that the monetary figures given by Iraq's government were bogus to throw off anti-dinar forces, and that George W. Bush said the Iraq War would pay for itself (note: he never said this) because he knew dinar riches were coming—and had already cashed out, along with his crony friends.[32]

Like Omega and NESARA before it, and Q after, the dinar depended on a magical event that would change everything for those who believed: "the RV," or the revalue. And like QAnon, that event was steeped in jargon, secret knowledge, and the feeling that "they" didn't want you to know about any of it.

When the RV was "released," the news first would go to "the mosques," so Iraqis could cash out their dinars. Then dinarians in the West would be provided with special 1-800 numbers to call and set up an appointment at their local bank or redemption center— "You do NOT want to just walk in and expect a bank to deal with you and give you the best rates," as one dinar update from 2013 put it.[33] To pull it off, you had to get dressed up, tell nobody where you were going (lest they try to steal your riches), and bring every form of ID you could find to a special entrance, where you were not to loiter. The bank would then provide you with a special account for your dinars where they'd be safe from US taxes—but only after you negotiated with the bank to get the best rate. Oh, and you'd sign an NDA vowing to never tell anyone what you did to become so rich.

The dinar exchange process was so complex, and the rewards so lucrative, that there soon appeared an anonymous e-book called *My Big, Fat, Wonderfully, Wealthy Life*, which told dinarians exactly how to get the most money out of the RV and all of the various legal instruments and tax shelters they'd need to protect it.[34]

"Have you considered that your CE [currency exchange] bank appointment will be the single most important financial event of your entire life?" goes one typically over the top passage in the book. "Bigger than your house. For most, bigger than your current net worth. Let that sink in. How much thought have you given to this CE? What if everything you thought about this moment came apart on you in that short 20 minutes? HOW?"

If dinarians, who had spent millions of dollars on the promise of a "wonderfully wealthy life," had truly thought about it, they would have realized they were being had. Currency doesn't "revalue" the way dinar gurus claimed it would, for one thing. Currencies can "redenominate," a process where hyperinflated currency is exchanged for bills of a lower denomination but the same value. Many developed nations have done that. But that's not the same thing as a "revalue," when a currency of little value suddenly explodes in value out of nowhere, with the holder left to negotiate what it's worth.

That doesn't happen. And even if it did, it wasn't going to happen with the dinar. One estimate from *Forbes* in 2014 said that there as many as 40 trillion dinars in circulation, with almost all of it floating around outside Iraq.[35] If the dinar were to revalue to its pre–Gulf War value, it would create $120 trillion of wealth—substantially more than the entire money supply of the planet, including money held in banks.[36] Some gurus promised "contract rates" of ten times even that—a financial catastrophe that would create quadrillions of dollars in wealth and immediately plunge the world into hyperinflation.

Beyond all that, though, the process of buying and selling dinars was unbelievably scammy. Most dinar brokers took about 20 percent off the top of any purchase, selling a million dinars for $1,100—when they were actually worth more like $900. And selling them back was nearly impossible. Not to mention that Iraq's economy continued to struggle with corruption, insurgency, and a lack of leadership.

All of it added up to a pernicious scam that defrauded countless people over the course of nearly two decades.

Even now, though, with all the arrests and disappointments,

these theories hang on, and have actually become more popular since QAnon arrived. Both NESARA and the dinar were specifically mentioned as defrauding several of the Q believers profiled in a 2021 *HuffPost* story.[37] All the while, they stay addicted to what skeptics deem "hopium"—the relentless and inexhaustible hope of a better future passed down through secret knowledge.

Like the promises of QAnon, that future never arrives. But unlike QAnon, the law could actually do something about these schemes. Clyde Hood and his acolytes went to prison, with Hood never leaving. Shaini Goodwin died with the IRS on her trail. And the numbers from various dinar prosecutions are sobering—a staggering $600 million defrauded by the dinar broker firm Sterling Currency Group, a $24 million dinar fraud in Ohio that went down in 2015, $2 million defrauded in a dinar scheme in Virginia that was busted in 2019, and the indictment of top dinar guru Anthony "TNT Tony" Renfrow for running a $1.6 million investment fraud scheme in 2015.[38] And many more that likely will never be known, thanks to the humiliation of their victims.

The minds behind creating and promoting QAnon didn't make these same mistakes. Q didn't sell currency or investments, but good feelings and community. It didn't promise vast riches, but the destruction of America's enemies. It didn't defraud you, it built you up and gave you a sense of purpose. And it evaded law enforcement by technically not doing anything illegal.

CHAPTER 5

We Are the News Now: QAnon Has a Big 2019

The first time President Donald Trump shared QAnon content, it was easy enough to justify.

On November 25, 2017, just weeks after the first Q drops on 4chan, Trump retweeted an account called @MAGAPILL, sharing a link to a site created by that account called "THE President Donald Trump Accomplishment List Website."[1] But @MAGAPILL was no ordinary red hat–wearing Trump disciple. They were also a supporter of the then-nascent QAnon conspiracy theory.*

Before his ban, Trump routinely used Twitter to praise himself, and to share praise from others—thousands of times over the course of his administration.[2] So if a "Presidential Accomplishment List" came across his feed, created by someone with "MAGA" in their handle, it's not shocking that he'd share it. For a while, the QAnon adherent in Trump's timeline appeared to be an outlier, and it would

---

* @MAGAPILL used #QAnon in a (now deleted) tweet just hours before Trump's retweet of the "accomplishment list" making a big deal out of Trump's claim that he'd "only stayed in Washington 17 times" before being elected president. Since Q is the seventeenth letter of the alphabet, Q believers thought Trump was shouting them out—despite there being no evidence that Trump or anyone in his orbit knew what QAnon was at that point. See Alex Kaplan, "Trump Has Repeatedly Amplified QAnon Twitter Accounts. The FBI Has Linked the Conspiracy Theory to Domestic Terror," *Media Matters*, August 1, 2019.

be almost another year before Trump would share material from another Q-linked account.

But by early 2019, Trump was routinely retweeting QAnon-promoting accounts, including an account whose avatar was a flaming Q wearing a MAGA hat. It was clear that the movement was getting in front of him more and more—to the point that by the 2020 election, Trump had retweeted hundreds of QAnon-promoting accounts, and was regularly sharing the memes created by members of the movement. And it wasn't just Donald Trump's Twitter that was becoming more receptive to Q and the ideas they were promoting. In the months after the Tampa rally, QAnon saw an explosion in growth across all platforms, with countless new members being pulled into Q's ever-expanding story of a secret and silent war between good and evil.

How big had Q gotten by spring 2019? As always with Q, actual numbers are hard to measure. Only abstract data points like hashtag uses and numbers of views on videos are available—both of which can be artificially boosted. But there are other, tangible events that happened around that time that show that the movement wasn't just growing, it was proving to be extremely durable.

By that point, Q had survived a string of failures that included the disaster in the 2018 midterms, the failure of any of the various memos or "real" investigations by Devin Nunes and other Trump supporters in Congress to hit pay dirt, and Robert Mueller failing to indict any pedophiles. Indeed, there were no indictments of anyone involved in the "deep state"—only of figures connected to Donald Trump. But the failures didn't seem to matter.

Q's presence itself even started to become obsolete. The timing and frequency of Q's posts were starting to become erratic and less frequent, often going weeks without word. But the Q movement was becoming increasingly able to subsist without the intel drops from its leader. The belief in Q's mythology, and the rightness of the cause they were supporting, was self-evident to its followers. Many believers were simply too far gone, adherents to a movement whose faith had become absolute. The *Vox* writer Jane Coaston described the movement as "[not] built on facts, but on almost religious fervor," taking on a messianic and unshakable faith in Trump, Q, and the righteousness of the plan.[3] Just after Trump retweeted the flaming Q–branded account, a Trump rally in Grand Rapids, Michigan, was swamped by QAnon followers to the point where one longtime Q watcher, the NBC "dystopia beat" reporter Ben Collins, tweeted that the size of the Q contingent in the crowd was "absolutely shocking."[4] The number of handmade Q signs and shirts was staggering—with rumors going around that the Secret Service had banned Q memorabilia from Trump rallies.[5]

"I just walked the entire line holding up this sign, full length uncut video upload late tonight or early tomorrow. Took over 20 minutes!!! Lots of noise!!! #WWG1WGA #QAnon #Qarmy #TrumpRally" tweeted the account @QuirkyFollowsQ, getting four thousand likes for their picture of a sign reading MAKE NOISE 4 Q.[6] Dozens of other rally attendees were shouted out in Q drops, with the "military intelligence team" spotlighting numerous individual believers there, calling them VIPs and patriots, and letting them know that they were seen and their efforts mattered.[7]

The buzz in the crowd, which was truly awash with Q gear, was that this was going to be the day that Trump would finally acknowledge the movement.[8] After all, he retweeted a video from the rally showing someone in a Q shirt.[9] Could tonight be the night? It wasn't, and he never mentioned Q in any way. But it didn't matter. It was clear by now that after a year and a half of growing adherence and huge Q attendance at Trump rallies, Q was here to stay. And if it wasn't clear from the hordes of Q believers showing up and representing at MAGA rallies, it would be clear another way: the top of the Amazon bestseller charts.

AN INVITATION TO THE GREAT AWAKENING

Who created the first piece of QAnon merchandise, and what was it? A bumper sticker? A flaming Q on a hat? Someone just grabbing a Sharpie and scrawling "#QAnon" on a perfectly innocent white T-shirt? It's likely lost to history. But whoever created it soon had a lot of competition—within less than a year of Q's first drops, there were thousands of Q branded items for sale on Amazon. The e-commerce giant offered everything from "coffee mugs, bumper stickers, mobile phone cases and grips, pet collars, books and rap songs," according to one *NBC News* story, with much of the gear eligible for free shipping.[10] Amazon made no effort at all to police this material until after the Capitol riot, pulling much—though not all—of it down. Nor did crafts giant Etsy, which had a huge array of homemade Q swag to offer, because none of it violated their anti-harassment policies. There were Q Patreon pages and GoFundMe campaigns. Q T-shirts were on Teespring, and there were Q apps on the Google Play Store.

Exact numbers of who made how much money are impossible to track. But it's clear that YouTube ad revenue, merchandise sales, books sales, and other income streams were making a lot of Q believers at least some money. And for a few, it was quite a bit.

Some Q believers were so devoted to cashing in on the movement that they actually attempted to trademark some of Q's most heavily used slogans.[11] Q promoter and new media content creator Dustin "Nemos" Krieger claimed to Reuters that he'd lost between $1 million and $2 million in potential sales from his Q merchandise stores being pulled down in the wake of the Capitol attack.[12] One of the biggest recipients of the generosity of QAnon believers was its hero, the gallant former general Michael Flynn. Facing legal bills which had ballooned to nearly $5 million while he went "deep cover" inside the deep state, Flynn profited immensely from selling QAnon merchandise and speaking at QAnon-related events.[13]

But no piece of QAnon merchandise would be as effective at "red-pilling" new converts—or drawing media attention—than one of the movement's first big hits: the hugely successful book *QAnon: An Invitation to the Great Awakening.* After all, plenty of books come out every week. But only a few hit the top of the charts—and maybe none quite so crudely written and utterly devoid of substance as this one.

The self-published work of an anonymous collective of a dozen authors calling themselves WWG1WGA, *An Invitation to the Great Awakening* hit Amazon in late February 2019 and immediately became the gold standard of Q books—standing out among a field of slapped together e-books and SEO grabs. Its chapters purport to do just what the title says: introduce new converts to the basics of how Q communicates, the messages that the Q poster is actually saying, how to interpret them, and why it all matters so much. "Our job is to generate a future that reclaims the reins of power from the forces that would abuse our children and enslave us," reads the book's introduction. "Our intention is to take them back and restore them to 'We the People.'"[14] Theoretically, at least.

The book's creators, speaking to Will Sommer at *the Daily Beast*, later revealed that the origins of the book aren't quite that lofty, residing not in a burning desire to wake up the masses but to get back at Reddit for banning the QAnon movement by putting their material in a collective form that couldn't be de-platformed.[15] "Nobody thought it would be a bestseller," one of the authors told Sommer.

So the book should be looked at less as an edification for readers, and more as an airing of grievances. This helps explain why this "introduction" to QAnon is so full of Q jargon that it would likely make no sense to outsiders. What it does contain is deep and detailed explanations of Q drops that are either hopelessly vague or cynically facile, and entire chapters padded out with transcripts of YouTube videos or interviews with people who have nothing to do with Q.

But like so much in QAnon, the accuracy or coherence of what was being said didn't matter—only that it was saying things that its believers agree with. And there were many people who agreed with it. The many, many people snapping the book up and leaving rapturous reviews didn't care that the book misspells Trump mentor Roy Cohn's last name, is full of citations to dead links, or goes off on wild tangents that have nothing to do with Q. A lot of people were getting turned on to Q for the first time, and to them, a book like this was everything they'd been looking for. And Amazon's algorithm made sure that it got in front of them, fueled by a huge clutch of initial sales.[16]

Almost at once, the book was deluged by hyperbolic five-star reviews calling it a masterpiece, a must-read, and "300 pages of amazing information." [17] (The book is 270 pages.) Many of the reviews, in turn, had hundreds of recommendations themselves. Could there have been artificial boosting going on? Maybe, but most likely, it was like-minded souls recognizing each other on the road to freedom.

Within days, the book shot to the Amazon bestseller lists—to number two in the automatically generated New Releases chart, to the top ten in Politics, and to the number-one spot in the Censorship section, ahead of *Fahrenheit 451* and *The Handmaid's Tale*. All told, of the almost twenty-four hundred reviews of the book by the end of 2020, 80 percent were five stars, and it was still a top one-hundred book in several Amazon categories until the site pulled it down in the wake of the Capitol attack. It was a legitimate hit, and a massive driver of discourse about the movement. A few other Q books have had some degree of success, including a book by stalwart Q promoter Praying Medic, which racked up over thirteen hundred positive reviews in less than a year. But none blew up to the degree that *An Invitation to the Great Awakening* did. Ultimately, the book was so successful that its creators started publicly fighting over the money they made from it while accusing each other of being grifters.[18] The WWG1WGA collective would never release another book.

The twin peaks of March 2019—the Grand Rapids rally and the success of *An Invitation to the Great Awakening*—proved that, far from being the flash in the pan of many recent conspiracy theories, Q had the ability to survive usually seen only in cockroaches. More people were finding something in QAnon that filled a need in their life—and Google Trends searches for "QAnon" spiked multiple times that month.[19] Maybe it was the promise of Hillary Clinton finally paying for her myriad (and unproven) crimes. Maybe it was the fun of decoding Q's drops and puzzling out their true meaning. Or maybe it was the friends they were making along the way. But it was clear that nothing negative could impact this movement. Any act of violence or negative coverage was dismissed as a false flag and a hoax by Q believers and Q themselves in Drop #3310:

Threat to Controlled Narrative.
Other than POTUS, can you name a group more attacked than 'Q' by the FAKE NEWS media.
Multiple tactics deployed including framing for crimes (think bridge, mob boss, etc etc).
DESPERATION.
Reconcile using logic.
THINK FOR YOURSELF.
DIVIDERS will FAIL.

The growth in Q's popularity and the matching growth of violent acts perpetrated by its followers (whether or not they had anything to do with Q) were forcing the mainstream media to give it credence. But this rapidly growing, enthusiastic, prolific group was also ripe for exploitation, like all cultic movements dependent on information passed down from top to bottom. And not all attention is good attention. These major events in the Q timeline brought publicity, but they also brought scrutiny.

With the combination of an increasing base of followers and more media focus, Q was needed more than ever. And Q continued to post intermittently, sometimes going weeks between drops.

This left space for the gurus and interpreters to assert themselves more and drive the direction of the movement's research efforts. The potential for misuse was about to be realized.

"FIVE JIHAD(S)?"

A former mining town turned tourist haven, Grass Valley is about sixty miles northeast of Sacramento, in heavily Republican Nevada County, California. With a population of about thirteen thousand, it's a hub for day trips and the local tech industry, but not exactly a strategic target to cripple financial or manufacturing sectors. In short, it's an exceedingly unlikely target for a false-flag attack by the deep state to sow panic and confusion in the population.

Or maybe that's what they want you to think.

Whatever the case, in April 2019, the intrepid Twitter user @TopInfoBlogs claimed that they were able to determine that a "jihad" against an innocent school event in tiny Grass Valley was on the verge of taking place. @TopInfoBlogs, an anonymous account whose job it was to "collect, list and participate in the Blogoshphere [*sic*]," took a break from their nonstop retweeting of pro-Trump and pro-Q posts to find a hidden message in a tweet by former FBI director turned Trump nemesis James Comey. Jumping on a perfectly harmless Twitter trend on April 27, Comey tweeted:

#FIVEJOBSIVEHAD

1. Grocery store clerk
2. Vocal soloist for church weddings
3. Chemist
4. Strike-replacement high school teacher
5. FBI Director, Interrupted[20]

Using powers of deduction that can only come from a highly attuned ability to see things that aren't there, @TopInfoBlogs figured

out that Comey wasn't just goofing off a bit on Twitter, but announcing an upcoming attack he was planning. How? By deciding that
"Five Jobs I've Had" was short for "FIVE JIHAD," then making an
acrostic of the first letters in the five jobs, and going with the first
thing that came up on Google. What came up was the Grass Valley
Charter School Foundation—which happened to be holding its Blue
Marble Jubilee auction and fundraising event on May 11.

The timing was unfortunate. @TopInfoBlogs made a meme that
declared "FF [false flag] ALERT??" and rather than go to the FBI
with their "research," they shared it with Joe M (@StormIsUponUs),
a prolific QAnon promoter and conspiracy theorist.* @TopInfoB-
logs wrote:

> Joe, have you seen this possible decode of Comey's latest
> "bizarre" tweet? It's possibly a coded FF message—and the
> possible "target" is a big school/family event at a Nevada [sic]
> fairgrounds.
> The date is around the time these things will be breaking
> also.😕😐[21]

Joe M, never one to find a conspiracy theory too bizarre to be
real, shared the meme and declared in a now-deleted tweet to his
hundreds of thousands of followers: *"Nothing better happen at Grass
Valley Charter School (@gvcharter) during their Blue Marble Jubilee
on May 11, Jim."*[22]

The tweet quickly got thousands of retweets. Joe M's many followers were convinced that one of Donald Trump's most powerful
enemies was tipping his hand in the open. And they started warning
Grass Valley Charter School. It was the deep, ugly concern of people

---

* The @StormIsUponUs account was eventually suspended by Twitter in April
2020 for telling their quarter of a million followers to "fire at will" at Democrats
supposedly behind the COVID-19 "hoax." See Mike Rothschild, "The Storm Is
(Not) Upon Us," *TheMikeRothschild.com* (blog), April 9, 2020.

who are determined to think you're in danger, and that it's their job to protect you, while the only real danger is their protection.

The emails and calls started coming in from Q believers to the Grass Valley Charter School, the local Chamber of Commerce, and to the fairgrounds where the fundraiser was set to take place. As president of the Grass Valley Charter School Foundation, Wendy Willoughby was the point person to deal with issues like this—but where do you even start?

"We received some emails that were disturbing and [the school] wanted me to know they all had been turned over to our District and our local authorities," Willoughby told me in an interview in 2020.[23] The deeper she went down the rabbit hole of Q and the emails, the more it physically got to her—her chest tightened and she sat reading in the dark, well past midnight. She read emails and tweets in her car outside her house, feeling more and more dissociated and overcome with emotion. How could this firestorm of nonsense possibly touch this tiny little event? What was going on here? Was there any danger?

Looking back on it a year later, Willoughby told me she was at first baffled by all of the attention suddenly swirling around her little event. But on realizing that this wasn't a joke, she burst into tears.

The next morning, concerned parents started calling the principal to figure out what was going on. What could administrators tell them? That an anonymous Twitter account told another anonymous Twitter account that James Comey tweeted in code that he was going to attack their fundraiser as part of his war against Donald Trump? And that online "digital soldiers" were afraid that the festival was going to be the scene of a massive child kidnapping? None of that is reassuring to parents.

Dozens of calls and emails were sent to various local figures, warning them of a terrorist attack. Several new videos were produced analyzing the Comey tweet for what it "really" meant—with some researchers mistaking Nevada County for the state of Nevada.

And freaked-out parents were demanding answers from office staff, who themselves had no idea what was going on. QAnon followers did not make any threats, but many expressed real concern for the safety of Grass Valley—one email to Willoughby pleaded her to increase security around the event or cancel it outright because "this kind of insanity is what drives mass shooters."

Another festival organizer, Kathy Dotson, told me in 2019 that by this point, because of the hysteria over the tweets and the reasonable fears of parents, "a successful and well-attended event was not a probability." So the Blue Marble Jubilee, a tiny fundraiser for a tiny charter school in a tiny town, was canceled. Because of a tweet from a QAnon guru.

In a twist of fate worthy of the best conspiracy theories, the Jubilee was canceled again in 2020, thanks to the COVID-19 pandemic. Willoughby told me afterward that with parents having lost two years of involvement in the school foundation, she wasn't sure if there would ever be another Blue Marble Jubilee. And she laid the damage squarely at the feet of QAnon and its followers.

Joe M, for his part, felt no remorse whatsoever, tweeting "I don't give a damn about the trolls attacking us for invoking the cancelation of this event, even if it was a false positive. Comey's Twitter account is definitely being used to transmit coded messages to activate cells."[24]

In fact, the false-flag believers decided they had evidence that proved they were right—after the event had already been canceled. On May 19, eight days after the Blue Marble Jubilee was to have taken place, the fifty-three-year-old Grass Valley resident Mary Lee Dalton was arrested after liquid explosive bombs were found in her closet. Dalton claimed they belonged to a tenant, and police couldn't find an apparent target for the bombs.[25] But Q believers discarded the inconvenient details of the arrest that would falsify their theory, namely that it took place a week after the event, and clung to the elements that matched up with what they believed. "Someone" was going to attack the Blue Marble Jubilee, and Mary Lee Dalton (who eventually pleaded guilty to the charge) was "someone." Therefore, the anons were right about all of it, even when most of it was wrong.

"Anons decoded the Grass Valley incident and prevented it while being labeled as a conspiracy theorist all while it was mysteriously true," gloated one anon on 8chan, while a Q believer on Twitter declared in a tweet shared over two thousand times: "Joe M vindicated! Patriots save lives! Suck it trolls!" and "Shout out to @StormIsUponUs Saving Patriots from another false flag!"[26]

But Wendy Willoughby knew the truth. "For those that believe that they thwarted a disaster, you saved no one," she told me in 2019. "If you want to make this country and the world a better place, then get off your screens and find somewhere to volunteer, maybe you could choose a school or organization that supports children. You need to make up for what you did."

For all of the attention the Grass Valley incident brought QAnon, Q didn't reap the rewards. The whole thing came during a fallow period for Q drops—just forty-two posts total from April to June. Q never mentioned Grass Valley, never directed their followers to research it, never encouraged anyone to report it. From Q's drops alone, which are theoretically the marching orders for this movement, you'd never even know it happened. It signaled a new and confusing stage in QAnon's development, one where Q's drops revealed less and were reactive, rather than proactive. They were commentary, not revelations. And sometimes, they didn't come at all.

Q had become a robust community that had survived countless disconfirmations, being kicked off its main social hub in Reddit, and numerous ugly national news stories. Indeed, it hadn't just survived, it had prospered, gaining a core of deeply dug-in patriots to follow it. There was money being made. Life, such as it is when you're sucked into a joyless conspiracy movement, was good.

"A CESSPOOL OF HATE"

Q seemed to be invulnerable. But the same could not be said for 8chan, Q's home since December 2017.

On August 3, 2019, twenty minutes before a twenty-one-year-old Texas resident opened fire at a Walmart in El Paso with an AR-15, killing twenty-three people and wounding twenty-three more, he uploaded his manifesto to 8chan. The incoherent screed, which touched on immigration and economics, was the third such document uploaded by a mass shooter to the imageboard, following those from the Christchurch, New Zealand, shooter who killed fifty-one people and the shooter who opened fire at a synagogue in Poway, California, and killed one person.[27] It also openly referenced both the Christchurch shooting and the unmoderated racist "discussions" that made up so much of 8chan's niche appeal.

Three manifestos by three alleged shooters, all uploaded to 8chan's /pol/ board, whose users had cheered on the Christchurch shooter as he livestreamed his rampage.[28] The imageboard wasn't just the home of racist memes and incoherent conspiracy theories—it was becoming part of the modus operandi of mass shooters. It was a place where these shooters were venerated as heroes and it had to stop.

"8chan has repeatedly proven itself to be a cesspool of hate," wrote Matthew Prince, the CEO of 8chan's security provider Cloudflare, in a blog post announcing the site's termination of service.[29] "We reluctantly tolerate content that we find reprehensible, but we draw the line at platforms that have demonstrated they directly inspire tragic events and are lawless by design. 8chan has crossed that line. It will therefore no longer be allowed to use our services."

When Cloudflare pulled 8chan's protection from hacking, a major denial of service attack by an unknown hacker immediately brought the imageboard down—silencing Q in the process. There was one brief attempt to resurrect the site a few days later when 8chan users founded a clone of the site on a peer-to-peer network, only to realize they were exposing their IP addresses and opening themselves up to "accidentally" downloading child porn.[30] It became clear that just as the racists on /pol/ would need to find something else to do, so would Q's digital army.

It was clear to everyone but Q acolytes, anyway. They kept the faith. After all, Q's silence that August wasn't all that different from the silences that Q had gone into before that. "Expect Q team to be 'officially' silent until 8chan is back online, which will only be AFTER congressional hearings on 9/5," declared one Q influencer on Twitter in late August, referencing the House Homeland Security Committee's subpoena of Jim Watkins.[31] And Watkins himself claimed in early September that the site would be back at any moment.[32]

It did not come back up right away, but it wasn't for lack of trying. Over the next three months, Jim Watkins and his son, Ron, tried a number of different avenues to get their board back up and running, rebranding it as "8kun"—a name change meant to denote that the "chan," an honorific used in Japanese to express affection for babies, children, and honored elders, had grown into a "kun," denoting an older and more respected person. And after a while the Watkinses finally found a new web host—a Vancouver, Washington, programmer named Nick Lim, who had founded the Internet service provider (ISP) BitMitigate, which also hosted the neo-Nazi message board the Daily Stormer.[33] Lim did business by the motto "If it's legal, I don't care," and evidently, he didn't.[34] Because 8kun—bringing with it all of the racism and anarchy of 8chan—was announced a few weeks later – with security provided by Lim's company. Lim claimed he didn't know what QAnon was, and only hosted 8kun and the Daily Stormer because others had tried to take them down.

But 8chan's founder turned Watkins family nemesis, Fredrick Brennan, didn't believe 8chan could grow up. Indeed, he believed it needed to die.[35] As soon as 8chan went down, and long before it found a home with Nick Lim's ISP, an enraged Brennan had been using his social media following and journalist contacts to publicly pressure networks into having nothing to do with the lightly rebranded 8chan. Every time 8kun found a new security provider, Brennan applied pressure. First it was a British web service company that took on and quickly punted 8kun, then the Chinese e-commerce giants Tencent and Alibaba, followed by a Russian ISP. Brennan pressured all of them: Do you really want to do business with these people, these arbiters of mass-shooter manifestos? And mostly, they didn't. In the next few months, 8kun was up and down over and over again—and Q was silent.

While the initial de-platforming of 8chan wasn't related to QAnon, Brennan believed the effort to resurrect it was tied up with the conspiracy—and that Q (whoever that was) was in direct communication with Jim and Ron Watkins.[36] It certainly wasn't the income from 8chan driving the duo's efforts—most of his finances were derived from other ventures. Maybe Jim Watkins really believed his website was integral to realizing "the storm." Or maybe the Watkinses knew that Q was the most consistent driver of traffic to 8chan that didn't involve the potential of mass-shooter manifestos. Both Jim and Ron Watkins have denied being Q on many occasions, and would continue to do so all the way through the Trump years.

In November 2019, Brennan told NPR's *On the Media* podcast that a top Watkins employee had told him that while Watkins believed 8chan itself was dead, its owner was focused on "getting the Q people back" on a new venture.[37] Ultimately, that new venture was just the old venture. While it's still not rock solid proof that Watkins is directly linked to Q, it is striking that Q stayed silent the entire time 8chan was down. Recall that in January 2018, right after Q's departure from Paul Furber's board, Q declared several times that there would be "no outside comms"—that is, Q would never post anywhere but 8chan – and was provided with extra security to confirm their identity by Ron Watkins in the form of a secure tripcode. So Q only existed on 8chan, and it appears that 8chan's new home needed Q to drive followers to.

Why a military intelligence group given a sacred task of liberating America and the world from a Satanic cabal would depend entirely on the availability of a janky message board owned by a porn maven in the Philippines wasn't a question that Q believers were interested in asking. Even when Q was silent for months, nobody in the movement seemed bothered by it. Maybe for those months the world just didn't need saving.

In any case, the battle continued—"8kun will be back, and stronger than ever before," tweeted Nick Lim in late October after yet another 8kun crash.[38] Eventually, it found a home with a Russian hosting site called Media Land LLC—a host credibly connected by cybersecurity researchers to a wide array of credit card fraud schemes, malware, and phishing scams.[39] So, thanks to a host located in the Russian port city Vladivostok and a few hours from the North Korean border, the great American patriotic icon Q was back. Drop #3579, on November 11, 2019, declared:

/agg_image_failure/
/route_DoD_11.11.18/
America Will Be Unified Again.
Future Proves Past.
Q

Despite 8kun's continued outages and hosting problems, including a period where Q could post but other 8kun users couldn't, Q seemed back for good by late 2019. The site eventually moved to Nick Lim's own host, VanwaTech, which he'd founded apparently just to host 8kun—and which Fredrick Brennan was convinced Jim Watkins partially owned, an accusation Lim has denied.[40] Since then, Lim has used a variety of IP addresses and hosts, all based in Russia, to ensure 8kun couldn't be taken down and Q could keep on being Q. And with Q back, things were looking up in MAGA world.

Trump seemed to be winning all over the place, with his enemies driven before him: the economy was on overdrive, the Democrats were courting disaster by pushing in all their chips on what the MAGA/Q community saw as a visibly ailing Joe Biden for president, and Trump's impeachment had failed to result in a conviction.

But the universe would have other plans for the Q movement. While Trump would stumble through the events to come, Q would only grow bigger, more violent, and into ever more of a conspiracy theory of everything—all thanks to the COVID-19 pandemic.

Whatever Q had been, whatever those 4chan anons had started, and what Jim and Ron Watkins and Nick Lim and the other characters in their orbit had resurrected, it wasn't going to be that again. It was going to be much bigger.

CHAPTER 6

God Wins: Why People Believe in QAnon

To any reasonable person, the failure of a long-foretold event erodes the belief that it will happen. But belief isn't reasonable. And this stubborn lack of logic isn't limited to people who think the deep state is trying to murder their children. We all have an innate need to believe in good things that are extremely unlikely to take place. It's the essence of hope. Chicago Cubs fans spent an entire century, one generation after another, insisting that maybe they'd win the World Series next year—and every year they were let down. Until the year they did win the World Series, that is. Most Christians wait for the Second Coming of Christ, and century after century, Christ does not come again. This is not a sign of lunacy, it's the way belief works. These things give people hope. And a life without hope is . . . hopeless.

Even when presented with crushing proof that they've been fooled, they still believe—often taking the proof that they're wrong as proof that they're actually right and are over the target. To do otherwise would be to give in to hopelessness.

That's how it's gone with Q's precursors. Even as local governments and law enforcement agencies put out notices warning people that the dinar was a scam, and after numerous dinar brokers were indicted, dinar-guru message boards still pumped out "intel updates." In 2018, the *Daily Beast* reported on Trump supporters who were making huge dinar purchases based on a cryptic comment from the president that "all currencies would be on a level playing field" in his dealings with China.[1] During the COVID-19 lockdown, hundreds of thousands of tweets mentioning NESARA were sent, while people claimed without evidence that their credit card debt and mortgages were suddenly vanishing, and that the CARES Act—passed by Congress in May to bolster the COVID-ravaged economy—was actually the long-awaited release of "prosperity packets."[2]

By the time of the COVID lockdown, Q had been exposed countless times as a fraud and a troll with no connection to military intelligence whose "predictions" were the same kind of rapid-fire guessing that a strip-mall psychic uses, while the movement's members were running into the law for their increasingly violent and untethered behavior. But to the faithful, these were all temporary setbacks, perpetrated by a bought-and-paid-for media. Everyone just needed to trust the plan and believe.

As Q would say many times, "Nothing can stop what is coming. Nothing."

ANOTHER NEW HOPE

To understand why QAnon followers believe in spite of everything requires understanding why people believe in conspiracy theories in the first place.

Human brains need to recognize dangerous situations, and we are hardwired to seek patterns, to find order in chaos, and to exert control where none can be found. Conspiracy theories, at their most basic level, assert that we are in danger from hidden forces. This helps give difficult questions and random events satisfying answers—and puts us at the center of those events. A person doesn't get cancer because of some randomly misfiring cells—they got it because of chemtrails or 5G Internet or microchips poisoning them.

Our beloved candidate didn't lose an election because they ran a poor campaign—they lost because of the conspiracy of a corrupt cabal to keep them from power. And on and on.

Our lives are often full of failure—personal, professional, and collective. We don't want to believe these failures are due to honest mistakes by others or random chance. And most of all, we don't want to believe that they're our own fault. To believe otherwise is to believe that either we screwed up, or that we have no control over what happens to us. And that's just too horrible to accept.

"Conspiracy theories resonate with some of our brain's built-in biases and shortcuts, and tap into some of our deepest desires, fears, and assumptions about the world and the people in it," writes author and psychologist Rob Brotherton in the introduction to his groundbreaking book *Suspicious Minds: Why We Believe Conspiracy Theories.* "We are all natural-born conspiracy theorists."[3]

Such beliefs don't begin with the Internet, nor are they more prevalent in the Internet age. Decades of polling consistently show that over half of Americans believe in some conspiracy theory, and that about as many people in 1963 believed that multiple assassins killed JFK as they did in 2013.[4]

As long as something major and unexpected takes place, there will be people who witness it and struggle to explain it. In his book, Brotherton goes all the way back to the years after the Great Fire of Rome in 64 CE to find the legendary Roman historian Tacitus writing up rumors that gangs of thugs kept citizens from fighting the fires, and that the corrupt emperor Nero had set the devastating fire for his own aims. Tacitus himself would have been around eight years old at the time of the Great Fire, so he would have been working with secondhand sources decades later. But it's clear that even as he and successor Roman historians contemplated "what really happened" in the Great Fire, the conspiracy was durable enough to stay with us two millennia later.

Conspiracy theories can be held by people who work normal

jobs, have loving families, and don't spend every hour of every day soaking in violent ideation. They can take the form merely of irritating our friends with *yet another* ramble about whatever hidden chicanery we've chosen to believe in—our phone breaking suspiciously just as the service contract expires so that we have to buy a new one, and so on. They can even be fun to speculate about—like the viral conspiracy theory about Chuck E. Cheese "recycling" unused pizza slices to make misshapen new pizzas.[5]

Notions that someone is trying to get something over on us go viral for a good reason: many times, someone *is* trying to get something over on us. Life is full of scams, rip-offs, fraud, small-time crooks, cheapskates, and shady types trying to make a buck at our expense. To assume that there are many forces out there trying to screw us or hurt us is not delusional. In fact, it might just mean your brain is working the way it should be. As the science writer and podcaster Brian Dunning put it in a 2011 episode of his podcast *Skeptoid*, while some conspiracy believers need help, most do not. Because there's nothing wrong with them.

"If you've had a conversation with a conspiracy theorist—and almost all of us have—you've met people who do *not* display symptoms of delusional disorder far more often than those who do," he said. "The ordinary conspiracy theorist is an intelligent, sane, and generally rational person. They are, in fact, unsettlingly less different from *you* than you may have thought."[6]

If you're hearing danger in a strange noise late at night, or looking at a world event and thinking that there must be more to it than what we're being told, you're just doing what your brain has evolved to do as a way to make sense of it. And we all do it. But some of us do it more than others.

CONSPIRACIES THAT CAME TRUE

The balance between appreciating danger in the world around us and the unswerving faith in a conspiracy theory comes to a head in the false equivalence between unproven theories and misdeeds that have been retroactively discovered. To conspiracy theorists the latter are considered "conspiracy theories that came true," and proof that whatever conspiracy currently being argued is also true. But there is a crucial difference between conspiracy theories and conspiracies.

Conspiracies, of course, are real. Nobody disputes that. To use the example of someone else's misdeeds giving us cancer, there have been plenty of instances when someone's else's misdeeds *did* give people cancer—but those misdeeds didn't involve chemtrails or 5G Internet poisoning, because those aren't real things. Toxic dumping, hiding carcinogens in food, polluting water, and the like actually give people cancer, and are carried out by major companies all the time. These are real things.

Even before Rome's burning spawned whispers of conspiracy, Julius Caesar was murdered by a group of Roman politicians conspiring together to both restore power to the Senate and to settle old grudges.[7] And 150 years before an attack on the Capitol that nearly culminated in the vice president being set on by a gang of insurrectionists, a conspiracy of killers attempted to assassinate the president, vice president, and secretary of war—with only one assassin, John Wilkes Booth, succeeding in killing President Abraham Lincoln. A conspiracy of German officers tried to kill Adolf Hitler in July 1944. And the US Public Health Service engaged in a grossly unethical four-decade conspiracy to withhold syphilis treatment from Black sharecroppers in Tuskegee, Alabama.

All of these are conspiracies. But they are not "conspiracy theories that came true" because none were theorized in any specific way.[8] Nobody knew about them, and many were only revealed thanks to whistleblowers, the revelation of legal documents, or the arrests of the conspirators. Likewise, none of the widely held conspiracy *theories* so popular in today's discourse, from the supposed poisonous spraying of chemtrails in the air to 9/11 being an inside job carried out by the US government, have ever been "revealed" as the truth. Their sheer size and scope make them all but impossible.

Despite this, QAnon posters like to use "true conspiracy theories" as a rhetorical trick to prove QAnon's plausibility. One of the so-called verified conspiracies of the past that is most referenced in Q's mythology is the supposed manipulation of the media by the CIA called Operation Mockingbird, which Q supporters take as evidence that the CIA paid journalists to write favorable stories about it. Another is the CIA's real and grossly unethical experiments carried out under the MKUltra banner to explore methods of mind control—which Q has hinted are still going on.

Even though such misdeeds by the CIA have been verified, they are often used in conspiracy theory circles to insinuate something much more sordid than the actual evidence corroborates. As far as Operation Mockingbird goes, the only documents available on it show it to be the surveillance of two Washington-based reporters over a few months in 1963—unethical, for sure, but not a massive and long-running conspiracy.[9] And that dubious venture was called "Project Mockingbird," not "Operation Mockingbird." Likewise, the government revealed that it had dosed unwitting people with LSD as part of a cluster of over 160 experiments during the 1950s and '60s collectively called MKUltra, but it abandoned the project and never achieved any measure of mind control over its subjects.[10]

But people believe the conspiracy theories because they fit in with the biases they already have about how the world "really" works. As we've seen, this is not necessarily a bad thing. But for many Q believers, that nebulous feeling that *They're all out to get me* becomes *They're all out to get me, and I'm gonna get them first*. This is the danger of Q—not that people believe it, but that believing it means that those who don't are the enemy. And as we've seen again and again, from Hoover Dam to the Capitol, it's extremely dangerous.

For the Q believer, then, Q is not a conspiracy theory—and many believers bristle at the term, calling themselves "conspiracy researchers" instead. And it provides its believers something nobody usually expects out of cultish conspiracy movements—hope.

GOOD GUYS DOING GOOD

For much of Q's existence, its stereotypical follower was a white American conservative driven to joylessness by their sense of persecution by liberal elites and obsession with Donald Trump's greatness. In other words, they looked and acted nothing like former QAnon believer Jitarth Jadeja. A progressive Australian of Indian descent, Jadeja has a booming, easy laugh and considers himself pro-choice, pro–drug legalization, pro–Bernie Sanders, and anti-establishment. He's the antithesis to the demographic that got caught up in an American conspiracy theory that is cheerleading a military takeover of the country after progressives are purged.

Yet he got caught up in it. Jadeja spent two years enmeshed in QAnon, to the point where he pushed away much of his social circle and found himself increasingly isolated and obsessed with what Q was telling him.[11] Before he got into Q, Jadeja had been baffled by the mainstream media's failure to see Donald Trump's rise coming, so he went searching for alternative explanations for the mainstream media's denial and ignorance. Naturally, he found plenty.

First came the conspiracy theory machine that was Infowars, and from Alex Jones, he got sucked into Jerome Corsi's breathless decoding of Q drops. In Q, Jadeja found not only better explanations for what was going on, but patriots pushing back against the darkness. As he told me, he found the good guys. His belief in Q, which lasted from late 2017 until well into 2019, wasn't "a logical thing." It was hope.

"I wanted to believe," Jadeja told me over a Zoom call that took weeks to schedule. His story of leaving Q had made him a momentary media sensation, as there were virtually no out-and-proud Q apostates at the time. And his story rang true for many people.

"I wanted to believe that the good guys were fighting the good fight, and in a better future," he said.

The story that Q laid out explained so much to Jitarth Jadeja. It explained why the Democratic Party in America had screwed over Bernie Sanders—Hillary and her cabal did it to stay in power. It explained why the media didn't see Trump's win coming—they were irredeemably corrupt and utterly blind to the "people's movement" that Trump had created. And it explained Trump's constant failure to deliver on his promises to lock Hillary up or reform the Federal Reserve or do any of the other "anti-establishment" things he promised to do—the deep state was thwarting him at every turn, or else he was failing on purpose in order to expose their evil. Q told him that a secret war was being fought to get rid of all these horrible people and fulfill Trump's divine promise. It was a war Jadeja wanted to fight.

It happened slowly, then all at once. At a low point after failing again to graduate from university and receiving an ADHD diagnosis, Jadeja spent months consuming Q media and interacting with fellow Q believers. He was soon on Reddit and YouTube all the time, watching endless streams of videos and reading the decoding threads of the Q gurus who could make sense of the cryptic messages. Q initially brought him a sense of joy and control, making him feel like he wasn't like everyone else. He wasn't a failure who couldn't move forward, but a warrior whose ADHD gave him an ability to hyperfocus. Q made him an asset, not a screwup.

"Q makes you feel important and gives you meaning and self-esteem," he told me, echoing a sentiment that current Q believers share on social media all the time. "You are saving the world when you're in Q, [it's] the highest way you can view yourself." And while Q believers immerse themselves in a violent and cynical mythology, they don't see it as anarchic or violent. They certainly don't see it as domestic terrorism. They see a secret war that must be won.

To Jadeja, Q believers "can only overcome [the darkness] by thinking they're doing the most important thing that can be done": literally saving the world. Looking back, his ADHD diagnosis and its ripple effects played right into this mindset, and had a major role in sending him running to QAnon. Many Q believers see themselves as "weaponizing" their lack of social skills, inability to read social cues, and repetitive behaviors—all of which are the classic symptoms of autism. These "autists" proudly flash their unique abilities by digging deep to solve Q's puzzles—the "corn code" and "dog code" seen in the tweets of powerful politicians who supposedly use anodyne pictures of pets or crops to signal major events in the war between good and evil, or the belief that typos in Trump tweets meant something more than a president who couldn't spell. They even explicitly label their skill set "weaponized autism," a term that took off on 4chan around the same time as Q did.[12] Jadeja began to see himself in the same light, with Q's cryptic clues allowing him to use his ADHD, something that the world saw as a crippling handicap, for good. He responded by pouring all of his time and effort into Q to the point of shutting everything else out.

Bit by bit, Jadeja transformed from an optimistic yet skeptical progressive into a cynical conspiracy obsessive, increasingly unable to talk about anything else other than Q. And he had no motivation to stop—not family, work, hobbies, nothing. Those people he remained connected to were either left in the dark or pulled down with him. While he kept his belief in Q from his extended family and friends—he knew how ridiculous it would sound to them—he did introduce it to his father, with whom he quickly formed a bond over the secret knowledge they were gathering. That bond became so strong that even after Jadeja left Q behind, his father was still a QAnon believer.

"Q cuts you off from society and uses that to draw you in and isolate you with likeminded people," he explained to me. "People can't leave, there's no incentive to admit they're wrong. [If you] admit [it] to friends and society, people don't look at you the same. People in your life drift away, with relationships damaged forever, and you did that, not Q."

The hope that fueled his initial belief turned into a type of addiction—an addiction to Q drops, to the discourse, to the special feeling of knowing something other people didn't. And ultimately, to that desperate need for something better. But no addiction can be this all-encompassing and not be harmful. Jitarth Jadeja's addiction would drive him to the edge of losing his family and his sanity in a swamp of conspiracies and cynicism. It took him two years and several undeniable disconfirmations that he couldn't explain away, but he eventually got out.

While his process of leaving Q and conspiracy theories behind isn't over, he's much further along than other people we'll meet. And the believers he left behind have no interest in joining him on the outside.

THE RIGHT JOURNEY, THE WRONG WAY

To the skeptic looking at Q from the outside, all of this seems absurd. And to be sure, many journalists and scholars have written the Q movement off as just that. "If it sounds crazy, that's because it is," wrote Jan-Willem van Prooijen, a Dutch professor of applied psychology, in an NBC opinion piece in 2018.[13] Some of the earliest writing about QAnon called it "an insane conspiracy theory tearing up 4chan," while *Buzzfeed* stopped calling it a conspiracy theory altogether and tarred Q with the inaccurate and unfair moniker "collective delusion," as if everyone who believed it were mentally ill.[14] Even journalists who write sympathetically about Q have a hard time resisting calling the movement's tenets ludicrous, and commenting on how bizarre it all is.[15]

Undoubtedly, at least some Q believers are mentally ill, to the point of being unable to stand trial for crimes. Others are probably in it for the trolling—or because they really hate Jews and Democrats, or worship Donald Trump to an unhealthy degree. But those extremes are out of the ordinary. Most are just people who passionately believe in a thing that isn't real. And while much of the press has written off Q believers as hopeless and unworthy of help, there is a strain of critical thinking and writing that sees Q believers not as mentally ill or even especially dangerous (even if some definitely are) but as searchers yearning for answers and authenticity when both are in short supply.

To Brian Dunning, the podcaster and science writer, Q believers see themselves victimized by the march of the progressivism that has been rewriting all the rules they once relied on. In this respect, Donald Trump isn't a reality show buffoon or a mediocre businessman possibly propped up by Russian money, but a messianic figure touched by God and chosen by the military to stop this forward march of alienating progressivism. The religious dimension of this embrasure of Trump is also important to understand. "They believe they're doing God's work," Dunning told me, echoing the messianic ideation so rampant in Q.

Dunning spends equal time demolishing liberal sacred cows as he does conservative ones on his podcast because conspiracy beliefs cut across all political movements and demographics. This helps him contextualize the appeal of QAnon. "Q [believers], antifa members, and Trump gun guys are cut from same cloth," he said. "They're looking for validation, and have a need to violently act out against their oppressors." But violent ideation and belief in a conspiracy that's often nonsensical don't mean that those caught up in it are necessarily bad or foolish people. "Most Q believers are as moral as any other group, but they've been given bad information that confirms their frustration with their lives," Dunning said.

Ultimately, Dunning looks at Q as "the right journey, the wrong way." For all of the terrible things about it, the Q phenomenon "exists for the right reason; it's made up of people looking for a solution—

it's just that the solution they've found is a terrible one," filling the hole in their lives with what Dunning describes as "BS." And while the idea that a science-minded person could find anything about Q less than completely toxic might seem shocking, it's an idea that other skeptics and critical thinkers agree with.

"Conspiracy theories are for losers," explained Metabunk founder and *Escaping the Rabbit Hole* author Mick West. West, an Australian transplant living in Southern California, has made a career out of empathizing with conspiracy theorists while meticulously demolishing their arguments, and wrote his book specifically to help people get out of conspiracy theories. So he's uniquely suited to helping figure out why people believe QAnon is real.

A conspiracy theory like Q "gives enfranchisement to people who want to be on the right side," he told me. The Trump years put these people in a position where they were actually in power, "but still feel like they're the underdog with the deep state in real power. It's the same as being obsessed with doing a daily crossword puzzle—it's fun, it exercises the brain, it gives a sense of accomplishment, and it's a ritual." To West, belief in Q can be a hobby, "but also something bigger and more important—a combination of a hobby and a quest, like a soap opera that makes a difference."

Like Dunning, West doesn't give any validity to the actual tenets of Q, calling it "insidious" and speaking out about its dangers at length.[16] But he's also fascinated by what it gives its believers. In particular, he seeks to understand the way it uses the Internet to indoctrinate and radicalize, "giving people a rich seam of content to consume, and a sense of purpose and meaning." Needless to say, all of those things are incredibly powerful drivers of thought.

"People are already into this, they are already susceptible to this," he explained further. "A huge percentage of the population already believes in conspiracy theories. Q is a self-reinforcing feedback loop, where the more people point out how ridiculous it is, the more publicity it gets." To West, Q is only unique in that it's constantly pulling in new material and reinventing itself, while most conspiracy theories consistently pile more ephemera onto a historical event, like JFK's assassination or the terrorist attack on the Twin Towers.

While most Q believers are just misguided people looking for a good answer to a difficult question, West believes that sense of "meaning and purpose" can also curdle into violence and anarchy when it becomes less of a journey and more of a crusade.

"That's how you get jihadists."

THE GLAMOUR OF HER OWN IDEA

Jihadists, of course, believe in what they're doing. You don't blow yourself up for a cause that you're only pretending to support. But do the people who are canny enough to monetize Q actually believe this stuff?

Asking such a question is usually pointless. What con artist is going to admit to you that he's a con artist and risk losing his con? On the surface, there's no reason to think Q promoters who have monetized their activities don't believe in their message. Sure, some of them are making money off of it—but that doesn't mean they don't believe it too. Why should Q's most vocal promoters somehow have more perspective or skepticism than the mass of its believers?

Generally speaking, Q believers are loath to talk to the mainstream media, who they see as the corrupt enemy of the people and an essential part of the conspiracy. Many fear their words will be twisted into fodder for the endless deep state–ordered hit pieces journalists write about Q—even complaining when they're directly and accurately quoted. Most of them either routinely ignore or publicly ridicule requests for comment.

Even so, there are a few telltale signs that these people really do believe in the mythology they've helped create—even if they do also profit off it.

One is the story of an aspiring screenwriter, who, after seeing his career stall out in Los Angeles, went home to reinvent himself as the Q influencer known as Neon Revolt.[17] Robert Cornero took his bitterness over what he saw as an alliance of Jews, gays, and people of color who had stunted his Hollywood dreams, and leveraged it into a hallowed role in the Q community. As Neon Revolt, Cornero would come to hold enormous sway over the Q community, becoming the admin for the biggest Q group on the alt-tech social network Gab and writing a prolific and verbose blog full of bizarre vitriol toward other Q researchers (whom he often singles out by name). He even self-published a book after raising over $150,000 to fund the project—and then sold the book back to QAnon believers.

Such a breathtaking grift brings up the natural question of whether Cornero believes Q is real, or if it is all part of a scam to use his genuine writing skills to make money in a way he never could as a screenwriter. Judging by what's left of Cornero's pre–Neon Revolt social media posts, he probably is a true believer. An acquaintance of Cornero who didn't wish to be identified described him as the type of person who believes himself to be the smartest person in the room, and constantly on the verge of success (to wit, he sold packages of "screenwriting consulting" despite never having actually sold a script). By the time of Trump's inauguration, Cornero's Twitter feed under his real name was showing signs of the Neon Revolt persona, including a tweet praising #GermanIdealism, retweets of Trump and Ann Coulter, and claims that "The Left has successfully, if inadvertently, 're-racinated' white people."[18]

While most of Cornero's Twitter presence under his real name is now gone, he was still using it as of May 2018—months after the first Q posts had gone up, and well after he'd adopted the Neon Revolt persona. And even though his tweets have been deleted, we still have records of the tweets sent *to* him as @RobertCornero—and they freely use Q slogans and mythology. The last contact Cornero appears to have had before completely giving over to Neon Revolt was a reply from a middle-aged woman saying simply "military tribunals and hang 'em."[19] At that point, Cornero appears to have completely drifted away from screenwriting, having been kicked out of writer Facebook groups after demanding on Gab that "globohomo"-infested (a portmanteau of "globalized homosexual") Hollywood be burned to the ground.

Clearly, Robert Cornero believed in QAnon enough to extol it under his real name, until he transitioned to a persona that was entirely about Q evangelism. And he wasn't the only one who appeared to absolutely believe what they were preaching.

I was contacted by a relative of one prominent Q influencer, a character who had over three hundred thousand Twitter followers until they were banned as part of the site's crackdown in early 2021. While this person didn't want to be identified for fear of provoking their relative, they made it clear to me that their relative's accumulation of a huge social media following was no grift or con, as they had no interest in monetizing their massive following. Nor was their family member an unwitting dupe of a foreign intelligence service. They were a true believer, not a clout chaser or scammer.

"He indoctrinated many family members," this person explained to me. "Luckily, there are several [of us] who have supported each other as we watch our Q family members spiral."

They also believe that he has merged elements of his real life with his online persona to the point where there is very little daylight between the two—while also suffering from what the relative believes are multiple mental illnesses.

"It blows my mind to see family members that are good people and intelligent become these characters," they told me in summary.

But while many, if not most, of the major Q influencers are true believers, some high-profile Q believers have turned on the movement. Both Alex Jones and Jerome Corsi, the two figures most responsible for Q's early spread, quit on Q, claiming the original Q poster had been "completely compromised" and replaced by "an overrun disinformation fount."[20] And Q lost @MAGAPILL, the first

Q believer that Trump retweeted, as a devotee as well. The anonymous Trump fan claimed in a now-deleted (though still archived) blog post that he was "very conflicted with QAnon and it's [sic] purpose" and hinted that QAnon was a psychological operation by the left devoted to erasing Alex Jones and other media "free thinkers."[21]

While it's hard to know what's in anyone's heart, there is one figure in the conspiracy world who didn't bristle at the idea of mainstream media coverage, but reveled in it—the Dove of Oneness, NESARA queen Shaini Goodwin. But even her most frequent interlocutor, the journalist Sean Robinson, never really knew the truth. Did Dove actually think NESARA would rain down riches on the earth? Or did she see what Clyde Hood had pulled off with his Omega Trust scam, and want to replicate it on a bigger scale?

Even now, years after Goodwin's death, Robinson doesn't know if she was a true believer or a scammer. Or both. Whether she believed in her own mythology or not was "the center of every inquiry I made," Robinson told me. "Based on my interactions with her and my research, I think she became caught up in the glamour of her own idea." But he says he was never able to clarify exactly what she believed, what convinced her, or, indeed, how she found the original NESARA proposal in the first place.

Goodwin denied being the leader of a cult. She maintained she was merely someone in tune to things that others weren't. Clearly, though, she got something out of it. And based on her precarious finances, it wasn't money. So what was it?

When Robinson interviewed Goodwin in 2004, she went to his office, "all gussied up and official," as Robinson put it. And there she proved herself to be just like everyone else, conspiracy believer or not. She was a person who needed to matter. She beamed when Robinson told her she had a gift a for writing, and that her ability to bring people together was a special talent. "I saw the need for approval and affirmation," he told me. She felt like she was part of something with the community she'd built, and in that, Dove came to believe NESARA—because it made her important and unique.

This is ultimately what brings people to Q, and what keeps them there. The promise of bad people being punished is one element of it, but the feeling of being part of something important and powerful is vastly underestimated. Q believers see themselves as soldiers fighting for the ultimate cause—and are surrounded by people who validate them, rather than insult them. Yes, Q makes mistakes and gets things wrong, and posts on a message board full of the worst people saying the worst things. But that can be explained away, or written off as just another attack by the enemy. What's real, what's tangible to Q believers is how it makes them feel. What questions it answers. What holes it fills that other aspects of life don't. For some, it's compartmentalized as that—good feelings shared with a community about something awesome that will happen to people they hate.

But for a few, it metastasizes. Sometimes it's due to mental illness. Other times, it happens because of need and anger curdling into violent resentment. No matter the cause, the end is the same: from the Capitol attack to countless tiny familial tragedies, the results are violence, pain, and shattered lives.

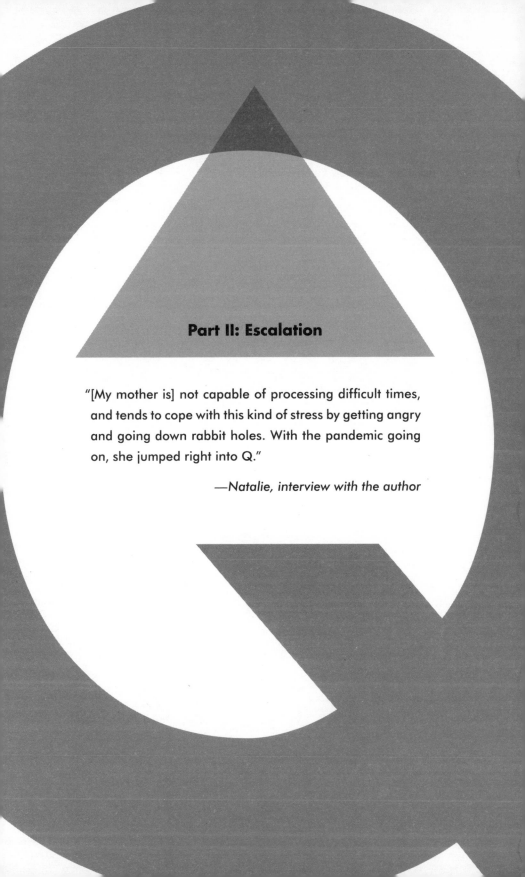

Part II: Escalation

"[My mother is] not capable of processing difficult times, and tends to cope with this kind of stress by getting angry and going down rabbit holes. With the pandemic going on, she jumped right into Q."

—Natalie, interview with the author

CHAPTER 7

This Is Not a Game:
The Many Crimes of QAnon Followers

"We don't want to die," the thirteen-year-old girl screamed.[1]

She begged the person imperiling her to stop. She cried, she argued, some reports even say she tried to throw open the door of the speeding van she and her brothers and sisters were trapped in. It was almost certainly the most terrifying moment she would ever face in her life, and she was barely a teenager.

Were this girl and her siblings the captives of a trafficking cabal? Potential receptacles for adrenochrome, mere moments away from a terrifying death at the hands of George Soros? No, they were trapped in a blue Honda Odyssey minivan barreling through Rockingham County, New Jersey, driven by twenty-nine-year-old Alpalus Slyman—their father.[2] With the classic-rock station WROR playing the hits in the background, Slyman was fueled up by the belief that Hillary Clinton was a baby-eating demon, the government was trying to murder him, and only QAnon and Donald Trump could deliver him from this horror. And the police were right behind him.

Slyman's police chase was just one of the many examples of Q's mythology spilling into the real world in the form of domestic terrorism and violent extremism. Long before Q-pilled insurrectionists sacked the US Capitol, Q believers were committing violent crimes, kidnapping children, and even killing people. The Capitol attack was far from the first sign of Q's potential for chaos. It was everything that came before.

GOOD AND EVIL

While Q believers deny it, there is a basic element of violence at the core of the QAnon mythology. How could any movement based around a "secret war" between good and evil that ends with military tribunals and summary executions be considered anything other than violent? In fact, the language used to describe the stakes of QAnon is strikingly similar to that used by terrorists.

In a prison interview with the University of California, Santa Barbara, professor of cults and religious violence Mark Juergensmeyer, the 1993 World Trade Center bomber Mahmud Abouhalima made it clear that he wasn't trying to enact social change or "raise awareness" of his ideals when he helped detonate an explosive-filled van in the basement of the World Trade Center, killing six people. He was fighting "a battle between good and evil and right and wrong," one that Juergensmeyer "just didn't see."[3]

An unseen war between right and wrong is pretty much the crux of QAnon. I reached out to Professor Juergensmeyer to ask if I was overreacting by drawing a parallel between QAnon and Al Qaeda or ISIS—and it turns out, he believes I wasn't.

While Juergensmeyer believes that most Q believers will eventually move on to something else, "the exceptions are the dangerous ones." Echoing the example of Mahmud Abouhalima, he continued that "these are the true believers who are willing to risk their lives to undertake an act, which we see as terrorism, [that's] consistent with their ideologies."

"The secrecy is part of the potency. It gives the followers a sense of smug satisfaction that they know something that everyone else does not know. Terrorist attacks are meant as much to assure the followers that there is a war going on as it is to shock the imagined enemy," he went on. And then he said something that made my stomach drop: "When the United States was attacked on 9/11 much of the impact was due to the surprise—not knowing who did this and why. It is not inconceivable that QAnon followers could commit acts of this magnitude."

QAnon has become both organized and violent much more quickly than any form of Islamic extremism. Al Qaeda had been around for well over a decade when its hijackers took control of four airplanes in the skies over the East Coast and used them to commit the worst attack on the continental United States in history. The Japanese doomsday cult Aum Shinrikyo similarly had been in existence for eleven years before its members attacked the Tokyo subway with sarin gas, killing thirteen and poisoning thousands in 1995. While nothing approaching this horror has come from a single or organized group of Q believers, the violent chaos perpetrated by Q believers at the Capitol proved without a shadow of a doubt that the potential is there. But it's not just mass casualty events within Q's grasp—smaller family tragedies happen all the time thanks to Q and the people who have given their lives to it.

"HELP ME, Q!"

From the breadcrumbs Alpalus Slyman left on Facebook through messages and livestreams (all of which are gone now), he seemed like a pretty ordinary guy who loved his family and video games.[4] He harbored some conspiratorial beliefs—9/11 trutherism, vaccine myths, belief in the Illuminati—but nothing that would seem to lead to a police chase and the potential death of his children.

But then came the COVID-19 pandemic, and a temporary layoff from his job as a baggage handler at Boston's Logan Airport. Videos he uploaded hinted at desperation and financial stress. He started bingeing conspiracy videos. And sometime around the first week of June, he found the viral ten-part QAnon video series *Fall of the Cabal*. Within days, he began to see himself as a target in Q's secret war. In the hours leading up to the police chase through Rockingham County, he'd been up all night, posting bizarre and troubling Facebook messages. He stated that Q was communicating with him through the classic hits playing on WROR ("I'm Still Standing," "Band on the Run," and the like). He claimed John F. Kennedy, Jr., had faked his death in a 1999 plane crash and would soon be returning to assume the vice presidency. And he appeared to believe that Barack Obama was born in Kenya and that Michelle Obama was actually a man posing as a woman—both common beliefs in the Q community.

The next morning, as his kids begged him to slow down, Slyman told both his children and the people watching his Facebook livestream that the police were trying to kidnap or kill him in a staged shooting and that "nothing was going to stop them." He told them that his oldest daughter and his wife, who had leapt out of the car to get help when it slowed down below one hundred miles per hour, were in on the plot to get him. He claimed their neighbors were spying on him. And as Facebook commenters begged him to stop the van, he, in turn, begged his two champions to come to his aid: "Donald Trump, I need a miracle or something. Somebody. QAnon help me. QAnon, help me!"[5]

Slyman was so new to the world of QAnon that he mispronounced it—"Q-AH-non," rather than "CUE-a-non." And he appeared to have some of the mythology wrong. But to the police chasing him, that didn't matter. All that mattered was saving five kids from their own father. Eventually, with his tires blown out, police say he rammed a passing car, then rammed a police cruiser before finally crashing into a tree. He was arrested without incident, and his children were, miraculously, unharmed. The legal case against him is still pending.

QAnon never did come to help him.

The story of Alpalus Slyman's chase and capture would play out repeatedly in the realm of QAnon. The basic pattern is the same: complete and nearly instantaneous radicalization into QAnon after being led to it by extant conspiracy beliefs. Slyman had lost his job because of the pandemic, and he needed someone to blame for it. As he dove into the conspiracy theories promoted in QAnon circles—that the COVID pandemic was both a hoax and bioweapon (conspiracy theorists often simultaneously hold conflicting beliefs), funded by Bill Gates and George Soros to exterminate the bulk of the population—his behavior escalated rapidly. He believed that soon, they'd take his life. So he did what a digital soldier does: struck back before he could be struck.

That path had already been paved for him.

THE DEATH OF FRANK CALI

Until March 13, 2019, the Gambino crime family boss Francesco "Frank" Cali was as attention averse as his most famous predecessor, John Gotti, had been flamboyant. He stayed low, quiet, and out of the papers. But Cali became a topic of national conversation because of what happened after a blue pickup truck rammed into his car, parked in the driveway of his home in the wealthy Todt Hill neighborhood of Staten Island.[6] Cali emerged from his house and exchanged words with the driver, who shot him between ten and twelve times, killing him. After Cali's death, Mafia watchers tried to figure out who might have killed him. New York's crime families had been at peace for years, and a family boss hadn't been shot dead since 1985. Not only that, but Cali had been shot outside his home, breaking one of the organized crime world's biggest taboos. Was it the start of a new Mob war? A power play from the inside?

It was neither. Police arrested Anthony Comello, a twenty-four-year-old Staten Island laborer whose attorney first claimed that Cali had disapproved of Comello dating the mob boss's niece. As the case wound its way through the courts, it would turn out that Comello, who had no mob ties, had much more in common with Alpalus Sly-man that he did with anyone in organized crime. He was a con-spiracy theorist and avid consumer of right-wing media, to the point where his lawyer claimed he had essentially been driven insane by it.[7] A few weeks later, seemingly desperate to communicate his right-wing allegiance to the outside world, Comello grabbed a blue pen during his arraignment hearing and started writing messages. Most were standard Trumpist fare: "MAGA Forever." "USA." "United We Stand." "Patriots in Charge."

But then came "Q Sent Me."

It wasn't the first killing committed by someone who appeared to believe QAnon was real. That dubious honor belonged to Seattle res-ident Buckey Wolfe, a member of the polo shirt–clad alt-right club the Proud Boys, who had also made a number of QAnon-related posts on Facebook before he "jam[med] the tang end of a four-foot long sharpened metal-bladed sword-like instrument" through the head of his brother.[8] As prosecutors would later allege, Wolfe called 911 and declared that his brother was a lizard who needed to die.[9] Wolfe's severe and obvious mental illness became the focus of the story, rather than his QAnon postings, which didn't seem to be the material motivation. Wolfe was found not guilty by reason of insan-ity, and remanded to a local mental health facility.[10]

Unlike Wolfe, Comello kept returning to major QAnon themes, including a February 2020 hearing where he declared, "I just want to say there is a lot on my phone and a lot of data about drug smug-gling, human sex trafficking all over the country."[11] Court docu-ments submitted a few months after the killing by Comello's lawyer attempted to have him declared mentally unfit for trial by paint-ing him as so broken by conspiracy theories that he believed well-known figures were members of the deep state were "actively trying to bring about the destruction of America."[12] Which is, of course, a central tenet of Q.

Before the murder of Frank Cali, Comello had already attempted citizen's arrests on supposed "deep-state" left-wing figures like New York City mayor Bill de Blasio and California congresswoman Maxine Waters. His attorney used this as evidence to argue Comello was making another misguided attempt at saving America when he backed his GMC Sierra into Frank Cali's parked Escalade. It was only after Cali made a "furtive action with his hand" that Comello allegedly feared for his life and shot Cali in the face, ten to twelve times.[13]

What's striking about both Comello and Slyman's cases was how quickly they both became radicalized—and how fertile the ground was for it to happen. Slyman began watching Q videos only days before his police chase, while Comello's lawyer claimed that "approximately five to six weeks prior to [the Cali shooting], Mr. Comello became increasingly vocal about his support for 'QAnon.'" His lawyer emphasized that "Mr. Comello's support for QAnon went beyond mere participation in a radical political organization, it evolved into a delusional obsession. . . . As part of his delusion, the defendant believed that he had been given secret knowledge about the Deep State, and that Q was communicating directly with him so that the defendant could play a grand role in the conflict to save the American way of life," which left him "unable to appreciate the wrongfulness of his actions."[14]

It's not clear why this "obsession" eventually focused on Frank Cali. Q had never mentioned the Mafia, nor had Trump undertaken any special effort to take down organized crime. In fact, Q drops made after the shooting called the incident "fake news" and claimed that the media had framed Q by using Comello as a stooge.

Regardless, the idea that conspiracy theories had shattered Comello's ability to tell right from wrong was compelling enough that in July 2020, a Staten Island judge found him mentally unfit to stand trial.[15] For as lurid and bizarre as the killing and its fallout were,

Anthony Comello's story was at least the work of a lone actor. When a group of QAnon believers started making the conspiracy real, things got even weirder—and more deadly.

SAVING THE CHILDREN BY STEALING THEM

Q had been calling some of the most powerful people in the world pedophiles, entirely without evidence, from the start. One of Q's earliest posts, Drop #153, even theorized that one of the reasons Donald Trump ran for president was "perhaps he could not stomach the thought of children being kidnapped, drugged, and raped while leaders/law enforcement of the world turn a blind eye."

In August 2020, the journalist and Q watcher Will Sommer at the *Daily Beast* reported on a clutch of QAnon believers, crank activists, and fringe legal theorists who had spent the last two years operating as a self-proclaimed Pentagon Pedophile Task Force, run by a former journalist named Timothy Charles Holmseth. Claiming to have been kidnapped and imprisoned by the deep state after supposedly uncovering an underground ring of child sellers at the Ukrainian embassy in Washington, Holmseth now declared himself to be the only journalist allowed to report on the task force—a handpicked team serving at the pleasure of President Trump to protect children who they believed were being delivered to state Child Protective Service agencies and sold into cabalistic sex slavery.

Holmseth and a few others, including an extremely prolific 9/11 truther named Field McConnell, made a seemingly endless series of rambling YouTube videos about the horrors of the cabal—some of which scored hundreds of thousands of viewers. And the people who saw the videos acted on what they were seeing. At least one video made by Field McConnell was in the YouTube watch history of Alpalus Slyman.

What did the "task force" actually do? Through a dodgy legal firm called E-Clause, two associates of Holmseth and McConnell named

Chris Hallett and Kirk Pendergrass bombarded family courts with sham lawsuits full of gibberish and fake or misused legal terms. This was a strategy frequently used by the sovereign citizen movement, whose members purposefully clog up legal systems by using linguistic tricks and incomprehensible legal filings to enforce their belief that they are exempt from US law. But the goal of the task force reached further: save children, by any means necessary. If that meant shooting CPS thugs when they came to your door to grab your babies, so be it.

Of course, there is no Pentagon Pedophile Task Force, as the Department of Defense confirmed to Will Sommer. There is no evidence that Child Protective Services in any state kidnaps children to sell to a blood-drinking cabal. The E-Clause "attorneys" Hallett and Pendergrass were not actually licensed to practice law. And no court in America has ever acknowledged that sovereign citizen tactics are legally valid.

But the alternate universe that QAnon had created was appealing to mothers who had lost custody of their children and were desperate to get them back. While there is no evidence of widespread kidnapping, child-custody disputes are rampant. Accusations that spouses are trying to steal the children to sell them to the child-torturing cabal have become frequent targets for QAnon believers who see CPS as a vehicle for the cabal to take their kids away.

The evil of government enforcers stealing children from aggrieved parents is a compelling story for QAnon believers, making the theories spouted by Holmseth and McConnell a lucrative profit center for the pair. E-Clause "lawyer" Pendergrass claimed in a livestream that he "live[s] predominately off donations" from supporters, and Field McConnell was able to raise over $44,000 for legal fees after a November 2019 arrest for stalking and harassment—a case still pending as of mid-2021. But like so much of QAnon, there was much more than grift going on here—these people truly believed children were in danger, and that they had to do something. The group would leave a trail of crimes and chaos in their wake, including multiple child kidnappings—not by the CPS goons that they made it their mission to stop, but by QAnon-pilled

moms in custody disputes. And all of it culminated in one of the
mothers "helped" by E-Clause allegedly shooting and killing one of its
"attorneys" in November 2020.

MOTHER AND CHILD REUNION

There is an irony in the rash of kidnappings QAnon mothers have
perpetrated in order to protect their children from kidnapping. One
such mother was Cynthia Abcug, a single mother of four. Abcug
moved to Colorado with her two younger children—eventually losing custody of the youngest child due to Abcug's alleged Munchausen
syndrome by proxy, a psychological disorder where a caregiver fakes
a child's illness in order to get sympathy or attention for themselves.[16]

Abcug's plight was exactly the sweet spot that Holmseth and McConnell preyed on—distraught mothers who couldn't understand why the
state took their kids away. According to police reports obtained by the
Daily Beast, Abcug got so caught up in the fiction that she enlisted the
services of someone police believed was a QAnon-believing "trained
sniper" named Ryan Wilson to concoct a plan to stage a raid and kidnap
her son from the deep-state pedophile cabalists who were holding him
in a foster home.[17] It was McConnell who was said to have arranged for
the hired gun. He also is claimed to have told Abcug that Trump would
protect her. The only thing that stopped the planned armed raid was
when Abcug's fifteen-year-old daughter informed on her mother.

Facing arrest, Abcug went on the lam in late September 2019, while
McConnell and Wilson weren't charged for their alleged roles in the
incident. Police had raided her home just before she vanished, finding QAnon paraphernalia—including blue bracelets featuring the
former Twitter handle of prolific Q promoter Joe M, who had championed the James Comey/Five Jihads harassment campaign.[18] Abcug
spent several months bouncing around the homes of various people in
this collection of Q-believing self-proclaimed child rescuers—all the
while giving interviews to friendly fringe media outlets to document

her plight. After landing at a burned-out house in Arkansas with a companion, Abcug was eventually taken into custody by the FBI in late December in Kalispell, Montana, and was charged with felony conspiracy to commit kidnapping.[19] She pleaded not guilty and was awaiting trial as of mid-2021.

Against all odds, Cynthia Abcug's story managed to end without tragedy—not counting her broken family and likely mentally scarred children. The same held true for another kidnapping driven by the Pentagon Pedophile Task Force. The Utah mom Emily Jolley abducted her son during a supervised visit, ostensibly to protect the boy from his father. Like Abcug, Jolley was a public devotee of QAnon and a sovereign citizen, and was also a member of the E-Clause Facebook group.[20] And like Abcug, this story also ended about as well as it could have, with Jolley arrested in Oregon and the boy returned to the custody his father, with Jolley claiming the warrant against her was fake, and her case awaiting trial. But another Pentagon Pedophile Task Force misadventure wouldn't end so tidily.[21]

Armed with a handgun and hopped up on conspiracy theories, Neely Petrie-Blanchard allegedly kidnapped her twin seven-year-old daughters from the rural Kentucky home of her mother, their legal guardian. But like Abcug and Jolley, she was no ordinary distraught mom. She was a devotee of E-Clause, acting as a moderator in their Facebook group.[22] She had a close friendship with one of its "lawyers," Chris Hallett, and even had a vanity license plate that read "ECLAUSE." She was also a hardcore believer in both QAnon and sovereign-citizen mythology, going so far as to declare on Facebook while on the run that the authorities had no legal jurisdiction over her. The authorities disagreed, and about a week later, Petrie-Blanchard was arrested.[23]

She resurfaced in November 2020 when she was arrested in Georgia for having allegedly shot and killed Chris Hallett at his home in Ocala, Florida. While out on $10,000 bond from the Kentucky kidnapping, Petrie-Blanchard began to believe Hallett had been conspiring with the government to hurt her children, who were still in the custody of their grandmother.[24] Things finally boiled over when, for unknown reasons, she confronted Hallett at home, and Hallett wound up dead. As one witness to the Hallett shooting told Police, Petrie-Blanchard held Hallett at gunpoint and declared "You're hurting my children, you bastard."[25]

At the time of the shooting, she had just been formally indicted in Kentucky on child-kidnapping charges—charges that Hallett and E-Clause likely couldn't do anything about.[26] Authorities in Florida believed the shooting was related to that case, but would not elaborate. Whatever the reason, now facing both kidnapping and potential murder charges, she ran again. And after again attempting and failing to use sovereign citizen tactics to avoid arrest, she was taken into custody, with her half sister blaming the Task Force for exploiting her mental illness to disastrous consequences. Petrie-Blanchard's lawyer told the *Wall Street Journal* that she doesn't dispute that she shot Hallett, and intended to use a temporary insanity defense at her upcoming trial.

While the one-off crimes committed by QAnon believers are a huge problem, it's in these planned and organized incidents that the real danger of QAnon as a movement becomes clear. It's very difficult to prevent a truly delusional person who thinks Donald Trump is talking to him through the radio from harming themselves or someone else. But these child kidnappings were carried out by groups of like-minded people sharing their belief in a powerful group of bad actors that had targeted their families. They had financial resources thanks to donations from other Q supporters, found safe harbors while on the run, were given material and personnel support by fellow travelers, and told their stories through Q-friendly streamers and fringe journalists. They even worked with fellow Q believers to create legal justifications for their crimes.

Like the Capitol attackers in 2021—or the large-scale terrorism of religiocultic movements like Al Qaeda or Aum before them—the Q child-kidnappings weren't random crimes by lone crazies. They were actual conspiracies put together by people who knew exactly what they wanted and had a plan to get it. And more often than not, those plans at least temporarily succeeded.

THE DIGITAL WAR GOES LIVE

Beyond the Hoover Dam standoff, the Cali and Wolfe killings, and the Capitol attack later, the blotter of alleged crimes that are seemingly Q-driven reads like the work of a movement infested with unstable and reactive personalities. To list a few:

- A chapel in Sedona, Arizona, was vandalized with Q slogans by a believer alleged to be "on a mission" to end human trafficking, with the case still pending.[27]
- A video maker pleaded guilty to threatening to carry out a massacre at YouTube's headquarters because his conspiracy-theory and QAnon videos were being delisted in search results.[28]
- The QAnon believer Jessica Prim livestreamed her attempt to board the NYC-docked hospital ship USNS Comfort with a bag of knives, claiming on the video that she was doing it because Donald Trump "talked to her" about saving the rescued children being held on the ship (her case is pending).[29]
- Cecilia Fulbright, a Texas Q acolyte, was arrested after police alleged she drunkenly tried to run multiple cars off the road in what she said was an effort to help Trump "[take] down the cabal and the pedophile ring." Her case is pending and she has pleaded not guilty.[30]
- Two armed far-right activists who drove an SUV with a Q sticker on its back window to the Philadelphia Convention Center were arrested allegedly trying to disrupt the vote count—and subsequently had their bail revoked for being caught on film participating in the Capitol attack. (Both pleaded not guilty.)[31]
- Cody Melby, a Portland Q believer, pleaded not guilty to allegedly firing two bullets into the side of that city's federal courthouse while attending a "Stop the Steal" rally to protest the 2020 election being "stolen."[32]

Eventually, the violent tendencies of QAnon believers got so bad that the FBI finally took notice. In a May 2019 memo that was obtained by Yahoo! a few months later, the FBI's Phoenix field office declared that "[domestic extremist] conspiracy theories very likely will emerge, spread, and evolve in the modern information marketplace, occasionally driving both groups and individual extremists to carry out criminal or violent acts." The memo identified QAnon by name as one of several high-profile "fringe political" movements that "tacitly support or legitimize violent action," and that attract "conspiracy theory-driven domestic extremists" who are motivated to act on their beliefs.[33]

But Q followers continued to maintain their movement was a peaceful digital gathering of researchers and patriots. Q didn't condone violent acts, and anyone who acted violently wasn't a real Q patriot. Plus, there would be a system in place to deal with the traitors and child killers when the storm came—indictments, followed by military tribunals.

This "no true Scotsman" fallacy, by which Q believers wrote off any violent action by their comrades as a false flag carried out to make Q look bad, powered virtually all of the discourse in the movement about the rot inside it. Nobody devoted to Q looked inward at what was powering this violence—only outward to who would want to hurt their movement. So Q believers claimed the FBI report was forged by Yahoo! in order to discredit Q, Timothy Charles Holmseth was a CIA plant with the job of fomenting violence in the Q movement, and Cynthia Abcug's case was merely a custody dispute and her link to Q was "propaganda and lies from the cabal's agents."[34]

"The media have no evidence that Q followers are violent," wrote prominent QAnon promoter David "Praying Medic" Hayes in a 2020 blog post that claimed the FBI bulletin was fake.[35] "Such evidence doesn't exist."

While Q believers find it easy to write off any violent episodes they encounter in the media as the product of the "fake news" media, there are countless unknown incidents that the media hasn't covered—tiny family tragedies that pit loved ones against each other.

One such story that's never been reported until now is that of Rick, a Midwestern man stalked and threatened with death by a former friend whose brain had been rewired by QAnon.

"MY FAMILY AND I ARE SCARED TO DEATH"

According to court documents Rick (a pseudonym) sent me, he'd been friends with Garth (also a pseudonym) for several decades. But recently, something in Garth changed. Garth had developed his own system for investing—a system that failed, costing him millions of dollars. Naturally, someone had to be blamed for it. And Garth thought he "had it all figured out."

"He thought the government was making countermoves to his moves," Rick explained to me. "If he made a stock trade, he thought it was being noted, and someone was trying to [hurt] his profit margin."

According to Rick, that's when Garth started putting tape over the camera on his laptop and removed the GPS from his car. He went on a gun-buying binge and loaded up on ammo and tactical equipment. By that summer, Garth had developed a system of graphs and charts that he believed broke open the government's entire plan to screw him. And Garth believed they would kill him before they allowed these charts to go public. Somewhere around that time, Garth had also found QAnon—a movement that directly and endlessly fed into the paranoia increasingly manifesting in his daily life.

"He was into [conspiracy theories] before, but not like when he found Q," Rick told me. And when Garth found Q, he got pilled fast. Garth started to carry multiple loaded guns and wore a tactical vest with knives and ammo. He believed he was going to be named secretary of defense and have high-level meetings with Russia and China, believed anyone who disagreed with him was committing treason, thought airplanes were flying over his house to spy on him, and told people Donald Trump was directly talking to him in his tweets.

Within a few months, the threats started. Court documents were filed alleging that, late that year and into the following year, Garth relentlessly physically and digitally harassed his immediate family with increasingly violent ideation and paranoia. Garth sent a deluge of threatening texts to family members, a local judge, and his friend Rick.

"Q is now after you. Good luck they are everywhere," read one text Rick showed me.

"So crazy that I get direct message communications with all top Q personnel for decodes. It is called intelligence beyond your comprehension and you burned your own son and destroyed his family. Your fate in my hands is unrelenting and unmitigated torture," went another. Garth claimed his oldest child would be a casualty, and tweeted that a judge he had gone before was "as good as hung." Finally, he started threatening to kill loved ones both privately and publicly on Twitter, saying over and over that he would shoot them in the head as punishment for their treasonous actions.

"He was threatening to kill us," Rick said to me, his voice shaking. "At that point, it wasn't if he was going to do it, but when."

Like so many tragic stories in the Q universe, this one didn't come out of nowhere. Garth had gone through a series of traumas, including a custody battle, significant mental health issues and the suicide of a close family member. But unlike the Q-pilled moms using fraudulent legal tactics to get their kids back, Garth didn't seem interested in regaining custody. Instead, his belief in Q manifested itself as simply wanting bloody revenge against his enemies— who, in this case, were the people closest to him.

"My family and I are scared to death," Rick wrote in a statement included in the court documents compiled by the state where Rick lives in its case against Garth.

"Three times we have fled our house, one time with supper being prepared, because of Twitter feeds, pictures of him outside of our house, or the last time because we were warned about threats.

"We are always looking over our shoulder. Our house is always locked and closed up. We feel terrorized. I am constantly looking out the window for him and his vehicle. We are losing money because of lost wages.

"We feel completely under his control and wonder when he might follow through with his threats."

Garth didn't get the chance to before law enforcement stepped in. After one of his children went to the police, Garth was finally arrested and charged with multiple counts of stalking, harassment, and making threats to a judge. It would take well over a year for Garth's case to go before a judge, due to the pandemic and multiple hearings regarding Garth's competency to stand trial, as well as him jumping his bail. But Rick made it clear to me that it all couldn't end fast enough. "We just want this over!" he emailed me right before Garth's competency hearing. And for Garth's victims, it might have been.

But for so many other victims of QAnon, justice would be delayed and the madness would continue as the conspiracy spread its tentacles into new radicalizing avenues—a vast menagerie of Facebook groups and Instagram pages devoted to alternative health, vaccine conspiracies, child rescue, and above all, COVID-19.

Q was getting worse before it was getting worse.

CHAPTER 8

Save the Children:
QAnon Transforms in 2020 with the Pandemic

When COVID-19 transformed the world in March 2020, Q suddenly became much less focused on indictments and much more wrapped up in the zeitgeist of the pandemic. Diagnoses were climbing by the day, major bastions of the social and entertainment landscape began to shut down, and Americans rushed to load up on supplies in depleted stores. It was a massive transformation that left tens of millions of people isolated, stuck indoors, and unemployed, with nothing to do, nobody to talk to, and nowhere to go.

With the population dependent on the Internet for a line to the outside world, the conspiracy theories seemed to spread as fast as the coronavirus itself. Did Bill Gates patent the coronavirus strain that was killing thousands? Was the virus actually spread by the mysterious 5G internet towers sprouting up everywhere you looked? Had the media and "Big Pharma" actually cooked up the entire coronavirus panic as a hoax to make sure Donald Trump didn't win a second term in November? Was it all fake? Just a bad flu? Or a planned genocide of the people the cabal discarded as "useless eaters?"

With these new themes circulating in the Q sphere, a new coalition of Instagram influencers, wellness devotees, and far-left anti-vaxxers flocked to QAnon's simple explanations for complex and fast-moving events. Many did not even know anything about the mythology underlying the group, but liked the anti-authority and anti-expertise messages they saw in it. Thus QAnon, a movement that had been founded on the promise of a great and bloody reckoning for liberals, somehow absorbed progressive wellness moms and Bernie Sanders voters.

Of course, the usual QAnon themes continued to circulate as well. According to one early strain of QAnon-driven chatter on social media, the lockdown wasn't in place to protect us at all, but because the US military was carrying out a secret rescue of children who had been sold into the sex-trafficking trade. To them, the lockdown was designed not to slow the spread of the virus, but to isolate the targets of the roundup. The biggest names in politics in business were rumored to be among those being taken out. Politicians, business tycoons, and celebrities—namely, Oprah Winfrey.

SOME AWFUL FAKE THING

Based on a grainy video of Oprah's mansion in Florida, Q believers posited that Winfrey was one of the key pedophile targets being grabbed. The video started making the rounds on conspiracy social media, in which, if you squinted hard, you could see her being dragged out of her compound by federal agents and see her assets being seized. Next stop for the Queen of All Media? A field tribunal held in conjunction with executive orders secretly signed by President Trump; a raised platform and a short drop by the neck at the secretly expanded Guantanamo Bay prison.

Overnight on March 17, 2020, while normie America fretted over whether they'd lose their job or die on a ventilator, #OprahArrested sped across the dankest parts of the Internet. It began on Facebook, when a user posted photos of supposed federal agents "excavating the property and digging up the tunnels" at Winfrey's house in Boca Raton. A short while later, a YouTuber narrated what he claimed was the arrest of "Hollywood pedophiles," with the shocking claim that the Boca Raton compound was "some kind of child trafficking location." It was all over Reddit, then it started trending on Twitter, and went viral on Facebook. It was so popular that *The Washington Post* felt the need to debunk it.[1] Their verdict: Oprah doesn't have a house in Florida. There were no tunnels and no secret underground lairs.

Ms. Winfrey herself waded in, tweeting in the middle of the night that she "just got a phone call that my name is trending. And being trolled for some awful FAKE thing. It's NOT TRUE," she reassured her 43 million followers. "Haven't been raided, or arrested. Just sanitizing and self distancing [sic] with the rest of the world. Stay safe everybody."

QAnon believers played a major role in creating and spreading conspiracy theories about the pandemic. Everywhere that fringe plots and theories emerged, whether it was about the effectiveness of wearing masks, videos of seemingly empty hospitals that theoretically should have been overrun, or the true cause of the outbreak, Q believers were making memes and sharing hoaxes. And it was radicalizing whole new swaths of people—many of whom simultaneously detested Donald Trump and agreed with some of his most radical and conspiratorial ideas.

Ultimately, the belief that the media lies to us is not partisan. And people of various political persuasions find Bill and Hillary Clinton loathsome, believe wealthy elites get away with immoral things, and feel that Bernie Sanders got screwed by pro-Clinton Democrats in 2016. There were legitimate fears that COVID-19 vaccines and 5G technology were untested and potentially dangerous, and that the COVID lockdown and mask mandates were either misguided or a form of massive social control. Liberals and conservatives alike believe these things—and Q acolytes were ready to welcome anyone with these inklings into their open arms.

So during the spread of COVID, Q was eagerly absorbed by a

nation locked down with nothing to do except go down Internet rabbit holes to figure out what the hell was going on and what they could do about it. And like so many people before them, they favored the conspiracy gurus giving them enemies to blame.

Q STAYS IN THE PICTURE

COVID-19 conspiracy theories started almost as soon as reports of the new illness surfaced. But there was one notable voice who was silent during the initial spread of COVID conspiracies: Q. Even though the first US COVID case was recorded in late January, it took Q until March 23 to even reference the pandemic in a drop.[2] Drop #3896, which echoed Donald Trump in referring to COVID-19 as the "China Virus," was simply a rehash of extant conspiracy theories about the virus—with Q adding a wrinkle about the virus being engineered to "shelter" a decrepit Joe Biden.[3]

When Q is absent for long periods of time, the major Q gurus tend to step into the void and take control of the "story," such as it is. So with Q silent as the pandemic took hold of the world, it was up to the biggest names in the movement to do the work. And that they did—using COVID to boost their social profiles, cause confusion among a population already soaking in it, and above all, sell things. And what Q gurus sold the most were quack cures and unproven treatments for an illness that nobody else seemed to be able to get a handle on.

What's usually known as the "Big Pharma" conspiracy theory had already been part of the Q mythology, with Drop #252 in December 2017 hinting that AIDS had been manufactured by "families in power," and Drop #693 a few months later rhetorically asking "When does big pharma make money? Curing or containing?" One of Q's strangest drops from April 2018, #1010, hinted at a vast pharma conspiracy in control of the household products industry, writing:

PHARMA [CLAS-D]
WATER
AIR
CHEMICALS PUSHED FOR HOME USE CLEANING
[CANCER] [BABY ON FLOOR-HANDS IN MOUTH—THE
START].
VACCINES [NOT ALL].

So there was a foundation for Q promoters to build on in the early days of the pandemic. Hence, Q gurus began to push a treatment that was already popular in anti-pharmaceutical circles: MMS, a "mineral solution" that when combined with citrus extract turns into chlorine dioxide—also the principal ingredient in industrial bleach.[4]

MMS was popular with conspiracy theorists and alternative health practitioners as a miracle cure for everything from autism to AIDS, with the usual hokum about it being suppressed by the bad guys in the FDA and the pharmaceutical industry because it was cheap and made their drugs useless. Even before COVID-19 had a real foothold in the United States, multiple Q-promoter accounts, including a budding anonymous influencer and "former police captain" called Chief Police 2, were pushing MMS as a preventive for COVID.[5] Q influencers touted its antimicrobial properties, claimed that spraying it on your skin or swishing it by mouth would kill the virus quickly (viruses and microbes are not actually the same thing) and that the media was lying about MMS being bleach in order to protect Big Pharma's profit margins, and claimed that as a bonus, taking it to prevent COVID would also cure a bunch of other illnesses.[6]

As a rule, the more conditions a substance claims to treat, the less it actually does treat. In this case, MMS not only does not treat various illnesses, but sickens and even kills people who take it.[7] Naturally, the government would rather you not take it for that reason. So multiple MMS pushers were sanctioned by the FDA, and the press viciously attacked it as a quack cure with serious potential for harm that was essentially the same as drinking industrial bleach. Which, to be fair, it was.

Meanwhile, Q began to claim that COVID-19 and the lockdown put in place to stop it were part of a strategy to get Joe Biden into office by cheating. Everything that was happening wasn't a once-in-a-century pandemic, but the deep state deploying "all assets" to win the election, as Q would claim in a number of drops in 2020. After all, it seemed like the perfect way to knock back Trump's chance for reelection, by saddling him with a pandemic and hobbled economy, then blaming personally him for it. But the initial rush of publicity over MMS had at least some impact on the Q poster, as one of their early COVID-related posts, Drop #3909, included the claim that the "FAKE NEWS" was colluding with the Democratic establishment to ban the use of the lupus medication hydroxychloroquine to treat COVID. HCQ, as it was known, had emerged early in the pandemic as a potential knockout punch for the virus when taken with zinc and the antibiotic azithromycin.

If MMS was a tough sell for a lot of people, the HCQ/zinc/Z-Pak cocktail wasn't. It took off like a rocket among right-wing pundits and mainstream conspiracy figures alike as a miracle cure that Big Pharma and their media lackeys wanted suppressed. The supposed potential of HCQ to end the pandemic and humiliate the anti-Trump "experts" on the left would become one of the biggest conservative talking points of the pandemic, and Q was right there pushing it all the way to the top.

Q would mention hydroxychloroquine a dozen times in April and May, and its rise in the QAnon mythology paralleled its rise in Trump's inner circle.[8] Trump himself touted it as a miracle that, at worst, would do nothing harmful. Or, as he rhetorically asked during an April press conference, "What do you have to lose" by taking it?[9] HCQ mania grabbed hold of the conspiracy theory community, with powerful figures touting its effectiveness, its inexpensive components, how much liberals didn't want you to take it, how you could make it at home out of tonic water and grapefruit peels, and even that it had pleasant side effects for one's complexion. Trump himself claimed to be taking it, and the drug became so popular that shortages of it put patients who had actually been prescribed the drug by their doctors at risk.

Eventually, the hysteria over HCQ faded out. The initial study that touted its effectiveness was widely condemned for not being based on solid scientific evidence—claims the report's author denies—and follow-up studies revealed that it not only had no preventive value against COVID-19, but it also had pretty serious side effects—including death—if taken in the massive doses that HCQ proponents were touting.[10] And if Trump had been taking it to prevent COVID, it pretty clearly didn't work, since he was eventually diagnosed with it in October. Or maybe that's just what the deep state wanted you to think.

QA-MOM

As the pandemic wore on, the novelty of Zoom meetings and socially distanced birthday car-parades faded away. People were tired of being inside, tired of the virus, and tired of their lives being turned upside down. Bored and isolated, they went looking for explanations, for enemies, and for entertainment. And conspiracy theories provided all three.

Among the new consumers of conspiracy theories about bioweapons and child trafficking and cabalistic plots were countless terrified and isolated mothers.[11] These theories were especially appealing to Instagram lifestyle influencers, a domain of attractive young mothers who build online brands by showing off their photogenic lives. Both high-profile influencers and their followers felt the same way— that something terrible was happening, and that raising awareness was the only way to stop it.

Just as QAnon is almost never someone's first conspiracy theory, many of the converts to "QA-Mom" found Q through other conspiracy theories in the social media influencer sphere. One was the viral video *Plandemic*, which claimed that the COVID outbreak was a plot between a shadowy cabal of scientists, foreign governments, and the pharma industry. *Plandemic* was a huge viral hit in May, racking up tens of millions of views and getting face time with everyone from Rush Limbaugh to Carmella Rose, a model and lifestyle influencer with 2.3 million Instagram followers who claimed "everyone need[ed] to check out" the video that "YouTube kept pulling down."[12]

The other viral conspiracy theory that scored big with the influencer community was the claim that the online furniture giant Wayfair was publicly (yet also secretly) trafficking children through listings of high-priced cabinets.[13] Even though there was no evidence to support it, the conspiracy theory was pushed by popular influencers with six-figure followings, several of whom pretended to call Wayfair and purchase the missing kids.

The viral success of *Plandemic* and the Wayfair conspiracy put far-fetched notions on the Facebook feeds of seemingly well-adjusted people all over the world, and it was a short leap from there to Q. By late summer, liberal-leaning influencers were routinely regaling their followers with brightly colored, Q-friendly phrases like "Where we go one we go all" and "#PainIsComing," tearful confessional videos about the horror of child trafficking, and inspirational messages geared toward young moms about asking questions and seeking truth.

These influencer accounts, which the QAnon researcher Marc-André Argentino dubbed "Pastel QAnon," piled up with followers.[14] Instead of pumping out the grotesque memes and incomprehensible charts usually found in Q discourse, they produced candy-coated paranoia and beautifully written-out memes about what horrors "they" were doing to us. And they were landing with a brand-new audience that wasn't primed for how to interpret these conspiracies or what to do with this "knowledge." Many of these lifestyle influencers, and the audiences embracing them, didn't mention Q or even appear to know what it was. But it didn't matter—they believed what Q had been pushing for two years.

The explosion of QAnon among the lifestyle-influencer community was so big and baffling that I immediately started asking the same question that I've asked about other QAnon promoters: Do they actually believe this? So I asked the *Atlantic* journalist Kaitlyn Tiffany, who had reached out to dozens of Instagram personalities and their followers in the course of her research for one of the first major stories about Pastel QAnon.[15] She made it clear that while these people were all over the place politically, with some liberal and others Trump-leaning, almost all outwardly put out signs that their belief in the tenets of Q was personal and deeply held.

"It's hard to say if they all believe it, since most are insistent on journalists being the devil" and had refused to engage with her, Tiffany told me. "But most probably believe it and take some care to mask it or apologize for it." Crucially, Tiffany pointed out that most of the influencers she approached for comment (almost always unsuccessfully) didn't post about Q on their permanent "grid," which would likely have been more lucrative, but in their Stories: short videos and photos that vanish after twenty-four hours. This gave their newfound embrace of Q less of an influencer sheen and made it seem more like a personal mission—and also suggested that they weren't doing it for money, which usually is made through posts on the grid. It wasn't about selling products, it was about sharing knowledge. Tiffany said that most of the messages she saw came couched with a disclaimer like "I know this sounds crazy, but this is my personal journey to accepting the truth."

And that journey was often simultaneously dark and paranoid yet sunny and optimistic. It was a view of the world that could be constructed by "doing the research." These were left-leaning moms with an anti-science and anti-vaccine mindset who believed Pizzagate was real, that children were being sexually and medically exploited by crooked politicians, that Jeffrey Epstein's downfall and death proved it all, and that feelings and emotional appeals were more valuable than actual learning and understanding.

"I don't get the sense that any of these women are learning how to use 8kun," Tiffany said, explaining that Pastel QAnon wasn't so much a Q offshoot as it was a movement of people who happened to believe what Q believed. "They're watching things shared on YouTube or Facebook, or seeing Instagram Stories from lifestyle-adjacent accounts. And they always say they did their own research, but that can't be true for all of them." Instead, many of these new Q followers were watching each other's confessional videos about how they "feel there's this horrible trafficking ring and the media is ignoring it," as Tiffany put it.

These weren't people looking to Q for guidance. In fact, many bristled at the idea that they could be lumped in with such a seemingly crazy group. And Tiffany wasn't concerned so much about violence from this cohort of believers either, but she was concerned about "Instagram's role in spreading the ideas of Q to a larger audience, and the destabilizing power of encouraging people not to trust science."

"A lot of women have been on Instagram for a long time and have been developing their audience for a long time. They really trust each other," Tiffany continued. "Hearing conspiracy theories from [someone you trust] holds more weight because you've been aspiring to this person's lifestyle for years." And in a movement where authenticity and relatability are prized, the goodwill these influencers have built up becomes a tight bond with someone you've empowered to speak the truth to you—even if that truth wasn't the truth but, as Tiffany put it, "a batshit conspiracy theory."

Led by a phalanx of influencers armed with candy-colored proclamations about child prostitution rings and the power of personal research, this legion of concerned moms wasn't alone.[16] And they weren't going to stay silent.

#SAVETHECHILDREN

Another factor that drove QAnon on Instagram and brought mommy bloggers into the fold was the fact that Twitter and Facebook were cracking down on Q iconography in the summer of 2020, leading Q followers to seek new strategies to keep their movement afloat. With the major traction of the Wayfair story, Q believers saw an opportunity to keep their story going without running afoul of Twitter's ban hammer.

The #SaveTheChildren hashtag began to appear in a number of viral posts by Instagram influencers with millions of followers that summer. These posts often took the form of simple videos, attractive memes, or frightening statistics that were often incorrect or taken out of context. But because child welfare is generally a thing people care about, they got serious traffic.

Seeing how popular the hashtag was getting, and conveniently having beliefs that dovetailed well with it, Q accounts hijacked #SaveTheChildren with Q-centric memes and slogans, along with links to actual news stories about the minimal work the Trump administration was doing to fight human trafficking, or conspiracy theories about Jeffrey Epstein and the Clintons.[17]

This effort, which had no drops from Q to guide it, quickly turned the concept of saving children from traffickers into an anti-cabal, anti-adrenochrome, pro-Trump rallying cry that could bring new cohorts of into the fold without running afoul of Big Social Media's "censorship"—because the social media giants couldn't do much about it. While it is not hard to ban hashtags or videos about Q—which are opaque and meaningless to all but Q believers—the idea of helping children was so anodyne and unobjectionable that it was essentially impossible to de-platform.

#SaveTheChildren exploded on Facebook especially, where hundreds of anti-trafficking, anti-vaccine, and anti-cabal groups saw their membership increase by thousands of percent. It provided an instant and obvious jolt to QAnon, with the hashtag used over eight hundred thousand times just in the first week of August, according to a report by the Associated Press.[18] Many of the people coming to Q from anti-trafficking posts through #SaveTheChildren had no idea what Q was or what it meant. Some weren't even Trump supporters. But fueled by pandemic fears and a genuine desire to "do something," they radicalized themselves quickly and efficiently.

So in the blazing hot months of late summer 2020, with the pandemic showing no signs of abating, the loose coalition of anti-vaxxers, anti-traffickers, anti-5G activists, COVID conspiracy theorists, anti-globalists, wellness advocates, terrified mothers, and crusaders for trafficked children hit the streets and began to march. They organized in cities all over America and around the world, often with little cohesion in their messaging, but with awareness and outrage in their hearts. And with QAnon slogans on their signs.

Video taken at a July 31 march in Hollywood showed less of a protest and more of a collection of people who were mad about various things.[19] Moms, twentysomethings, students, and hardcore conspiracy theorists slowly walked down a mostly empty street carrying signs reading EXECUTE ALL PEDOPHILES and BILL GATES IS EVIL and WE DEMAND JUSTICE and DEFUND HOLLYWOOD and GET PEDOS OUT OF GOVERNMENT and chanting for CNN executives to come down from their offices (which they likely weren't in because of the lockdown). Many people caught in the slow-moving mass were simply walking with the crowd, or looking around seemingly confused about how a protest works.

There were hundreds of rallies in other cities, many organized by Q promoters, and all were a similarly confused mishmash of politics and philosophies. Anti-trafficking protestors at a Chicago rally chanted "ICE loves our children," an image totally at odds with what Immigration and Customs Enforcement was actually doing to children at the US-Mexico border.[20] Video of a tiny rally in Sandusky, Ohio, saw a heavily armed man with an AR-15 and a skull mask standing at a socially distanced interval from a middle-aged woman holding a sign reading CHILDREN ARE NOT PROPERTY.[21] COVID masks were common at some rallies, and others were so driven by conspiracy theories that marchers were questioning whether Donald Trump faked his COVID-19 diagnosis.[22] Other #SaveTheChildren gatherings were indistinguishable from Trump 2020 rallies, pro-police "Back the Blue" gatherings, or groups of anti–Black Lives Matter agitators looking for someone to punch.

But there were two things that characterized the rise of a #SaveTheChildren movement in the summer of 2020. One was that they seemed to have little interest in helping extant groups already fighting child trafficking.[23] In fact, one such group, the Polaris Project, put out a press release saying that the recent activity had led to a flood of bogus trafficking tips, which was making it "more difficult . . . to provide support and attention to others who are in need of help."[24] The other was that the rallies were awash in QAnon iconography. In fact, QAnon-related social accounts accounted for the vast majority of #SaveTheChildren traffic on Facebook and Instagram.[25] Everywhere you looked at these rallies you saw evidence of Q's penetration. There were references to Pizzagate and adrenochrome, #wwg1wga and giant flaming Qs on signs, and artwork full of winks and nods to Q.

But Q seemed either unimpressed or unaware of the movement's growth among the young yoga moms and crystal healers of America. Q never mentioned *Plandemic*, the Wayfair conspiracy theory, adrenochrome, the supposed "tunnels" that kids were being moved through, or anything to do with the #SaveTheChildren marches. As with the beginning of the pandemic, Q believers were running in the direction they wanted to take the movement, not the direction Q set down—because there wasn't one. Some die-hards were dismissive of the new converts. The QAnon influencer (and prolific pitchman for the quack COVID cure MMS) Jordan Sather claimed on Twitter that the "Save the Children movement [was] being infiltrated and co-opted" by the deep state, and that a skull-masked Portland area marcher had "never read a Q drop in his life."[26]

And it was true that many of the people who got involved in the #SaveTheChildren movement either didn't know much about Q or actively claimed they wanted nothing to do with it. The organizer of a protest in Kansas City specifically told the marchers and biker groups planning to attend that "talk of conspiracy theories and QAnon are NOT something that should be consuming this protest. If you choose to talk about those topics, know that you are selfishly taking away from the whole point of this event."[27]

GOING GLOBAL

The QAnon movement was growing exponentially, while Q's role directing that movement was shrinking. Even as #SaveTheChildren was drawing in millions of new members through Facebook and Instagram, the Q poster made no real effort to consolidate this growth, or even acknowledge it. By that fall, the number of Republicans who believed the conspiracies spun by QAnon were at least somewhat real had exploded to over 80 percent, even as Q was leaving the trappings of QAnon behind altogether and becoming a true conspiracy theory of everything.[28] As evidenced in the #SaveTheChildren movement, QAnon symbolism and ideology was worming into the mainstream GOP and conservative orthodoxy, providing beliefs to a wide range of political persuasions and demographics, many of whom had no idea what they were getting into—but agreed with it nonetheless. But in August 2020, #SaveTheChildren went global, and Q was nearly silent.

So QAnon was growing up and sustaining itself without the "leader" at the head of the movement. And it wasn't just growing in the United States.

QAnon-driven marches took place around the world that summer, and over seventy different countries developed organized

QAnon Facebook groups throughout 2020.[29] QAnon had once been a mostly US-centric phenomenon, seeing as it dealt with the minutiae of American politics and the insider fights within the Trump administration. But during the worst of the lockdown I personally spoke to journalists in the United Kingdom, Poland, France, Germany, Finland, Spain, and Japan who were all baffled at how a movement that holds the internationally unpopular Donald Trump up as a messianic figure could take off in their particular country.

The entire world was stuck at home and grappling with economic disaster and personal uncertainty. While certain aspects of Q appeal to fringe dwellers around the world (fear of all-powerful cabals, a vague sense that the media is lying to us, opposition to global banking, etc.), each country where QAnon flourished embraced a slightly different version of the conspiracy, sanding off certain aspects and playing up others based on that country's politics and social media trends.[30] It wasn't unusual for one country to pick up on Q as a political movement, and another to embrace for its anti-science elements.

Members of Germany's far-right *Reichsburger* movement embraced Q's rejection of globalism, while it was also picked up by the French yellow vest movement, which had adherents in both the far left and far right fighting against what they saw as systemic government corruption. The United Kingdom in particular found itself with a rapidly growing #SaveTheChildren movement that meshed well with extant anti-vaccine groups and conspiracy theory movements. In Japan, Q believers inexplicably embraced Michael Flynn as a hero, while Brazilian Q believers merged their fervent adoration of far-right president Jair Bolsonaro with New Age beliefs about alien federations and mysticism.[31]

In particular, Australia struggled massively with QAnon, to the point where it had the fourth-highest QAnon social media traffic in 2019 and 2020, behind only the United States, the United Kingdom, and Canada.[32] Q mythology worked its way into anti-lockdown protests and conspiracy theories, becoming one of the biggest drivers of in COVID-19 vaccine refusal and hampering what had been a strong overall response to the pandemic.[33] Australians found their prime minister, Scott Morrison, embroiled in a scandal after he was publicly revealed to be friends with a prolific Q promoter named Tim Stewart who went by the handle BurnedSpy, and whose wife was on the PM's staff. Even two years after the connection between Morrison and QAnon was revealed, he still refused to discuss if Stewart's beliefs had influenced his governing.

Around the world, people of widely varying political creeds and locations on the spectrum of conspiracy theory belief all found the same thing in Q: "the real reasons" why the COVID-19 pandemic was going on. Those reasons and their details fluctuated among believers—a pinch of Jewish machinations, a dash of Bill Gates genocidal ideation, a sprinkling of Chinese Communist chicanery—but Q provided them with an outlet for their anger and a community of fellow travelers. And there was plenty of anger. As the pandemic ground on and more of the population became tired of complying with lockdowns, public displays of rebellion against mask mandates and social distancing began to go viral on social media. And Q believers were at the center of several high-profile public blowups.

A video of the Arizona PR firm owner Melissa Rein Lively destroying a display of masks at Target while screaming that she was the "QAnon spokesperson" racked up tens of millions of views and resulted in Lively being institutionalized for a week.[34] Like so many others, Lively had been driven by pandemic fears and exhaustion into a massive network of Facebook groups spouting conspiracy theories that gave comfort to the struggling and disconnected. Involvement in those groups led quickly to QAnon videos and the belief that she not only was watching the world "wake up," but she had a role to play in it. And Lively, who has since disowned QAnon and started treatment for bipolar disorder, wasn't alone. Other anti-mask demonstrations involved people spouting Q-approved conspiracy theories, harassing store employees, and coughing on bystanders.[35] A Palm Beach County Commissioners meeting devolved into chaos when a participant began ranting about Bill Gates, 5G towers, and "citizen's arrests" coming as soon as the people woke up.

Stateside, as the summer of #SaveTheChildren turned into a dark winter of 2020, the COVID-19 outbreak tore a hole in the fabric of American society. Q believers worked hard to create an alternate reality where the virus was under control, the people who died from it had really died from something else, and masks were a slaver tool designed to keep the population docile. They trended conspiracy theories about Trump's COVID diagnosis and hospitalization being a ploy to expose the deep state, about COVID deaths only afflicting the elderly and those already sick, and about the potential COVID vaccine being far more harmful than the virus. It was all lies, put out by the deep state and their media lackeys to do one thing: keep Donald Trump from winning the 2020 election.

The Q poster had stayed mostly quiet about the Democratic primary, essentially lumping all the prospective nominees together as a faceless blob of leftist corruption whose eventual winner wouldn't matter, because Trump would easily be victorious in November. As Biden and Trump found themselves more or less unable to campaign because of the virus, Q's narrative coalesced: Biden was propped up by Ukrainian money and Chinese vote-stealing; he and his family were hopelessly corrupt; his son Hunter was a malevolent child molester; and Joe himself was so spent that he was being hidden from view with COVID-19 serving as a convenient excuse for his lack of public appearances.

But when the unthinkable happened and Donald Trump lost the election, Q believers were left with a choice: accept that they'd been misled from the beginning, or concoct an even more complex conspiracy theory to explain the failure of their last one.

You can guess which one they chose.

CHAPTER 9

Memes at the Ready:
The War Between QAnon and Social Media

Before the Internet, believing in a conspiracy theory took work. You had to know which dank bookstore to patronize and which gun show or truck stop was selling the hot new anti-Clinton video, or find the right shortwave radio broadcasts about UN storm trooper invasions. None of those limitations did anything to impede belief, of course. But it at least formed a barrier to entry for potential believers. And it made spreading these theories to the uninitiated more difficult.

Popular conspiracy theories from pre-Internet times usually unfolded slowly, often starting with a single radio broadcast, tabloid story, or newspaper column, some of which even had elements of fact in them. They were passed around, rewritten, and expanded for years. Like any oral history or unwritten legend, each individual teller embellished it in their own special way. But unless you wanted to publish your own books or pamphlets, they were passive experiences—a conspiracy theory was a thing being done to you, that you learned about only after it happened, with the materials you consumed only providing insight on the various players, who all remained far out of reach.

As the Internet moved from experimental to omnipresent, conspiracy theories were suddenly much easier to find and spread. Fringe beliefs were a natural fit for early bulletin board systems and Usenet newsgroups, as Internet pioneers shared everything from clues in the popular early alternate reality game *Ong's Hat** to much darker stuff—rumors of gun confiscation and dissenters being thrown in FEMA camps and of Bill Clinton destroying his septum from his operatic cocaine use as governor of Arkansas.[1] There were anons even back then, such as MI5Victim, a UK information technology worker who was so relentless in spamming Usenet groups and message boards with lurid tales of being persecuted and threatened by British intelligence that he was banned from almost every major early Internet communication service.[2]

As early Internet journalist and angel investor, Esther Dyson, told *Wired* magazine in 1997, "the Net is terrible at propaganda, but it's wonderful at conspiracy."[3]

Social media, particularly the explosion of Facebook as a tool for baby boomers to stay in touch with their families, was the next natural step in the evolution of conspiracy theories in the digital age. But it arrived with a twist: it not only allowed easier access to conspiracy theories, it allowed users to build up their own audience—and tell them anything they wanted. Conspiracy theories already moved much faster online than in the real world, but social media allowed them to be created out of nothing. You didn't need to wait for a survivalist newsletter or anti-Illuminati blog post to land in your inbox. You could just film yourself trying to melt tightly packed snow and claim it wouldn't melt because it was fake or full of microscopic robots. And if you got a bit lucky, your theory could go viral, land-

---

* *Ong's Hat* is an early alternate-reality game seen by some experts in that field as a forerunner to QAnon. It was a collaborative fiction based around a supposed multidimensional time travel device hidden away in the thick forests of Pine Barrens, New Jersey. Most of the complex fiction surrounding *Ong's Hat* started on early internet message boards in the 1980s, and was compiled and expanded upon by the author Joseph Matheny, who refuses to disambiguate which aspects are real and which are fictional.

ing on the Facebook feeds and Instagram grids of people all over the world, as that one did in early 2021.[4]

QAnon was a perfect fit for social media. It was active rather than passive; it was driven by decoding clues and solving puzzles; it was visually interesting; it was open to any number of interpretations; and it was spinning a web of lies that its believers were perfectly happy to fall into. QAnon certainly wasn't the first conspiracy theory to harness the power of the Internet for easy communication and propagation. But it was the first to exist almost entirely online, with no scientific knowledge or military expertise needed to understand it—just a hatred for the people Q hated, and the need for an online community that gave you praise and good feelings.

As a movement that began entirely online, QAnon probably wouldn't exist without social media. It certainly wouldn't have spread so easily without the tireless "work" of its biggest Twitter and YouTube influencers. And it wouldn't be so viral in the mainstream Republican Party if it hadn't been allowed to grow unchecked on Twitter, the platform of choice for Donald Trump's own conspiracy theory ideation. It's impossible to understand Q without understanding how it uses social media—and how social media giants spent years allowing it to flourish without oversight or accountability, only to see their laxity blow up in their faces.

MEMES LOCKED AND LOADED

Most conspiracy theories start off with a real-world event and transform it into something unrecognizable. QAnon is different in that it started with nothing and went from there. From the very first Q drop, Q was about a nonexistent arrest of Hillary Clinton, and only added more fake details to the already fake event. There was no apocalyptic event like a pandemic or assassination that Q was trying to explain at the outset—only an endless series of clues to future events that never came true, all building on top of each other.

And it moved fast. As soon as Tracy Beanz started making videos, and Paul Furber and Coleman Rogers launched the first Reddit forum devoted to Q, it found an audience ready to see Hillary Clinton punished for her "crimes." Multiple videos besides the first Tracy Diaz decodings of Q drops had cracked the six-figure mark in views. Searches on Google for "QAnon" spiked on November 18, 2017, then again right after Christmas of the same year.[5] The #QAnon hashtag first emerged on Twitter on November 2, 2017, the same day that a Canadian 4chan user dubbed the poster "QAnon," and it took off from there. And a now-deleted thread on the imageboard Imgur that told the story of "the coming storm" got well over one hundred thousand views by December.

Ironically, some of Q's earliest drops hinted that Google, Facebook, and Twitter were untrustworthy and part of the deep state's media arm. But Q began to generate a serious amount of traffic on Twitter, about 5 million tweets from just late October 2017 to the end of February 2018.[6] According to data from the Concordia University PhD candidate Marc-André Argentino, by 2018, the major personalities of the Q movement—promoters like Dave "Praying Medic" Hayes, InTheMatrixxx, and QAnon76—were all among the Twitter accounts most mentioned by Q believers, alongside luminaries like Donald Trump, Sean Hannity, and Michael Flynn. And there were 55 million hashtag mentions of Q in 2018, with 23 million uses of #QAnon itself.[7] Q was clearly breaking out on Twitter, and Twitter wasn't taking any notice. It was a major mistake that would have profound implications for Q and for US politics.

But for all the gains Q was making, the movement suffered a setback in March 2018—Reddit presciently banned the original home of non-chan Q discussion, r/CBTS_stream, along with its creators, Furber and Rogers, for "repeated violation of our content policy, specifically, the prohibition of content that encourages or incites violence and the posting of personal and confidential information."[8] But in another scene that would repeat itself constantly over Q's lifespan, Q followers found ways around the ban.[9] Another subreddit, r/GreatAwakening, exploded in membership, quickly getting to over seventy thousand members. And Coleman Rogers and his wife would launch Patriots' Soapbox, a twenty-four-hour, all-Q-all-the-time YouTube channel (it still exists as its own website, with far less traffic) that fostered endless QAnon discussion and allowed minor right-wing celebrities to sell Q believers on whatever scam they were running that day.

Rogers's success in making Patriots' Soapbox was so complete that the channel survived even after he made what looked like a hugely revealing mistake. While sharing his desktop on a livestream, he appeared to accidentally log in to 8chan using Q's tripcode and post something, before quickly cutting out the live feed from his computer and declaring, "Sorry, leg cramp."[10]

"How did you post as Q?" one viewer asked Rogers in the chat window that ran over the endless livestream. Nobody answered, and while some Trump supporters used the incident to write QAnon off as a joke (the rabidly pro-Trump subreddit r/The-Donald would auto-delete all mention of QAnon as a rule), the channel quickly piled up almost fifty thousand subscribers and ran for several years as a safe space for minor right-wing celebrities to spew conspiracy theories.

Despite Q's success on Twitter and YouTube, at that point, there was little mention of it on other platforms, particularly Facebook, where its presence was negligible. Google search traffic for QAnon was low in those first months, and the mainstream media coverage of Q was mostly of the "How can anyone believe this nonsense?" variety, mocking its reliance on Donald Trump's supposed super-genius, dismissing it as a goofier version of Pizzagate, and calling it crazy and a "rage-fueled fever dream."[11] And, to be fair, it was all those things. But Q believers took it all in stride, slowly building followings and dispensing their mythology to new converts. And their diligence paid off. Over the next two years, before social media companies decided that enough was enough, Q had almost free reign on every major social media network.

Long before the COVID-19 pandemic, QAnon had a major footprint on Instagram, building a younger audience that would bloom tenfold during the time of coronavirus.[12] Facebook groups devoted to Q and Q-friendly subjects had millions of members before Mark Zuckerberg's people finally took action against the conspiracy theory.[13] And as we've seen from the @MAGAPILL saga, Q was so popular so quickly on Twitter that President Trump retweeted a public Q devotee just weeks after the first drops—with its growth skyrocketing during times of political controversy. Q continued to pick up tens of thousands of new believers on the site even before the pandemic—with over 68 million uses of QAnon hashtags and slogans from late October 2017 to March 2020.[14]

While it would still be several more months before Twitter would take any kind of real action against Q, Q made inroads on every social platform where people could spew conspiracy theories, from the secure messaging app Telegram to the video platform TikTok. If you built it, the storm would come, and fill it with racist and anti-Semitic rants about George Soros, conspiracy theories, and inflammatory memes.

DIG, MEME, PRAY

Unseen by the media and unchecked by the social platforms, Q believers were developing a method of communication that was simple and clear to people who spoke the language, while being totally incomprehensible to outsiders. In particular, Q acolytes mastered the use of memes, the jokey images spread around the Internet as shared cultural touchstones. Memes have been part of the Internet since modems had enough baud to download them—going back to the mid-1990s, when a creepy, blocky dancing baby went from an awkward internet meme to a running gag on *Ally McBeal* as it gyrated to "Hooked on a Feeling."[15] And they're a hugely important part of the discourse in places like 4chan, popularizing everything from goofs like LOLcats and Rickrolling to horribly destructive movements like the harassment of women journalists under the GamerGate banner.[16]

As someone versed in the speech patterns of the chans, the Q poster clearly knew the importance of memes in communicating the mythology. In turn, Q drops are full of exhortations to readers to make memes and disseminate them as a way of avoiding Big Tech censorship and algorithms, going all the way back to Drop #532 in January 2018:

MEMES/POSTS.
Organized and coordinated?
POTUS may reTWEET [sic] one or more.
READY FOR LAUNCH?
SHOW the WORLD.

Q fanatics were, indeed, ready for launch. They spoke extensively on 8chan about the importance and power of memes to share the narrative, wake "normies" up to the corruption of the deep state, hijack trending hashtags, disseminate research, and of course, make liberals cry. "Strategically, these type [sic] of memes are VERY important," declared one anon a few days after Q's call for memes, continuing,

WE NEED TO PREEMPTIVELY DEFUSE THE
FALSE FLAG NARRATIVES BEFORE THEY START—

1. Because it shows foreknowledge and validates Q/POTUS intel if they *do* roll them out
2. Because it may save innocent lives if (((they))) [the three-bracket symbol used on chan sites as a code for Jews] are forced to discard the strategy
3. Because forewarning the people (and comforting them

that the military, intel and law enforcement are on the job)
will truly offer calm if that part of deep state's strategy *is*
employed in the storm.[17]

Another 8chan poster commenting in response to Q's initial call
simply declared, "We have a lot of memes to create!"[18] Q would extol
the power of memes to spread the message and defeat censorship
many times, with followers responding to the call every time. And
it made a certain amount of sense. Q's mythology of an all-powerful
deep state at war with a cadre of woke patriots was hopelessly insular and extremely difficult to describe in words without seeming
like a crank. But attention-grabbing memes depicting Democratic
luminaries in prison with the text of a Q drop or Oprah Winfrey
exclaiming "you get to go to JAIL!" could be interpreted by anyone.[19]
This is how Q presented itself to people finding it for the first time:
not as red-string-on-corkboard conspiracy madness, but the vague
dread that "they" were doing terrible things and didn't want you
asking about it.

Pictures are a universal language. And memes in particular are
so easily shared and understood that formerly anodyne message
boards and Facebook groups dedicated to sharing mildly amusing
pictures became infested with Q images and iconography. One was
Giggle Palooza, a Facebook meme group with over 1.5 million members that was radicalized into a dumping ground for right-wing conspiracy theories during the pandemic, transforming from a space
for harmless memes about coffee and grandchildren to ones screaming about Hillary Clinton and martial law.[20] All of it was driven by
a page owner who identified as a pastor and QAnon believer—and
the newly "awake" posts routinely got thousands of likes and shares.
In QAnon, there was no room for puns or images of Garfield complaining about things—it was all digital war, all the time.

As the relationship between Q and Trump became more obvious in public, Trump would routinely share Q memes and slogans,

often acting like he had no idea what they were about. Even in early March 2020, as COVID-19 panic began to settle over the country, Trump responded to the chaos and fear not with a speech or a rhetorical exhortation for Americans to socially distance, but with a meme—of him playing a fiddle with the text "MY NEXT PIECE IS CALLED . . . NOTHING CAN STOP WHAT'S COMING," with Trump himself adding, "Who knows what this means, but it sounds good to me!"[21]

Plenty of people knew what it meant. By that point, memes weren't just a communication tool or a way to proselytize—they were a weapon. In Drop #2189 Q would order followers to "lock" memes "on target," and to "fire at will," viewing them as important to a digital war as bombs and bullets were to a physical one. Even social media companies making token efforts to stop Q memes were folded into the Q mythology, with 2018 drops pointing out software that Facebook started using to filter out conspiracy and inflammatory memes—which Q "autists" (their preferred term) attempted to defeat with blurred fonts and reversed pictures.[22] Memes were a critical tool for harassment, and they could easily be spread by bot networks and burner accounts. And anyone who ran afoul of Q or its believers could expect to find themselves on the wrong end of a firehose of social media–driven harassment and graphic memes. It's happened to me, and to a lot of other people as well.

THE BATTLE OF SB 145

QAnon-driven brigading over social media has fallen on the heads of a number of prominent liberals and outspoken Trump opponents. Using old jokes, out-of-context tweets, and manipulated images, Q believers painted the comic and actor Patton Oswalt as a pedophile who openly spoke of his attraction to children without fear of repercussion.[23] They tarred the model and influencer Chrissy Teigen as a top-level cabal operator and pedophile who attempted to flee the country in advance of "the storm" with her husband, only to be caught and sent back for a public execution that never actually took place. They went so far as to mercilessly troll her with accusations and memes after she announced the stillbirth of her child.[24] And Tom Hanks was hit with so many baseless allegations of pedophilia and murder by QAnon believers that it goosed Google and You-Tube algorithms into putting far-right links at the very top of search results for the actor before the mistake was corrected.[25]

But far from the lofty perches of stars like Hanks and Teigen, a vast engine of harassment, trolling, and threats can be turned on anyone who the Q movement deems to be the enemy.

And in August 2020, as #SaveTheChildren mania was sweeping the conspiracy world at large, that engine drove straight over Catie Stewart in the battle not between good and evil, but over the arcana of the California state legislature: State Bill 145.

As the communications director for California state senator Scott Wiener, Stewart was not in a position that usually merited much scrutiny. Wiener is a gay, Jewish Democrat representing San Francisco, one of the most liberal enclaves in America. He's well-liked, visible in his community, and routinely advocates for marginalized groups in his city.

But that summer, threatening messages started coming for Wiener. They were full of graphic depictions of violence, accusations of child rape, and disgusting memes. And as part of her job, Catie Stewart was the first set of eyes on most of them. A few messages seemed like genuine questions from concerned people who didn't seem to know what they were talking about—people Stewart was able to speak to personally and sometimes correct on their mistaken beliefs. But those were outnumbered by gleeful proclamations from middle-aged women hoping Stewart and her boss would get raped and murdered.

The source of the onslaught was a recent bill introduced in the state congress. Wiener had been one of the driving forces behind SB 145, a measure meant to fix a loophole in Section 290 of the

California penal code, which dealt with judges automatically adding people to the state's sex offender registry for acts outside vagi-
nal intercourse when one of the parties was underage, while having
the discretion not to for "traditional" sex between a man and a
woman—disproportionally requiring LGBTQ people to register as
sex offenders, even if the minor was 17 and the offender was 18 or 19.
It was a standard bill that went through the standard markup process. But when you're putting the words "juvenile" and "sex" in the
same sentence, there are people who are going to notice and think
it's their job to stop whatever is happening. A large and vocal cadre
of citizens suddenly and wholeheartedly became concerned that the
state of California was about to legalize pedophilia, and they took to
social media to register their outrage.

After SB 145, "if you are between fourteen and seventeen and have
consensual sex with someone within ten years of your age, a judge
[has] the discretion [whether or not] to put the older partner on the
sex offender registry," Stewart told me. Before SB 145, a judge could
only use their discretion on heterosexual intercourse—an oversight
that imperiled countless young members of the LGBTQ community
who were in consensual relationships with someone near their own
age. The bill certainly wasn't "legalizing pedophilia" or turning a
blind eye to child rape. "Even with the new law, no criminal punishment has changed," Stewart said. "And if the sex wasn't consensual,
it's still automatically rape."

But the people sending the messages to Catie Stewart and Senator Wiener either didn't see the distinction or they just didn't care.
What they did care about was saving the children—and killing the
people endangering them. The social media harassment "started out
of nowhere," Stewart said, when a Q-believing Instagram influencer
found an old article on a right-wing website about SB 145 and posted
about it, claiming it would legalize pedophilia. According to Stewart, the initial Instagram post got nearly five thousand comments
almost right away and the flood of messages began just after that.

"Did you seriously pass a fucking bill lowing [*sic*] the penalties for having sexual relations with willing children? CHILDREN CAN'T FUCKING GIVE CONSENT," screamed one of the messages Stewart forwarded to me, as I attempted to understand how a state senator's staffer got embroiled in a national news story. "You're a sick fuck" another simply declared. Another called Wiener a "creepy little man" and hoped "his kids don't ever get anal raped since you made it legal." (Senator Wiener has no children.) Stewart had to take interns off phone duty due to the volume of inflammatory calls and death threats coming in, while she instead argued personally with outraged believers. Wiener was even doxed by a fanatical #SaveThe-Children believer—his personal information and address made public for the whole world to see.[26]

All of this was driven by QAnon believers, almost entirely through social media. Twitter, Instagram, and Facebook helped transform a procedural bill meant to close a legal loophole into liberals legalizing pederasty. Tweets sent by a conservative California state senator who opposed SB 145, claiming the bill would "lower penalties for adults who have sex with children," got thousands of shares.[27] Pastel QAnon moms and influencers spread the same disinformation to their followings, while YouTube videos opposing the bill got hundreds of thousands of views. "One account posts it and it goes viral on Instagram," Stewart said, adding that YouTube videos were the worst drivers of the harassment. Ultimately, Wiener's office got over one thousand death threats, and Stewart had to work with California State Police to ensure the safety of his staff—all while Stewart dreaded the moment that Donald Trump himself would tweet about it.

That tweet never came, as Trump himself never weighed in on the matter. But Donald Trump, Jr., Rush Limbaugh, and Texas senator Ted Cruz all got in on the act, with Don, Jr., getting nearly six thousand retweets accusing "Joe Biden Democrats [of] working in California to pander to the wishes of pedophiles and child rapists." Cruz retweeted a photo of Scott Wiener and baselessly claimed that "today's CA Dems believe we need more adults having sex with children, and when they do, they shouldn't register as sex offenders."[28] On and on it went.

All the while, social media companies were painfully slow to abate the harassment—some of the threatening and misleading posts would stay up for years. Like so many other conservative culture war campaigns, the attacks finally ran out of steam as the Q harassment machine found a new target. But the slowness of Facebook and Twitter to act on this ghoulish, violent harassment and overwhelming flood tide of fake news wasn't new. The campaign against SB 145 was simply one example of what had proven by then to be a glacially slow reaction by the tech giants to QAnon activity—which would eventually have horrific consequences long before the attack on the Capitol finally forced them to do something about it.

ROWING A LEAKY BOAT

From the very start of QAnon, the social media titans seemed baffled by what role they should play in stopping its spread, instead allowing QAnon hashtags, slogans, and memes to radicalize more and more people with almost no oversight. All the way back in January 2018, before some of the biggest gurus had begun evangelizing Q, Facebook posts about Q-driven concepts like the "16 Year Plan to Destroy America" (Drop #570) were drawing scores of commenters demanding the execution of Hillary Clinton and Barack Obama by firing squad. Twitter had the same issue on the same timeline: countless tweets going back to the very beginning of Q calling for Democrats to be executed, and "hashtag rallies" publicly organizing and directing harassment.[29] And nobody in a position to abate it did anything.

For as much as Q grew on Twitter, Facebook was even worse, with QAnon influence in the site's hugely popular groups increasing well into 2020—170 QAnon groups, pages, and accounts across

Facebook and Instagram totaled more than 4.5 million followers in that year alone, according to research by *The Guardian*.[30] This was long after the first violent crimes had been committed in Q's name, and this continued as the pandemic converted anti-vaxxers and wellness devotees into Q acolytes. Individual posts would be removed, but only if they blatantly violated a site's harassment policy—which many were deemed not to. According to interviews by *The Washington Post*, executives at these companies knew they had a problem fairly early on, but didn't take action for fear of "policing beliefs," as one executive put it, or "taking sides" against Trump supporters already aggrieved at what they saw as liberal companies censoring conservatism. All of it was part of a Facebook policy revealed in 2021 that showed they changed their rules and enforcement policies in the lead-up to the 2020 election in a way that went easy on conspiracy theory purveyors, particularly Alex Jones, who Facebook employees claim had his ban personally reduced by Mark Zuckerberg.[31]

But outsiders with links to the company could see there was a problem long before then. One was Brooke Binkowski, the former managing editor of the fact-checking mainstay Snopes, who vocally rebelled against Snopes entering into a partnership with Facebook—recognizing Facebook's potential for radicalization and conspiracy theory growth. And she was right, speaking out publicly against the hypocrisy of the site setting fact-checking standards as its own users pushed out the very rumors and smears that she'd been tasked with debunking.[32]

"I'm desperately sad," Binkowski told me. "I never wanted to be right. In fact, I was hoping I could be seen as a mildly alarmist whackadoodle who was spreading rumors to chase clout." In particular, Binkowski was especially alarmed at the explosive growth of rumors and violent hate speech on Facebook related to the Rohingya genocide in Myanmar.[33]

"I spent a couple months weighing out the pros and cons of coming forward about Facebook in 2018, after all this crazy shit came out about Myanmar," she said, realizing that for her, the worst thing that could come of speaking out was that she would lose her job at Snopes because of the bad press for Facebook. "[I realized that] was a desirable outcome—it would remove a lot of the pressure and the scrutiny."

She and a number of other anonymous fact-checkers did eventually come forward, blasting Facebook's laxness and inconsistency in an article in *The Guardian*. "But to no avail."

Sure enough, Binkowski says she was soon pushed out at Snopes, suffering tremendous guilt for what she felt like was her accidental role in backstopping the worst abuses of social media. She would later write an op-ed for *Buzzfeed* comparing the experience of fact-checking an endless storm of Facebook hoaxes and harassment to paddling a sinking boat in a storm, beset by ever-changing rules, an endless need for clicks, and indifferent executives.[34] Meanwhile the problem of fake news and conspiracy theories driving violence was no closer to a solution, with Q continuing to gain converts among isolated and terrified populations beset by COVID-19.

When asked what Facebook had done to curb QAnon before it really took off, Binkowski, in the weary and furious voice of a frustrated Cassandra, pulled no punches.

"They could have listened to me in 2016 and 2017," she replied. "But now I know they didn't, because as we now all know, that was their business model. They knew what they were doing all along. They'll try to say they didn't, but they knew. I can tell you this with authority because I told them. I begged them to listen to me when I, as a Snopes employee working with Facebook on their fact-checking enterprise, had unique insight into what was happening thanks to their platform."

But the site that responded earliest to Q continued to recognize new and dangerous developments and do something about it: Reddit. In late August 2018, subscribers on the successor subreddit to r/CBTS_stream, called r/GreatAwakening, publicly misidentified and doxed a Minnesota resident as the gunman who shot and killed two people at a video-game tournament in Florida.[35] The wrongly identified "shooter" was the subject of a brief smear campaign by far-right media outlets before the mistake was finally discovered. Reddit responded not with warnings or suspensions, but owing to both the doxing and a general uptick in violent threats and ideation against regular Q targets, closed r/GreatAwakening and a dozen other Q forums, and banned all organized discussion of QAnon.[36] By quickly de-platforming the movement and following up with rigorous banning of forums that tried to evade the ban, Reddit's leadership effectively rendered Q invisible on one of the world's biggest social media outlets.

Reddit didn't want Q, but Q didn't need Reddit. They had the rest of the social media landscape at their beck and call.

BAN HAMMER

Without any consistent help from the social media giants, it fell to users on these same sites to take matters into their own hands. Liberals on Twitter routinely reported ban evasion (which the site did not even provide as a cause for complaint in its abuse reporting options) and would often get the same accounts suspended over and over, only to see these posters go to Twitter alternatives like Parler to complain about their ban, announce their new Twitter handle, and go right back to posting.

There were more organized efforts as well, such as the concerted effort to expose not only major Q gurus, but the operators of Q-drop aggregator sites as well. These sites, places like QMap.pub and QAgg.net, served as waystations for Q believers to get the latest drops without having to navigate 8chan, and were a major part of Q's information ecosystem. Independent outlets like the British fact-checking site *Logically* went after these aggregator sites, with a summer 2020 story exposing the operator of QMap, the most popular aggregator and the only one endorsed by the Q poster, as an IT executive at Citibank who soon found himself out of a job.[37]

Twitter, Facebook, and YouTube finally took serious steps against Q and its gurus around that same time. In July, Twitter banned about one hundred thousand Q accounts, blocked the use of Q-related URLs, and de-boosted Q in search results.[38] Facebook took similar steps a month later, scourging many of the groups that had grown so much because of the pandemic. Over the next few months, everyone from TikTok to Etsy took steps to definitively curb Q's growth on their various platforms.[39] But numerous major accounts, video channels, merchandisers, and influencers remained—and the most influential personality of all, Donald Trump, continued to tweet conspiracy theories and Q memes with no meaningful pushback.

Ban evasion became so much a part of standard operating procedure with Q that the Q poster made reference to it, asking followers in Drop #4734 to "Deploy camouflage. Drop all references re: 'Q' 'Qanon' etc. to avoid ban/termination."[40] The branding change never really stuck, but then again, neither did most of the bans. Most followers suspended from Twitter that summer, such as major influencers like Joe M, along with many others, came back again and again. And Facebook continued to struggle with disinformation, with Q-driven concepts like child-trafficking hysteria and antifa starting forest fires in the Pacific Northwest easily jumping from social media to major right-wing pundits.

Finally, January 6, 2021, came, and with it, the nightmare that disinformation specialists and extremism researchers had feared. Social media played a huge part in coordinating the attack, and ginning up the anger and conspiracy theories that led to it.[41] Conspiracy theories about Biden stealing the election and how the results could be overturned exploded in the two months between the election and the attack, turning Trump-world figures into media stars—with Trump amplifying all of it on Twitter. During the attack itself, insurrectionists posted so much incriminating material on social media that Virginia senator Mark Warner formally asked the telecom and tech companies to preserve what was essentially a digital crime scene.[42]

Facebook and Twitter responded by cracking down hard on QAnon. Facebook, which had resisted wider bans on Q groups due to fears that conservatives would see them as overly limiting free speech, as revealed by the *Washington Post* in March 2021, closed tens of thousands of groups and pages. And Twitter executives realized their limited ban of QAnon that summer "wasn't sufficient," according to a CBS News story that same month, and banned over seventy thousand users, including major influencers.[43]

Among them was Donald Trump, who was suspended from a dozen platforms, including his beloved Twitter.[44] After over three years of handwringing, and a laundry list of crimes, Q was no longer welcome on Big Social Media, sending believers scurrying to conservative echo chambers like Gab and Parler, or to secure messaging apps like Telegram—where they'll stay until the inevitable moment when the bans loosen up. To Q followers, mainstream social media sites are the battlefields in the digital war. They won't abandon Twitter and Facebook forever.

But can the next Q be prevented through diligent de-platforming and keeping an eye out for warning signs? Can Facebook do anything to make it right when the time comes? To Binkowski, who tangled with the social giant again and again over these issues, it's possible—but unlikely.

"They can give up their technology and infrastructure to the people of the world and make it open-source," she told me when asked what Facebook could do going forward, adding that setting up a foundation to hire journalists purged from digital media sites "pivoting to video" based on flawed Facebook metrics would help as well. "It won't make them as much money, which is why they of course won't do it, but it's the only right thing to do. Their closing down groups is tantamount to closing the barn doors after all the rabid bulls have escaped to wreak havoc on the public at large.

"They really fucked up."

CHAPTER 10

Change of Batter Coming?
QAnon and the 2020 Election

Ashli Babbitt voted for Barack Obama, but she died for Donald Trump.

On January 5, 2021, the thirty-five-year-old Air Force veteran and QAnon believer declared on Twitter that "they can try and try and try but the storm is here and is descending on DC in less than 24 hours . . . dark to light!"[1] It was the last tweet she would ever compose. A day later, she was dead, having spent the last moments of her life taking up arms against her homeland.

Her death marked the end point of a journey through a pipeline of radicalization that ultimately affirmed QAnon, not the Constitution, as her guiding light.[2] Babbitt had once been a liberal Obama voter, according to her social media posts and interviews with family members. But like so many others, she began to radicalize with the prospect of the hated Hillary Clinton winning the 2016 election, embracing Donald Trump in the process. By November 2019, she was tweeting about Pizzagate. QAnon hashtags followed within a few months. By the time of her death, her Twitter feed was a firehose of election fraud conspiracy theories and "stop the steal" memes, the same ones being pushed by Q promoters, Trump inner-circle members, and the president himself.

Her misguided zeal to save Constitutional freedom by destroying it led her to the second floor of the US Capitol, where the windows leading from the Speaker's Lobby into the main House chamber were being smashed. The goal of her insurrectionist mob: find Mike Pence and make him pay for his treachery.

Pence, interrupted in his constitutional duties of accepting the certified votes of the Electoral College, had just been evacuated from the House chamber. But other House members were still there, guarded by a crude barricade and a few armed officers who were on the verge of being overrun. Ashli Babbitt never laid eyes on Pence or any member of the House, though. She only found the Capitol police officer who, fearing for his life from the horde bearing down on him, shot her dead as the glass shattered around her.

What put Ashli Babbitt in the company of that mob was her belief that the deep state had stolen the 2020 election. And that with every other legal tactic exhausted, only patriots brave enough to take up arms, including the digital soldiers of QAnon, could steal it back by force. Q's prophecies of Trump winning in a landslide over a decrepit Joe Biden had fizzled, but those who believed in them weren't going to melt away, as the Seekers UFO cult had done in the 1950s.

It was time for blood to be spilled. It was time for action. The Capitol attack was the final act of QAnon's complete enmeshment in conservative orthodoxy, a takeover by radical nihilists, clout-chasing grifters, and conspiracy-theorist bomb throwers that the mainstream Republican establishment didn't denounce until they were already assimilated deep in its fabric.

By the time Joe Biden took the oath of office, QAnon was just as much a part of GOP orthodoxy as Benghazi and Hillary's emails— or the Clinton "Body Count list" and Barack Obama's supposedly fake birth certificate. The Republican Party was the party of Q.

RED WAVE RISING

4chan culture had long ago embraced Trump's nihilistic approach to governing by trolling. But it took longer for the rest of the Republican

Party to join in. Even as Q exploded into the media eye after the August 2018 Tampa rally, the rest of the GOP kept the movement at arm's length—careful not to endorse its tenets while also careful not to push away its believers and their precious votes. It's a dance the GOP would continue to perform well into 2020—which led straight to disaster.

The only QAnon-aligned candidate of note in the 2018 midterm cycle was Nevada Republican Joyce Bentley, running in the state's deeply Democratic First Congressional District. Just weeks before the election, Bentley endorsed Joe M's "Plan to Save the World" video, full of claims that "our world has been under the growing influence of a vast transgenerational criminal mafia that was able to rise up to the highest levels of power."[3]

Bentley's endorsement of QAnon didn't help her—she was wiped out in November.[4] And QAnon didn't do the 2018 GOP any favors in general. Despite Q's lofty claims that the election would be a "red wave," the party lost forty seats in the House. In the days that followed, believers swarmed onto 8chan, Twitter, Voat, and other social media venues to vent their frustration. Some called for the military to take over; others argued over what happened next, declared they'd been duped, looked for shills in their midst, and fantasized about "citizen militias" taking to the streets. The media was quick to proclaim the nascent Q movement was falling apart.[5]

But the Q movement didn't fall apart. Believers dug in, reloaded, fired up new memes, and got back to work making "the Great Awakening" a reality. Soon, Q began claiming that the "Senate was the target" of the midterms, in a shift typical of the Q poster every time a prediction failed to come true. According to Q, a firm grip on the Senate would prevent Trump's removal via the phony impeachment charges Democrats would inevitably level. Furthermore, it was okay, according to Q, for so many Democrats to have won in the House, because they were all about to be arrested, and the subsequent special elections to fill their seats would see control revert to Republicans. Q implored believers to "trust the plan."

There were two developments from Q's drops immediately after the midterm debacle that would have chilling ramifications for the years ahead.

One was Q's claim that members of anti-fascist groups would be brought in by the busload, making an "organized push" to intimidate conservative voters, rig or destroy voting machines, and steal the election.[6] The media and social media pundits wrote it off as a joke at the expense of Trump voters, mocking the misery of Q believers and tweeting jokes about conservatives believing in absurd "antifa super soldiers."[7] Two years later, as Capitol insurrectionists blamed nonexistent antifa and Black Lives Matter activists for carrying out a "false-flag" attack, it wasn't so funny.

The other was that just days after the election, Q began hammering an already familiar Trump-world trope: voter fraud. Q played up Trump's already extant tendency to see fraud in any election in which he didn't overperform, making claims in Drop #2479 of "blank ballots" being held "under lock and key" to be counted later and fraudulently added to Democratic tallies. Through it all, Q implored believers to hang in there, because "TOGETHER WE WIN."

Q believers did hang in there. They stayed strong and trusted the plan, ensuring Q wouldn't fizzle out, but prosper in the years ahead. And a strange thing started to happen in Republican politics in general in the aftermath—Q believers stopped just voting for MAGA candidates, and started becoming them.

"A PATRIOT WORTH LISTENING TO"

The earliest Q candidates to emerge for the 2020 cycle were not entirely impressive. The first to get national attention was Danielle Stella, a Minnesota Republican who proudly declared she "stood 100% with QAnon" when she announced her campaign to unseat the Democrat Ilhan Omar in the House in the summer of 2019.[8] Later suspended from Twitter for claiming Omar "passed sensitive info to Iran," for which she said the House member "should be tried for #treason and hanged,"[9] Stella managed to parlay a year of press coverage into just twenty-two hundred votes in the GOP primary. But more QAnon-endorsing candidates would join her, with considerably more success.[10]

Beyond Stella's misbegotten campaign, nearly ninety Q believers launched campaigns for the House alone, with additional candidates running for Senate and gubernatorial races. Some of them had merely shared a video or used a Q catchphrase, typically claiming they "didn't know what it was." Others were full-throated evangelists for "the storm," proudly taking the "digital soldier oath" and pumping out an endless stream of QAnon content on their social feeds. There was Johsie Cruz, a Georgia House candidate who vaguely threatened Jeb Bush with QAnon on Twitter and called Q "a new type of war"; Catherine Purcell, an independent candidate for Delaware's House seat who made truly frightening videos claiming that "Democrats eat you for adrenochrome"; and New Jersey Republican Billy Prempeh, who posted pictures of himself at Q rallies and claimed the Great Awakening was "going on right now."[11]

Two Q-linked House candidates, Indiana's Dion Bergeron and California's Reba Sherrill, even accepted support from 8kun owner Jim Watkins's "Disarm the Deep State" SuperPAC. Watkins's fundraising effort, such as it was, flopped badly—the PAC distributed just $600 of the $5,400 it raised, and the candidates it made videos for lost their primary elections.[12] So did Cruz and Purcell. Prempeh did make it to the general, where he lost by thirty-four points. Most Q-endorsing candidates struggled to gain a footing, and some dropped out before their primary. A few, such as Florida Independent House candidate K.W. Miller, clearly were in it for the publicity—Miller brought viral traffic to his doomed candidacy by making hysterical claims, for example tweeting that Beyoncé Knowles was actually a very tan Italian woman, rather than a Black American.[13] Candidates with links to Q didn't fare much better at the local level.

But they didn't all lose. Two picked up enough support in the primary to advance to the general election in districts where they had a chance to win. One was the Georgia CrossFit enthusiast and business owner Marjorie Taylor Greene, who called Q "a patriot worth listening to" among what would be revealed as an absolute blizzard of conspiracy theory posts on social media.[14] The other was the pistol-packin' Colorado restaurant owner Lauren Boebert, who had made the rounds on conspiracy theorist media after having public confrontations over COVID-19 restrictions and guns. Her views on Q came out soon after, with Boebert explaining on hardcore Q believer Ann Vandersteele's YouTube show *Steel Truth*, "Everything that I've heard of Q, I hope that this is real, because it only means America is getting stronger and better, and people are returning to conservative values."[15]

Boebert and Greene were inexperienced newcomers who ran on a more local version of Donald Trump's outsider populism. They won with small vote totals in their primaries, running campaigns based on conspiracy theories and fear of an onslaught of socialism. They even both explained that they are not Q believers at one point—though not convincingly, given that they continue to express support for some of the conspiracy theories that make up Q. But their districts were solidly conservative, with Greene's so deeply red that a Republican pudding cup would win an election there. With onlookers shocked that two devotees of a crazy conspiracy cult could join Congress, that's exactly what they did. Nobody should have been shocked at this point.

"CLEAR COGNITIVE DECLINE"

For an insider plugged into the highest levels of military intelligence, QAnon didn't see Joe Biden's electoral victory coming. Far from it.

Despite Biden's polling numbers against Trump looking strong enough to win, it took until July 2019 for Q to begin really hammering the former vice president, mostly getting in a few shots at Biden's son Hunter—a drum that both the liberal and conservative media had already been pounding for months.[16] In April 2020, after COVID-19 had thrown any notion of a traditional campaign cycle out on its ear, Q finally turned both barrels on Biden, insinuating that the seventy-seven-year-old nominee was mentally spent, physically shot, corrupt to the bone, and being hidden from public view.

Over hundreds of drops, sometimes dozens per day, Q hammered away at Biden. Q went after the former vice president's age, mental health, financial dealings, and supposed role in helping his son beat corruption charges leveled by a Ukrainian prosecutor (the same claim that had been made by Trump, and which had played a major role in his impeachment at the end of 2019). According to Q, Democrats and their lackeys in the mainstream media were pulling out all the stops to, paradoxically, either protect him or deny him the nomination at various points in the following weeks. As drop #4014 put it:

> Why are they pushing back the [D] convention?
> COVID-19 concern or strategic for last minute change?
> Change of Batter coming?
> Why was she 'saved' from officially announcing?
> Why was she 'reserved' for a last minute change?

In this case, "she" likely refers to either Hillary Clinton or Michelle Obama, both of whom were being tossed out by Q believers as the eventual "real candidate" in the "change of batter" (which is not an actual term used in baseball) that the Democrats had planned to screw over both their primary voters and Trump.[17]

"HOW DO YOU SHELTER [BIDEN] FROM DEBATES? HOW DO YOU SHELTER & PROTECT [BIDEN]?" blared Drop #4245 in May, backing up the claim that the Democrats would "change out" the nominee in a convention moved as close as possible to Election Day. A long Q drop in June, #4545, was even more inflammatory, accusing the COVID-19 lockdowns of purposefully sapping the hope and energy of Trump voters. In a clear echo of Trump's continual claims that the election was going to be rigged, Q claimed that the mail-in voting push being driven by the pandemic was part of a massive scheme to steal the election through "harvesting," that the polls were rigged to show support for Biden, and that China would be participating in the fraud by "cloning" ballots from battleground states.

And Biden himself was a wreck, hidden away to prevent "self-embarrassment" and to sweep away news of "family bribes and corruption." Q later claimed in Drop #4657 that Biden was in "clear cognitive decline," and that Biden's team would "find excuse/reason to terminate" the presidential debates, while also being "provided the questions ahead of time and assistance in the form of a special communication device." Biden didn't "terminate" the debates, and actually held his own quite well in a chaotic scream fest against Donald Trump.[18] Ironically, the only one of the three debates that did end up being "terminated" was due to Trump's COVID-19 diagnosis.

As the slow march toward the election ground on, and Biden's "clear cognitive decline" never quite manifested, Q switched targets to join in on the far right's relentless assault on Joe's son Hunter. Through it all, Q stuck to the same message: Biden was a worthless and barely functional puppet candidate who would be tossed off the ticket at the last second, while the deep state and its Chinese allies simultaneously rigged the election for whichever sap the cabal picked in his place. The expectations on Trump couldn't be higher, and for Biden, they couldn't be lower.

THE QUESTION, ASKED

Just as Q dismissed Biden, so too did QAnon promoters and believers. Chief among the Q devotees who wrote Biden off as a decaying cinder of a man was Donald Trump himself. Echoing the language of Q's drops, Trump blasted Biden over the course of a year and a half as "sleepy," "creepy," "creepy sleepy," "slow," "corrupt," "China Joe," "Hidin' Biden" and rhetorically asked both "Where's Joe" and "Where's Hunter?"[19] Like Q, Trump singled out mail-in voting, calling it "a fraud like you've never seen" and making bizarre claims that poll workers were "selling ballots."[20] He claimed Biden was hiding "in a basement" while Trump went out to meet the people at rallies (rallies that often ended in explosions of COVID-19 diagnoses for attendees), and slammed Hunter Biden's business dealings and well-known drug problems.[21] And Trump gleefully retweeted Q-driven conspiracy theories about Biden's brain "freezing," repeated Q-driven claims that Biden was a pedophile, and pumped out countless accusations about voter fraud and rigged voting machines.[22]

Likewise, Trump's inner circle and mainline Q believers alike spread breathless conspiracy theories about the COVID-19 lockdowns being designed to hurt Trump, claimed Biden had been wearing a hidden earpiece to feed him answers during his debates with Trump (recall Q's drop that Biden would get "assistance in the form of a special communication device"), and regurgitated smears about Hunter Biden's drug use and alleged child abuse (which nobody had ever actually alleged).[23]

For a while, Q's insults and Trump's insults moved together on parallel tracks. It was impossible to tell which one inspired which, though it's not like Trump suddenly discovered the power of a crushing put-down delivered to a rabid rally crowd. This is, after all, a candidate who called the 2016 election rigged and fraudulent *after winning it*. It was a potent and consistent message delivered from multiple vectors—corruption, fraud, decay, and a deep state pulling out all the stops to stop Trump, just like they'd tried the last time.

In summer 2020, the two tracks finally came together. For years Q believers had demanded that the media "ask the question" about QAnon directly to the president so that he would be forced to explicitly acknowledge it. By their logic, Trump being asked about QAnon would somehow require him to admit that the previously secret Q team was real, thereby "ending" the conspiracy and handing victory to the deep state. Why the media, which Q believers thought were facing execution in "The Storm" for their corrupt links to the deep state, wouldn't want to "end" the Q movement before that is another seemingly basic question that nobody bothered to ask themselves. Nor did anyone involved with Q wonder why Trump couldn't simply volunteer to talk about Q, or why his answer wouldn't be anything other than his usual word salad. But that summer, with QAnon driving story after story in the media, someone finally did "ask the question." Trump's support for Marjorie Taylor Greene, and her belief in Q, came up at an August news conference, and Trump said of the people who had spent almost three years idolizing him as a god: "I don't know much about the movement, other than I understand they like me very much, which I appreciate."[24]

"QAnon believes you are secretly saving the world from this cult of pedophiles and cannibals," a reporter followed up.[25] "Are you behind that?"

Given that few people would willingly admit to not being behind a group fighting "pedophiles and cannibals," the moment of truth that Q believers thought would "end" their conspiracy movement turned out to be as slow and easy a softball as anyone could possibly ask for.

"I haven't heard that. Is that supposed to be a bad thing or a good thing?" Trump replied, hitting the easy pitch out of the park. "If I can help save the world from problems, I am willing to do it. I'm willing to put myself out there. And we are actually, we're saving the world."

Naturally, popular Q promoters rejoiced on social media.[26] InTheMatrixxx declared "Thank you, Mr. President!" while Major Patriot pointed out how Trump said "NOTHING BAD" about the Q movement. Others believed Trump was covertly shouting out the Q movement in the coded language of his response.

Regardless, that October, Trump praised QAnon again, telling the NBC host Savannah Guthrie that he knew nothing about it, but "what I do hear about it is they are very strongly against pedophilia, and I agree with that."[27]

Trump's conspiracy theories were now indistinguishable from QAnon's. The president kept tweeting about fraud and rigging, and shared an absolutely unhinged conspiracy theory being promoted by Q followers that as vice president, Biden had helped organize the mass killing of the Navy SEAL team that had killed Osama Bin Laden—just one of the 315 separate times Trump would retweet or boost content from a QAnon believer before his eventual banning from Twitter.[28]

With the election approaching, Q and Trump had told a compelling story to millions of pandemic-weary, conspiracy-believing, Biden-hating Trump voters: Trump was a hero saving the world from pedophiles through his army of Q believers, Biden was a barely functional puppet of the deep state and Chinese money, COVID-19 was being exploited (or had even been created) to hurt Trump, and "China Joe" would never and could never be president.

Above all, Trump had no chance of losing as long the election was conducted fairly and legally. If Biden won, it meant the election was stolen and illegal.

Millions of Trump voters heard the message as clear as a bell.

STOP THE STEAL

Even with all the insults and allegations and conspiracy theories and smears and boasts and wild claims put forth by Trump and his camp, one inescapable fact began to dawn as 2020 election night sunk into blackness: Donald Trump lost.

After a few late swings of close red states to blue, it was all over. That Saturday, Joe Biden and Kamala Harris stood in front of a Philadelphia rally ground full of COVID-restriction compliant Democrats sitting in their cars and declared victory. Except to millions of Trump supporters, they hadn't won. It was fake. Phony. A fraud. Trump had been deprived of victory by giant middle-of-the-night dumps of fake mail-in ballots that swung red states to blue as America slept. Republican votes had been changed or thrown out thanks to foreign plots, complex CIA vote-harvesting programs, and the machinations of a truly evil election administrator—the voting-machine company Dominion.

The election was being stolen from the god emperor and handed to the decrepit basement-bound mummy Joe Biden, right in front of the world's eyes. Just like Q and Trump had said would happen.

The explosion of conspiracy theories after the election is impossible to separate from QAnon. It represents the movement's biggest success in its quest to troll the deep state into submission. 4chan and Twitter immediately became hives of disinformation related to voter fraud and ballot rigging, shooting the "best" theories straight up the right-wing "disinfo" pyramid.[29] Q promoters on Twitter (of whom there were still hundreds, despite the site banning some in July) spun a new great hope: Trump not only had won, but won in a four hundred–plus Electoral College vote landslide. But pretending to lose was necessary to sniff out and crush the fraud of the deep state. Once the fraud was revealed, everything would be fine.

Absent in all of this was Q, beyond a couple of meaningless drops a few days after the election. It was a cold and unforgiving silence that left Q's countless acolytes desperate for answers and reassurance that everything would be okay. And into that silence screamed Q's biggest gurus—grabbing control of the movement for good and never letting go.

"We're in day 2 of Joe Biden thinking he is president," declared Q promoter CJ Truth to hundreds of thousands of followers that Thursday, with "firefighter prophet" and Trump acolyte Mark Taylor claiming confidently that Trump would be "the next president" (he was already president).[30] Joe M went even further, saying Biden was a fascist working for "hostile foreign forces," Trump won in a landslide and would stay in the White House, and that "everything you thought you knew was a lie."[31]

These messages of grievance and determination, and countless others just like them, got tens of thousands of shares and likes over the next few days. Every day after Biden's win, Q promoters relentlessly held the line: Trump had won massively, Biden would never take office, and the corruption would be so obvious that Biden would concede and present himself for execution.

The churn of "Trump actually won" conspiracy theories was a storm of purposeful disinformation so thick that at one point, 5 percent of *all tweets* about the election were coming from Q-linked Twitter accounts.[32] And they weren't congratulations to Joe Biden for a well-fought campaign.

At the very center of the orgy of conspiracy theories was Ron Watkins—who claimed to have resigned from running 8kun on Election Day to pursue woodworking.[33] Watkins didn't reach for a lathe or a saw, though, but for an owner's manual for a Dominion voting machine, tweeting after the election that he had figured out how the machines could be rewired to change votes—a possibility that no voting machine company in their right mind would ever put in print. Watkins, who lived in Japan at that point, began billing himself as something called a "large systems technical analyst" and an expert in US election law, going on a relentless binge of tweets "proving" Dominion's role in boosting Biden to victory. The tweets caught the eye of the Trump-slavish One America News Network reporter Chanel Rion, who featured Watkins's nonexistent expertise in a TV segment claiming that millions of Trump votes had been "deleted" by the company. Nothing else could possibly explain how Joe Biden won.

That segment, featuring Watkins wearing a black cowboy hat and a red flannel shirt and rambling straight to the camera, went straight into the eyeballs of the holder of America's nuclear codes, with Trump retweeting it using the segment's title: "Dominion-izing the Vote."[34] It made no sense, of course. Dominion was only one of many companies who administered voting machines, and the counties in Georgia it did administer actually went on balance to Trump.[35] But by then, the ship of logic had sailed. We were in Q land, and we weren't getting out alive.

Ron Watkins, a figure credibly linked to the direct posting of Q's drops, was tweeting his way to superstardom. In that, he was joined by other major Trump figures who were putting out endless conspiracy theories about Dominion changing votes using software developed by the Venezuelan strongman Hugo Chavez—who had been dead since 2013.[36] Ron gained half a million Twitter followers, and some very powerful new friends in the Trump-world sphere, including Trump's shame-free legal consultant Rudy Giuliani. He and other Trumpists heaped so much abuse on Dominion (all of it based on lies and conspiracy theories) that his followers doxed and threatened to hang a twenty-year-old Dominion employee who was recorded putting a flash drive in a computer in a short "bombshell" video that Watkins tweeted, "proving" the votes had been deleted.[37]

And he wasn't the only hero birthed out of the slime of the post-election, pre-inauguration disinformation frenzy.

Just as Ron Watkins reinvented himself as an election-fraud expert and sold his theories to the most powerful man in the world, so too did Trump-world lawyers L. Lin Wood and Sidney Powell. Both were already part of the right-wing ecosystem, with Powell acting as Q hero Michael Flynn's attorney, and Wood serving as a campaign lawyer for Trump.[38] Both had subsequently made themselves part of what their fellow Trump lawyer Jenna Ellis dubbed the "Elite Strike Force," the team that lost dozens of sloppy and misspelled lawsuits attempting to overturn the election.[39] And both had aligned themselves with Q believers, with Powell sharing Q content on Twitter and appearing on Q-friendly livestreams, and Wood including #WWG1WGA in his Twitter bio while shamelessly pandering to Q believers on social media.[40]

Wood, Powell, and Watkins all became field marshals in the fight for Trump to stay in the White House, relentlessly urging Trump to take drastic measures and invoke the Insurrection Act or martial law to seize voting machines and overturn the results. They claimed over and over and over that Trump won, Biden lost, the election was rigged, and the country was in peril if drastic action wasn't taken *right now*. And they were finding huge new audiences, with Wood quickly racking up half a million followers on Parler alone, and Watkins at nearly 580,000 on Twitter before he was finally banned.[41]

As if throwing a lit match into gasoline, Q resurfaced one last time on December 8, making their final drop of the Trump years. It was, as with many other recent Q drops, unfathomably lazy. But in light of what was about to happen, it was also one of the most prescient: a link to a YouTube video, which shot up from around ten thousand views to over 1.5 million in the days after the drop, of Trump rally footage set to Twisted Sister's 1984 hit "We're Not Gonna Take It."

#CROSSTHERUBICON

As the already infinitesimal hope of a Trump miracle victory faded into nothingness, the tweets of the Elite Strike Force and their Q-believing members took on the cryptic end-times sheen of Q drops, like this Ron Watkins tweet from December 18:

> When the process has been rigged and corrupted.
> When SCOTUS fails to take action.
> POTUS @realDonaldTrump must stand up to DEFEND
> THE REPUBLIC.
> He is SWORN to protect us from enemies both FOREIGN
> and DOMESTIC.

The similarity to Q's writing style was so striking that I actually reached out to Ron Watkins to ask him about it—to which he replied, "I don't know enough about Q's writing style to comment on that."[42]

What Watkins did know about was getting traffic. In a massively viral Twitter thread, (like all of Ron's tweets, everything he tweeted after the election was erased when he was banned from Twitter) Watkins declared that Trump must do what Julius Caesar did when he invaded Rome and "cross the Rubicon"—use executive orders to invalidate the election and make bloody war against the domestic enemies threatening his reign.[43] The #CrossTheRubicon concept took off immediately among Q believers on social media with tens of thousands of similar tweets taking up the hashtag.[44] Watkins put out a poll asking if his fans would support a "limited martial law" and got over ninety thousand "yes" votes. Fake-news sites and Q promoters got in on the act, rumormongering about Chinese soldiers massing on the Maine-Canada border, earthquake weapons being deployed, Supreme Court Chief Justice John Roberts caught on tape angrily refusing to put Trump back in office, and troops preparing to go into the streets of America's cities. All of it stoked a digital frenzy of millions of Americans demanding that their beloved president plunge the country into a dictatorship and crush his enemies—their enemies.

Unsurprisingly, the concept of a peaceful transfer of power is not compatible with an election loser calling up the military and forcibly seizing control. And as the hope of a civil or legal miracle ebbed, violence became more and more inevitable. In fact, it had already started—two men were arrested outside the Philadelphia Convention Center with guns and Q merchandise several days after the election for allegedly conspiring to try to stop the vote count.[45] It was, of course, just a taste of what was to come (ironically, one of them would be arrested again for violating their bail conditions after being caught at the Capitol insurrection).[46]

As the weeks between the election and Biden's assumption of the office wore on, Trump's offensives were thwarted at every turn. His Elite Strike Force lost its great hope of the Supreme Court taking up their case. Every county certified its vote tallies, with every state, in turn, certifying the Electoral College voter slates their citizens had lawfully chosen. Audits and recounts turned up nothing in terms of voter fraud. The process went forward as it had every four years since the first competitive presidential election in 1796. Biden went about his business as president-elect.

So Q believers put their faith in one last desperate gamble: "the Pence Card."[47] Pence had mostly stayed out of the president's fight to stay in power, content to make a few speeches and keep his head down. But in the fantasy world of #CrossTheRubicon, Pence potentially could swing the whole thing back to Trump thanks to an apparently undiscovered bit of electoral magic. During the January 6 joint session of Congress, at which the vice president was presented with the electoral votes, House and Senate members could legitimately team up to challenge state vote tallies, and many "stop the steal" devotees believed Pence could take those challenges as the impetus to throw out the results of any state whose votes were successfully challenged. This would either invalidate Biden's win or throw the election to the House of Representatives, where Trump would be picked by a majority of state House delegations.

This was never an actual possibility. The VP's role in accepting the Electoral College voting slate is entirely ceremonial. And while challenging state vote totals is a constitutional practice, Pence had no more power to snap his fingers and reelect Trump than any previous vice president in history. If they did, wouldn't Al Gore have tossed out Florida's disputed electoral votes in 2000 and made himself president?

Despite there being no possibility of "the Pence Card" being played, January 6 became the Last Stand of Last Stands, a rally and protest outside the Capitol where thousands of MAGA die-hards would implore Pence to sweep America's electoral process into the trash can of history. Extremists of all stripes openly plotted what they'd do if Pence didn't follow their orders—with 1,500 violent posts by QAnon believers alone flagged in the aftermath.[48] They brought guns, flexible handcuffs, and rope for a gallows. Having been sworn in just days earlier, Marjorie Taylor Greene objected to the vote while wearing a black face mask that proclaimed TRUMP WON.

"Be there. Will be wild!" Trump tweeted a few days before the ceremony.[49] And it was.

What happened next was entirely foreseeable—QAnon had spent a year putting out drops claiming that if Biden won, it was because the election was rigged. It happened because of Trump's amplification of those conspiracy theories, and their spread by Q-believing right-wing media stars with huge followings. It happened because of the social media kingpins letting those statements metastasize with little pushback. It happened because of the years of "Great Awakening" rhetoric pumped out by Q and its biggest promoters promising the destruction of Trump's enemies. It happened because of the "god emperor of the United States" ideation that took over 4chan and far-right social media before the election.[50] And it happened because of the mockery and dismissal of QAnon as a crazy cult for boomers.

Four attackers died on January 6, including Q believers Ashli Babbitt and the thirty-four-year-old Rosanne Boyland, a Georgia woman whose social media showed her to be deeply sucked into Q's mythology.[51] A Capitol police officer was also killed, with several others taking their own lives in the aftermath. It was the worst assault on America's seat of power since Redcoats burned the White House in 1814—a disaster that could have easily ended with the deaths or kidnapping of Mike Pence and Nancy Pelosi, the first and second people on the presidential line of succession.

Even so, democracy survived that day. The votes were counted after police and the National Guard retook the Capitol. Mike Pence took no action to thwart the process. Hundreds of insurrectionists, the bare-chested Q Shaman and many of his Q-believing brothers and sisters among them, were easily identified by open-source intelligence on social media, and indicted. Twitter and Facebook finally did the right thing and cracked down on both QAnon and Trump's allies. They banned Trump himself.

It was over. Two weeks later, even as Q believers still clung to the desperate hope of something—anything—happening to stop it, Joe Biden took the oath of office. There was no storm. There was no Great Awakening. There were no mass arrests. The booms promised by Q never came. The Q movement took its best shot to "save the world," and failed.

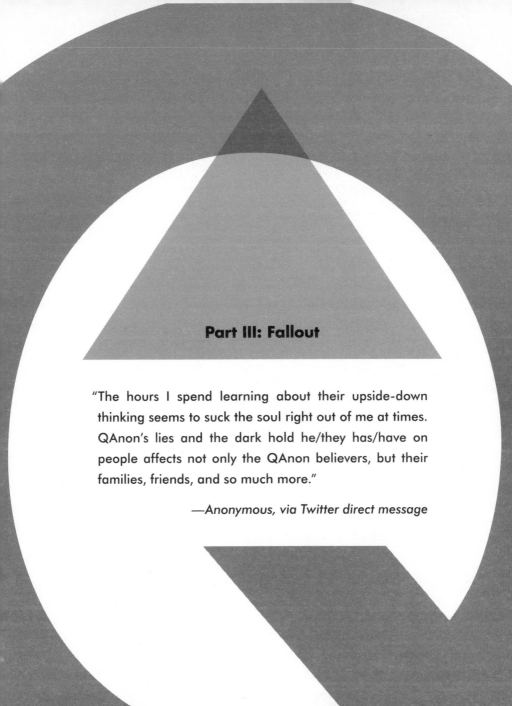

Part III: Fallout

"The hours I spend learning about their upside-down thinking seems to suck the soul right out of me at times. QAnon's lies and the dark hold he/they has/have on people affects not only the QAnon believers, but their families, friends, and so much more."

—*Anonymous, via Twitter direct message*

The Only Cult That Teaches You to Think for Yourself: What Experts Think QAnon Is (and Is Not)

One of the most frustrating aspects of telling the story of QAnon is that Q isn't just one thing. It touches numerous different areas of culture, politics, sociology, and technology. Q's origins are completely rooted in American hucksterism and evangelical tropes—yet it can trace its lineage to both English and Russian anti-Semitism. It's often called a cult, but has no real leader. Others see it as a new prophetic religion—but it has no clergy and relies on New Testament scripture as much as it does classified intelligence. It has puzzles to solve, yet offers no hint as to when you've solved them, nor does it eventually reveal those solutions. Q claims to be a military intelligence figure "saving the world," yet vanishes for months at a time. It's a marketing grift that doesn't do enough to be effective at either marketing or grift. It's very slippery to pin down, but also fairly easy to understand.

To truly get Q means understanding it holds aspects of all of these different disciplines—and more—without being any single one of them. But why isn't it any single one of these things? And if it's not, can we ever have any hope of really understanding it? What do the experts *in* those fields think of Q?

TERROR AND LOVE

From the beginning, the word "cult" was an easy shorthand to describe QAnon. Media outlets wrote of "the cult of QAnon," described its destructive mind-control techniques, and wrote its believers off as the digital version of drooling zombies in beige frocks, stripped of agency as they fought for scraps of affection from a god figure.[1] But Q's followers are far more complex and human than those crude tropes allow for—and Q is too multifaceted to simply call it a cult and pat ourselves on the back for being smarter than the people who fall for it.

As it turns out, even experts and professionals who study cults and cultlike movements are divided on whether Q can really be defined as a cult, or if it is merely a movement that exploits the same foibles that cults do. Many experts struggle openly with the question. And none could provide a simple answer.

As director and founder of the Cult Education Institute, Rick Alan Ross would be among the foremost people to be able to ascertain whether or not Q is a cult based on the criteria he's developed through his decades of research—as well as his countless interventions to help people get out of coercive groups. When I spoke to him, he walked me through how there are three basic aspects that determine whether a movement is a cult—and how QAnon does and doesn't fit into them.

"One is a charismatic leader who becomes an object of worship," Ross told me. That leader is typically totalitarian and demands total control over believers, rewarding belief with praise and punishing failure by withholding it. "Two is a deliberate effort to employ thought reform or coerce persuasion," he continued, pointing out how Q has created an alternate universe online where people can cocoon with like-minded believers who swiftly attack opponents, and who wave away uncertainty with calls to trust the plan and hold the line. "And three, is this group destructive? And I don't think there's any question that [in this case] the group is destructive."

But because Q doesn't quite fit into all of those categories, when I asked Ross if Q was actually a cult, even he could only say "yes and no."

"The only way it's not a cult is if it can be argued and proven that it's a leaderless group. Which is not the case," he said, because Q, of course, has Q—and Trump. And yet, Ross continued, "where there's a problem with Q is establishing who is in charge." As Ross puts it, cults typically have a charismatic leader who becomes an object of worship. "[But] Q can go quiet, which [makes QAnon] a movement that's taken on a life of its own without directives" from the top. We've seen from Q's silences during the pandemic and after Joe Biden's election that Q believers can happily go on fighting against the deep state without orders from a leader. This allows Q promoters to fill that void—something no cult with a charismatic figurehead at the top would ever allow.

So with a charismatic leader who takes long breaks from actually leading (and appears to have completely disappeared now), can the QAnon movement be considered to actually *have* a leader? And if it's a leaderless movement, can we call it a cult? This genuine confusion about what to label Q—a cult, or just a gathering of people who think something you think is weird—extends to other experts in the field of coercive moments.

Mark Juergensmeyer, the religious studies scholar who helped me make the connection between the "battle between good and evil" rhetoric of imprisoned Al Qaeda members and that of QAnon, was similarly ambivalent as to the issue of how accurate it was to call Q a cult. Some of it has to do with the very word "cult" being a term that carries too many inaccurate and simplistic connotations to be useful.

"In general, sociologists and scholars of religion have avoided the term 'cult' since it has been used pejoratively in the popular media against any religious group or movement that one doesn't like," he explained, referring to the scorn and derision that members of such groups are reflexively treated with. "So if you use the term you'll have to define it. If you mean by that term a secretive, authoritarian movement with a strong boundary maintenance between who is in and who is out, then yes, from what I understand, QAnon would qualify." But of course, it's not that simple.

With what Juergensmeyer denotes as "mechanisms to reward or force compliance with the rules and beliefs of the movement," he prefers to see Q as simply a worldview rather than as the stereotypical definition of a cult. He believes that Q's embrace of Trump as a charismatic leader has less to do with thought or behavior control than it does with the rejection of traditional political norms and authority. Q believers wholeheartedly embrace neo-nationalist rhetoric, full of secrecy and paranoia about enemies lurking everywhere—which is cultlike in its fear of outsiders, but far more patriotic and jingoistic than a traditional cultic movement. And it was Trump, not Q, who was already offering all of that—an "America first" ideology that cast foreigners as a caravanning horde slowly creeping toward the border, with "enemies of the people" in the liberal media acting as their mouthpiece. Q didn't invent that. And neither did Trump. These are the hallmarks of mass movements going back generations.

Dr. Alexandra Stein, one of the United Kingdom's foremost experts in social psychology and totalitarianism, was another top-tier thinker I went to in order to find a simple answer for this complex question. And just like Ross and Juergensmeyer, she didn't have one.

"I don't know," she explained with a smile when I asked her if QAnon was a cult, revealing how she herself was struggling with how to think and write about the Q movement. Stein touched on the same problem others have had: the issue of whether or not Q has a charismatic and authoritarian leader. Because we can't assess the leadership structure of Q—and it's not clear that there is actually one—Stein believes that if Q is a cult, we're only seeing it from the outside. This makes it very difficult to discern what's happening in the hearts and minds of its members. But on the surface, at least, all the trappings are there.

"Q's discourse and ideology are extremely cultlike," Stein said. "It's totalistic, it's them versus us, it's fiction, [and] it must be dissociative," she continued, referring to what she sees as believers attempting to escape reality through Q. And echoing Juergensmeyer's exhaustive work trying to understand the motives of Al Qaeda members, Stein connected the graphic violence fantasies of Q and its believers to the internal social media indoctrination of ISIS—a combination she defines as "terror and love."

That particular death cult is known for showing new converts what she describes as "brutal imagery interspersed with utopian, North Korea–style" images and propaganda about the beautiful land they're helping to create. And this same strain of violent utopianism is all over QAnon, which has a central belief that a storm of mass arrests and public executions will usher in a new era of peace and freedom—with a special emphasis on punishing child abusers, a group that pretty much everyone agrees deserves punishment. All in all, it adds up to what Stein refers to as a "mindfuck" for anyone pulled into it—one that's possible to leave, but doesn't make it an easy or desirable choice. Don't you trust the plan? Why would you walk away from it if you did?

Like QAnon, most cults don't make it impossible to leave, instead casting the outside world as an evil and dangerous place that you don't want to reenter. "The driving force of a cult is fear, and Q is full of fear," she continued. "It keeps you revved up in chronic anxiety, and you're isolated, so you can't go outside the system to a rational person." There's a nameless terror outside the closed circle of Q, "and even if you can't name it, it's a feeling. The outside isn't a safe place, this is the only safe place."

The feelings of fear are never relieved or allowed to be processed in a healthy way, only intensified with more memes, more conspiracies, and more enemies. And the Q believer has pushed away the loved ones and friends who *could* help calm those feelings, leaving "rational people unable to think for themselves."

Stein goes on to describe another element of a cult that other experts have touched on: the secrecy. The very core of QAnon is so-called classified information being dispensed by an anonymous figure in the form of riddles and codes that make no sense to an outsider—all leading up to a great event that only Q knows the date of. What could be more compelling and secretive?

"It's structured like an onion, with the least crazy parts on the outside, and getting more and more separated from reality" as you get inside it, she explained, a trait found in other fringe movements that depend on secret scripture or revelations from a god figure. "You have a porous external layer [of social media posts], but deeper down, it's super-secret, and that's a highly cultic phenomenon."

Stein paused, as if she had finally found the answer to the question she'd been asking herself since we started chatting.

"It looks like a cult, doesn't it?"

THE GOSPEL OF Q

Just like it's easy to write QAnon off as a cult, it's also easy to write it off as a New Age religion, a young Scientology based not in the self-healing of Dianetics, but the good feelings pumped out by Q.

Q is already deeply evocative of the Christian Identity movement, the nebulous mass of white supremacists, sovereign citizens, and militia members who preach holy war through violence and law-breaking, endorsing everything from evading taxes to killing judges.[2] Could Q take the tenets of those movements, merge them with the scriptures provided by Q in the form of the drops, and eventually become its own religion?

It seems like a possibility, given Q's impact on the evangelical community. But Q has no physical church, no codified structure, no clergy, and no real spiritual element that's not cribbed from evangelical Christianity—tropes that the Q poster was easily able to exploit. Q believers also don't engage in large-scale proselytizing, preferring to "red-pill" new converts personally by sending videos or guides to them, rather than simply spamming out links to "decodes" that will make no sense to an outsider.

So the key to this possibility lies not in the trappings of a church, but in the movement's devotion to prophecy. Like its predecessors NESARA and the dinar scam, Q is a movement that, at its core, believes in the ever-approaching Great Event, though in this case, it's the mass purging of progressives, rather than a large cash payment.

Q began with such visions in the form of Donald Trump prophesying a coming storm—and that we were only in the calm before it landed. Over and over, Q promised great change, an event that would forever alter the course of the world by eliminating the bad people and rewarding the good. And like any good prophecy, it was always on the verge of happening, always delayed, and always back on track through the combined efforts of the figurehead and the followers. As far back as Drop #778 in February 2018 Q declared:

> TRUST THE PLAN.
> WE ARE WINNING.
> ARRESTS WILL COME.

What was Q's foretold event if not another version of the arrival of a messianic figure that so many religions feature—something wonderful and life-changing that will pay off the faith you've shown and cast those who scorned your belief into the Lake of Fire?

But unlike the Second Coming of Christ, or the prophecies in the scriptures of Judaism and Islam foretelling events in which billions of believers still put their faith, Q's prophecies can definitively be dismissed as false.[3] The arrests didn't come. The "calm before the storm" never begat even a light mist. When a prophetic movement fails in its telling of the future, results can vary.

Sometimes these failed prophetic movements are resigned to history after falling apart—the most famous relevant example might be the Seekers UFO cult meticulously chronicled in *When Prophecy Fails*.[4] Over Christmas 1954, a small group of Seekers, led by a seemingly meek housewife who claimed she was a vessel for alien communications, spent night after night in the biting cold of a Chicago winter, waiting for a ship to pick them up and spirit them away from a world about to be flooded. The "spacemen" never came, despite believers giving them multiple chances to fulfill the prophecy. Some Seekers reacted to the multiple failures of their leader's foretold events by declaring that their faith had saved the world and the UFO didn't need to come, or that the "spacemen" were in the crowd waiting alongside them for deliverance—but more of them simply went home. The Seekers were soon no more.

But there are also numerous instances of a prophetic movement turning its leaders' failed visions of the future into a legitimate faith that survives to this day. Seventh-Day Adventism traces its roots to the failed end-times prophecies of Baptist preacher William Miller, who declared to a massive and soon-to-be-let-down flock that the last day was nigh, based on his personal interpretation of the Book of Daniel in the Bible—first in March, then April, then October 1844.

None of them happened, of course. But while many of Miller's followers eventually abandoned the movement, others believed *something* had at least begun, even if they couldn't articulate what it was or when it would happen.[5] Powered by their faith that the end-times weren't upon us, only their *beginning* was upon us, a small core of Miller's followers shook off what became known as their "Great Disappointment" and soldiered on—and the Seventh-Day Adventist church was formed two decades later, becoming the spiritual home for as many as 20 million people. Likewise, the Latter-Day Saints founder Joseph Smith had a slew of failed prophecies to his name, as did Charles Taze Russell, the spiritual founder of what would become the Jehovah's Witness movement—which would continue spewing missed end-times dates well into the twentieth century, including a disastrous failure in 1975 that sent church membership plummeting after believers walked away, having spent years preparing.

Three legitimate religions, all with their roots in failed prophecy, all full of members able to reconcile the endless delays of a Great Event that would change everything.

So if Q is heading toward some sort of retroactive erasure of its past prophecies in favor of future legitimacy, it wouldn't be the first fringe movement to make that leap. And the ground is already prepared. Concepts of "spiritual warfare" and donning "the armor of God" are already all over the mythology of both Q and the increasing number of evangelical churches that have found solace in preaching the wisdom of Q alongside the Gospel of Christ. The anti-progressive, anti-science, pro-Trump mores of evangelical churches fit perfectly within Q—and their members have radicalized at a brisk pace. An American Enterprise Institute survey from early 2021 reported that 27 percent of white evangelicals—a number far higher than any other religious cohort surveyed—believe that QAnon is either completely or mostly accurate.[6]

"I find QAnon consistent with many other extremist religio-political movements that I have followed over the years, including those that have arisen in response to the recent global crises of mass migration, economic globalization, and now a global pandemic," Mark Juergensmeyer said, citing the explosive growth of ISIS in the Middle East and the rise of far-right populist movements in Europe as examples of holy crusades against evil wedded to violent politics—with terrible results for the innocent people caught in their blast radius.

"If QAnon was only interested in becoming legitimized as a tax-exempt religion, this would be the mildest outcome we could foresee," he continued, citing Scientology's claims of being a legitimate faith as an example. "It would make it more controllable," he added— but cautioned that this was just one direction Q could go in. Others would combine prophecy and faith in far more disturbing ways.

"A more likely trajectory is for the movement to remain sub rosa,"

Juergensmeyer predicted, sketching out a darker potential path for Q. "It could be a de facto religion without being an institutionalized one. As a secret religion it could possibly spawn overt acts of violence," he said, though he believes that if the acts of violence committed under the banner of Q are "horrendous [enough], they may frighten its own followers and they may back off."

That pathway for Q, a religiously tinged political movement that has never gotten all the way to being an actual religion, is also where Tyndale University professor James A. Beverley has landed. Beverley is associate director of the Institute for the Study of American Religion, and the author of the first book to seriously examine Q's enmeshment with organized religion, called *The QAnon Deception*.

Beverley looks at Q as a political and social movement that lacks a coherent religious message, rather than as a potential new religion in the making. But while he sees the appeal of Q in evangelical circles, he sees that more as a reflection of their embrace of Trump rather than any sort of belief in Hillary Clinton sustaining herself with adrenochrome.

"The language of spiritual warfare would appeal mostly to charismatic or Pentecostal Christians attracted to QAnon," Beverley said. "I doubt if talk of the 'armor of God' means much to anons who don't care about Bible verses or [have a] spiritual focus."

Notions of warfare, battle, or even scrambling the radar of the enemy can have both religious and secular overtones, he pointed out. Beyond that, the "holy lingo" used by Q in a number of drops, and by followers of Q-believing churches, might actually be a turnoff for many QAnon believers who see Q as a military intelligence unit, not as some kind of evangelical hit squad. Many truly believe themselves to not be racist or fascistic—something that can't be said of Christian Identity believers. While many of these people might, to use a lazy stereotype, cling to their Bibles as tightly as they cling to their SUPPORT THE TROOPS bumper stickers, they might not want to hold them in the same fist.

One former Q believer, Serena (a pseudonym), told me as much over the phone months before the Capitol insurrection.

"I didn't sleep, it's all I did," she said, fondly recalling how she stumbled onto Q in late 2017 after losing her home in a natural disaster. She was "learning 4chan and 8chan, all the different platforms. Learning to stay ahead of the hopeful stuff." She "just wanted the power to be for the people and not the criminals." To Serena, Q was cool and exciting, and made her think she was a warrior on the verge of changing the world.

But all that went out the window when Q began to post Bible verses—something no US military official would ever do publicly – even if they were already violating their enlistment oath by leaking classified information. "I felt crestfallen," she said, her voice filling with anger at the idea that Q "would risk [a] military leak channel with Bible verses."

"I thought it was an alliance between Trump and military intel. Now I know it was just a scam," she told me—still audibly upset that the conspiracy she wanted to be true had gotten religious, as it were.

It might simply be incompatible for a prophecy-based religion based around Q to have any appeal to anyone other than evangelicals—who themselves don't seem entirely comfortable with it.

RUSSIA, RUSSIA, RUSSIA

If it's still not clear what QAnon really is, could that be by design? Could a foreign power or domestic conspiracy have created or hi-jacked QAnon, and used it to drive believers toward extreme ideologies as a way of harming the great democracies of the world in a psychological operation? Could Q be a weapon used either by a domestic conspiracy hoping to overthrow legitimate democracy and install Trump as eternal president, or a Russian active measure that succeeded beyond the Kremlin's wildest dreams?

Both theories have their proponents.

The theory that Russia has some hand in QAnon is usually brought up in conjunction with Russia's many other documented attempts to influence American politics and culture, particularly the 2016 election. If those are Russian active measures, why can't this one be that too?

On the surface, it's not an idea that can be dismissed outright. Paul Manafort, Trump's former campaign manager and a prolific lobbyist for Russian interests, was indicted on charges of money laundering and criminal conspiracy by the Special Counsel's office on October 27, 2017, and the first Q drop was made the next day—theoretically the perfect distraction to keep the spotlight off Russian meddling. News broke just days before the 2020 election that Russia-backed Twitter accounts had been among the earliest boosters of Q, using sock-puppet accounts to praise videos by early Q YouTube star Tracy "Beanz" Diaz and sharing Q hashtags.[7] The thousands of tweets these accounts put out represented some of the earliest public acknowledgement of Q, with some made as early as a week after Q's first drops.

We already know that the Pizzagate and Seth Rich conspiracy theories were heavily promoted by the Russian disinformation machine, and many of the same figures targeted by QAnon were linked to those earlier theories.[8] As Twitter finally began cracking down on troll and bot accounts, Russia still had public links to Q—the de-platformed 8kun was only able to find hosting in Russia after being rejected by British and Chinese ISPs, for one. And many of the figures who have benefited from Q have links to Russian interests or money. Roger Stone has consistently boosted QAnon, and also has deep ties to WikiLeaks, the destination for the stolen emails that Russian hackers grabbed from the Democratic National Committee.[9] And QAnon hero Michael Flynn is so entangled with Russia that his own indictment by Mueller came as a result of lying to the FBI about his interactions with Russia's ambassador.[10]

Not coincidentally, Stone and Flynn are often seen as leaders of a more domestic version of this conspiracy, working with people like

Steve Bannon and a dizzying array of trolls and hackers to steal the 2020 election for Donald Trump—which they came uncomfortably close to actually doing.

But to the cybersecurity researcher Brian Krebs, framing Russia as the driving force behind Q's success "seems like a pretty weak argument."

Through his blog *Krebs on Security*, Krebs keeps tabs on the latest developments in hacking, cybercrime, and the goings on of the shadier parts of the web. Krebs has already exposed at least one Russia-linked Q event, 8kun's move to a "bulletproof" Russian host that served as the point of origin for a wide range of malware, credit card fraud scams, and phishing schemes—so he'd theoretically be in a position to uncover more.[11] But if Q, who by this logic, moved 8chan to a domestic host as a way to protect their investment, was really linked to Russia, Krebs isn't seeing it. "It doesn't seem like a Russian influence campaign," he told me.

"When the Russians are involved in something, they have a clear sense of who should benefit from it. Russians excel at selectively leaking information that's damaging. They support publicizing and fanning the flames of things that are already divisive." Essentially, Russia finds extant trends—whether they're real stories like the Seth Rich murder, or 4chan goofs like Pizzagate going viral. Russian trolls and bots work to boost these, rather than creating their own from scratch. The polarization of social media and the instant spread of conspiracy theories ensures they don't have to do more than grab onto the suspicions and fears already taking hold in our society.

And Russia's "psyops" have a goal, an objective beyond simply "causing chaos" or getting people to vote for Trump. Q doesn't have that kind of objective—remember, it's based in a prophetic vision, not an action plan to bring that vision to reality. Its believers up until COVID-19 were almost entirely already rabid Trump supporters, and that only changed with the pandemic—an event even Russia couldn't forecast.

Other experts in the cybersecurity realm have said essentially

the same thing—that Russian trolls and domestic political operatives will amplify what's already out there, but that only Americans
can create conspiracy theories that will sucker in Americans.[12] And
no American has suckered as many of his countrymen and women
than Donald Trump. As the former FBI counterterrorism special
agent Clint Watts said in a 2020 NPR interview, "Russia doesn't have
to make fake news. They just repeat what conspiracies are coming
out of the White House and the [Trump] administration."[13]

While Russia-linked accounts did boost QAnon early on, there's
no evidence that Russian operators had anything to do with the
earliest posts on 4chan, or the later posts on 8chan or 8kun. These
posts are far too fluent in the specific tropes of chan trolling, evangelical hucksterism, and far-right conspiracy theories to not have a
deep understanding of how these worlds fit together—and how their
members can be exploited. A Russian ISP hosting 8kun, or 8kun's
eventual host VanwaTech using Russian IP addresses, are not the
same as the Russian *government* hosting 8kun or having a hand in
Q's drops—it's merely signs that Russia has less oversight of its Internet hosting structure than most Western nations. And the people
who were pretending to be White House insiders and secret agents
on 4chan weren't spending any time worrying about distracting the
public from Paul Manafort's indictment, as some have suggested.
These aren't exactly the people who would have required a "distraction" from mainstream media by Russia.

We've already seen from accounts like FBI Anon and HighwayPatrolman that a compelling story told to a conspiratorial
audience can find sympathetic ears and go on to prosper—especially if it involved Hillary Clinton getting a short drop from a
gallows. And online hoaxes have accelerated into a deadly real-
world phenomenon without a political valence before, such as the
meme of the supposedly real horror monster Slender Man, a tall,
thin ghostly figure in a black suit, which started on the Something
Awful forum in 2009.[14]

Despite having a clear point of origin as a piece of artwork with no greater meaning and that was itself a clear takeoff of the men in black of 1950s UFO lore, anonymous users gave Slender Man such an involved backstory that he essentially became real to those who decided he was real. It took just a few years for Slender Man to become so accepted by his believers that films and TV episodes were made that centered on Slender Man's "real" origin, and two tween girls stabbed a friend to demonstrate their loyalty to the ghostly figure. QAnon has even been referred to as "Slender Man for Boomers"—an obvious hoax that was nonetheless so compelling that believers disregarded its obviousness in favor of the blind belief that was all real.[15]

Even without past examples of hoaxes making the swamp-to-nightly-news jump, it's also important to remember that Russia amplifies everything that might prove useful to its interests—from racial divides in 2016 to COVID-19 conspiracy theories in 2020.[16]

And Russia's early amplification of QAnon played only a minor role in the movement's overall growth. There were over one hundred thousand tweets with QAnon hashtags sent just in the first weeks that Q was posting, and Russia-linked accounts only accounted for about 10 to 15 percent, with all of those accounts apparently suspended by 2019, when Q was at its zenith on Twitter.[17] It's clear that Q was growing on its own, not because Russia was pumping it up, but because nobody was stopping it.

Moreover, the impact of various forms of Russian trolling isn't even all that significant compared to other Russian efforts, such as the hacking and dumping of documents—or simply having political opponents shoved out of windows. The Internet Research Agency, the troll farm that ran Q-boosting bots in 2019 and whose leaders were indicted by Robert Mueller, was the least effective of all of Russia's interference in the 2016 election, making no measurable impact on American voters, despite its outsized press coverage.[18]

Other similar theories that contend Q is a psyop run by American traitors, and/or by Trump acolytes ready to form an army to fight and die for him, fall apart under examination.[19] These theories, which often spin out into a torrent of thin evidence implicating dozens of hackers and trolls (who habitually lie and feud with each other too much to actually conspire together) lack coherent and compelling evidence.[20] And these sorts of theories appeal to both sides of the political divide, looking to blame each other—liberals who think Q is a Republican op, and conservatives who think it's a Democratic op.

A theory of this sort is unnecessary to explain Q's success. Q has no coherent plan, no grand design, and no apparent operational structure. If it did, Q would have been making drops hand over fist as Trump was in the throes of his attempt to steal the election. But Q said nothing. Plus, a real conspiracy to harness Q believers as some kind of mind-controlled MAGA army wouldn't depend on a rickety message board for its existence, and would drive specific and actionable goals, not post cryptic nonsense and vanish at random. It would also likely have a more difficult password to crack than "Matlock."

A GAME THAT PLAYS ITS PLAYERS

QAnon is a cultish movement that's not quite a cult, a movement with prophetic elements that's not quite a religion, and a recipient of Russian boosting that's entirely American. And despite being descended from long-running frauds, it's not really a scam. Q's creators and exploiters have evaded any kind of legal jeopardy for exactly this reason—it's not illegal to pretend to be a prophet or digital warrior online, as long as you aren't promising financial returns or specifically exhorting people to commit crimes. And despite Q mythology having a major role in the lead-up to the Capitol attack, it's a stretch to say that the Q poster directly ordered anyone to do anything.

Q also has elements of a game—puzzles to solve, enemies to fight, goals to achieve, characters to play. But even the designers of alternative reality games (ARGs), the kinds of difficult and fragmented interactive puzzles that have been on the Internet for decades, disagree on how "gamified" Q is. One, Adrian Hon, who created and ran one of the most popular ARGs of the early Internet, says flat out that "QAnon is not an ARG. It's a dangerous conspiracy theory," while another game designer named Reed Berkowitz claims in a blog post that Q not only *is* a game, but is a "game that plays people" and is designed to further the aims of its creator—whoever those people are.[21]

Many of these arguments over what QAnon actually is—is it a psyop or not, is it a cult or not, is it a game or not?—depend on the profession of the person making the argument. Cult experts tend to see Q as a cult. Game experts tend to see Q as a game. Cybersecurity experts tend to see Q as a cybersecurity issue. But Q believers see it as a plan to save the world—a plan being carried out by Donald Trump, his handpicked advisors, and his millions of digital soldiers.

It doesn't matter that whatever that plan was, it failed. No powerful liberals have been rounded up for arrest and execution, and Donald Trump lost the 2020 election to Joe Biden. The issue is that Q's adherents don't believe either of those things, and that lack of belief in the basics of reality has had devastating consequences for American politics.

Experts and scholars can have endless Twitter fights over what Q is and isn't—but to a terrified GOP mainstream, beset by conspiracy theorists and Q acolytes stringing up a noose on the Capitol front lawn, Q is their worst nightmare. It's a political movement that revolves not around patriotism or traditional conservative values, but bloody revenge against diabolical enemies. Its voters demand loyalty, fealty, blood in the streets, and the total overthrow of the political norms of the past.

CHAPTER 12

Mathematically Impossible:
Debunking QAnon and Its Prophecies

It should have never gotten this far.

The idea of a high-ranking team of military intelligence operatives, the silent tip of America's spear, using memes and riddles to leak their operational plans on a message board best known for Japanese fetish porn should not have found paydirt in American politics. QAnon believers should have been dumped alongside flat-earthers, moon-landing deniers, people who think missiles disguised as holographic airplanes hit the World Trade Center, or people who think they had sex with aliens.

Yet there are people who truly, earnestly believe the Earth is flat. There are people who will swear on a stack of Bibles that we never went to the moon, that no planes hit the World Trade Center, or that they're in a passionate relationship with a being from the star Sirius. While these people don't take violent insurrection into their own hands, and there aren't a lot of them, they exist. They are people we know and love. And there's almost nothing in the way of debunking or fact-checking that will make them change their minds. Probably just the opposite.

There are likely millions of people who believe QAnon is real, and far more who believe parts of Q's mythology without identifying as Q believers. Exact numbers are impossible to pin down, but even the lowest polling numbers taken after the Capitol insurrection are disturbing. There's the poll that showed well over a quarter of white evangelicals believe QAnon to be at least somewhat correct. And the lowest polling numbers agree, showing that around 8 percent of Americans believe the QAnon conspiracy theory to be "very accurate" and 10 percent more find it "somewhat accurate."[1] Going beyond Q itself, a December 2020 poll by NPR/Ipsos found that about a third of Americans believe in the existence of a shadowy "deep state" pulling the strings of international politics, and that 23 percent of Republicans believed in a pedophilic ring of "Satan-worshipping elites" who are "trying to control our politics and media."[2] Finally, though the site has methodology problems, a late 2020 YouGov poll found that some 30 percent of Republicans had a "favorable view" of QAnon.[3] And there's even less polling on the spread of QAnon around the world, with the only significant poll taken of Q belief in the United Kingdom finding that as many as one in four Britons believe some aspect of Q.[4]

As of the 2010 census, there were about 280 million adults in the United States. Taking the absolute lowest number of people who find QAnon to be "very accurate" against that total population gives us over 22 million people. Even boiling it down to just a percentage of the 74 million people who voted for Donald Trump in 2020 results in almost 6 million Q believers. This is a lot of people. The number of people who believe in *some aspect* of Q without identifying as believing in Q is likely far higher. And it's possible that QAnon believers are actually underrepresented in these polls, according to preliminary data from a University of Southern California study done in the immediate wake of the 2020 election.[5]

There are more measurable signs, too: the hundreds of thousands of followers many Q gurus had on Twitter before their accounts were banned, the explosive sales of *An Invitation to the Great Awakening* and other Q books, the million-plus views an obscure YouTube video could get in days after Q linked to it. Clearly, this mythology has crawled into the brain of America and the world in a way nobody could have possibly foreseen even at the onset of 2020.

But with Biden in office and "the storm" no longer seeming to be upon us, is that mythology worth debunking anymore? No movement based on the prophecy of a purge of the deep state carried out by Donald Trump can remain unscathed now that Donald Trump is no longer president. Does this mean that the Q drops are still applicable? Is there any point to actually getting into why QAnon itself is a hoax?

If the answer lies in the number of people who believe it—with millions more mystified and abandoned loved ones they've left behind—then the answer is yes. Those loved ones, the people struggling to understand Q, need to know why QAnon fails at every level to stand up to critical examination. Debunking and fact-checking might not sway extant believers, but it might provide a shaft of illumination to believers who have even the slightest doubt. And it might serve as a first line of defense in the future, years from now when Q has turned into something even worse.

It also matters because Q gurus on far-right social media sites like Gab and on Telegram's Q channels are still exploiting the drops, still using them as the center around which their mythology revolves. Finally, even though the last Q drop of the Trump years was in December 2020, there's no telling if or when Q might come back. By the time this book is out, Q might have made hundreds of new drops, rehashing old drops or creating new conspiracies out of the events of the day. It's worth showing in detail why Q, no matter who makes the posts, is not who they claim to be, has no secret knowledge or clairvoyance, and is wrong about almost everything all the time.

THE GOSPEL OF Q

The closest thing to a founding document or scripture for Q are Q's drops themselves. There are 4,953 of them posted just during the

Trump years, totaling 60,000 more words than the New Testament.[6] While not all of Q's mythology stems from the text of those cryptic posts, they are the foundation of that mythology. The cumulative weight of their secrets is what makes Q special and unique from all other conspiracy theories and "insider" anons on 4chan. Some have spilled secrets, and some have lasted a long time—but only Q broke out into the mainstream.

This book has already examined quite a few of the individual drops, but not the corpus of drops as a whole. If Q's entire movement revolves around the veracity of the information locked within these posts, then we need to examine that body of text. And if the Gospel of Q, if one can call it that, isn't a truthful peek into what the deep state doesn't want us to know, then what is it? Parables? Discussion prompts? Puzzles to solve? Trolling?

In late 2020, *Insider* sifted through the entire block of drops to find the most widely used words ("people," "POTUS," "control"), whose names Q uses most (Hillary Clinton, then Barack Obama, followed by Robert Mueller), what time of day they're posted at (between 9:00 a.m. and 1:00 a.m., Pacific Time), their median length (105 characters or 12 words long), and even their use of capital vs. lowercase letters.[7] But while that story helped put a lot of the pieces together about what an average drop might look like, it didn't tell us anything about the texts themselves, or who wrote them. Another study, carried out by a Swiss research firm, used machine learning to determine that the drops almost certainly were written by two different people—a finding entirely consistent with Q's journey from long 4chan thrillers to short blobs of capitalized text on 8kun.[8]

But this type of statistical analysis is only one way to look at Q's drops. Another way is just to read the texts. And a thorough read of them reveals a "military intelligence team" that is, to put it mildly, not especially good at its job of "saving the world." Q's drops veer wildly in subject matter, tone, and complexity. They can be hypocritical, contradictory, and incomprehensible—or fairly straightforward and predictive. Hundreds are just links to long-gone tweets, conservative media stories, or removed YouTube videos. A few, such as Q's claim that a "change of batter" would knock Joe Biden off the Democratic presidential ticket in Drop #4014, seem unfamiliar with American idioms—you'd say "pinch hitter" when talking about substituting a batter in baseball.

Some almost salivate for violence ("These people need to ALL be ELIMINATED. Those who know cannot sleep," screams Drop #2051 on August 31, 2018) while others specifically claim that any violent act committed by a Q believer is fake (Drop #1797, posted just weeks earlier, calls media stories about crimes committed by Q followers a "false 'violent' narrative push"). They are nakedly anti-Semitic and racist, referring to Barack Obama only by his middle name of "Hussein." But Q also declares on seven different occasions that patriotism has no skin color, and anyone who loves freedom is welcome to join them in their quest. And as we'll see below, they are full of false and vague claims, failed predictions, and assertions that are so bizarre and counter to publicly known information that they specifically defy evidence and proof.

Taken together, the drops conjure a team of warriors fighting an unimaginably difficult battle against evil—who happen to take months off at a time and never actually accomplish anything of note. At the darkest hour of the Q movement, when Trump looked to have lost the election, Q literally did nothing but post a Twisted Sister song—after a year of pumping up that Biden could never and would never serve as president. If Q is a field marshal leading an army of digital soldiers, then by extension, Q abandoned them in the field and rode off into the sunset with the wounded and dying left behind.

This is the paradox that Q lays out—a figure at the center of power who does nothing with that power other than tease that one day, they'll actually do something with their power.

And for an elite team of operators, Q is also sloppy, making typos in drops and needing other drops to correct their mistakes, with the excuse that they are "on the move." Some drops have been deleted altogether, or double posted. Q posts long strings of random letters and numbers that are meant to be taken as secret formulations— primers like "Code: AB-aKd&Egh281Q" that are almost certainly just random bangings of closely situated letters and numbers alternating with the left and right hands.[9] Beyond errors, Q repeats drops or phrases used previously, like a video of an AC-130 gunship firing its weapons, which Q has used seven different times. And the Q poster—supposedly an oracle of truth—has been hoaxed several times, including once right before the election when Q shared a fake-news story about James Comey's daughter investigating Jeffrey Epstein's death for the FBI, which they subsequently disavowed by admonishing followers for "taking the bait."[10]

Believers even think that drops signed "Q+" were personally posted by Donald Trump—despite Trump famously being computer illiterate and not even knowing how to send his own emails.[11]

The truth about Q's drops is that they are, on balance, meaningless fragments of nonsense. Yes, when taken together they tell a compelling story full of twists and turns, secret and lies, heroes and villains. But so do Dan Brown novels and *Star Wars* movies. And nobody thinks George Lucas is a secret intelligence agent with top-secret clearance fighting a war against Satanic pedophiles. Anyone with enough time and imagination could have posted the first drops. And once you embrace the idea that the drops could have come from anyone, then who they came from suddenly matters a lot less. They mean nothing and deliver nothing.

Not one thing Q has ever posted requires any kind of special access—only an active imagination and a following willing to forgive their lapses. And at that, Q believers excel.

NO PROOFS, NO PUDDING

Just as observant Jews no longer stone those who violate Deuteron-omy 22:11 by wearing "clothes of wool and linen woven together," Q believers think that not all of Q's drops are accurate, but the ones that are accurate are so mathematically impossible to write off as coincidences that they prove Q is who they claim to be. This is the same view that powers much of the cult of personality around Trump: heads, he wins; tails, you lose.[12]

To backstop this view, believers have created a genre of Inter-net memes known as "Q proofs." Proofs provide just that for believ-ers—evidence that Q and Trump are intimately connected, and that there's no way anyone could post what Q posts without that connection.

"#Qanon's intel drops are approved by President Trump and the proofs provided here will debunk any claims otherwise," reads the introduction to QProofs.com, one of the many sites where these memes are collected (like many of the sources used in writing this book, QProofs went down, but is still easily accessible on the Inter-net Archive).[13] "Examining these proofs provided by Q and Presi-dent Trump will convince the most skeptical person who takes the time to examine them. The proof of Q's legitimacy is undeniable and the information these drops have yielded is shocking beyond belief."

Q proofs work under a principle that Q created, "Future proves past," a phrase used three dozen times in Q drops. This holds that events that will unfold later will serve as evidence of Q having been correct beforehand. It's a form of retroactive prediction that can turn the most innocuous bit of text into incontrovertible evidence once something comes along that matches up with it—which, given the vagueness and sheer amount of text Q has written, is always eventu-ally going to be something.

They're often connected to events in popular culture or politics, or Trump using something in a tweet that Q once used in a drop, such as particular phrase or misspelling. A typical Q proof found on QProofs and other sites goes like this:

> Drop #1077, posted on 4/7/2018, has the following text—
> *Night [4]*
> *Increase in chatter.*
> *Auth B19-2.*
> *Sparrow Red.*
> *Prevent at all costs.*
> *Good.*
> *Castle_Online.*
> Q

Gibberish, right? Except that was posted the same day that the Syrian government used chemical weapons in an attack on rebel forces in the city of Douma—an act that one week later, brought military intervention by the U.S. in the form of missile strikes. On the 15th, two days after American bombers fired missiles at Syrian military targets, the Department of Defense's official twitter account posted the following:

> "A @28thBombWing #B1B Lancer takes off on a strike mission April 13, in support of the multinational response to #Syria's recent use of chemical weapons. Two B-1Bs employed 19 JASSM-ER, the first combat employment of the weapon."[14]

When you take those two posts and combine them with a Trump tweet from April 11 proclaiming that the United States would be firing "nice and new" missiles at Syria in retaliation for their use of gas, you have a Q proof in the form of confirming Q's use of "B19" and "two"—and Trump seeming to leak that these new missiles would be used for the first time. Future proves past.

NATIONAL DOG DAY, AND OTHER CONSPIRACIES

But what does that mean? In all likelihood, nothing. Most Q proofs are extremely tenuous, and most only serve to add weight to the already extant belief that Q is right, not to actually prove it. You can debunk this one, for example, by pointing out that the phrase "B19-2" doesn't mean anything (searching for it on Google brings up only the medical billing code for "unspecified viral hepatitis C"), and if the Air Force fired eighteen or twenty missiles, Q would be able to find a proof for that as well. But thin gruel like this has a purpose—it adds to the collective weight of the "proof" of Q's veracity, even if it's easy enough to dismiss in its own right.

There are hundreds, maybe thousands of Q proofs floating around on 8kun and various other sites—far too many to debunk one by one. This, of course, is the point. But a few stand out above the others. If you spend enough time in the Q ecosystem, you'll probably encounter them, and it's worth knowing what makes them bunk.

One of the most popular is that over several different drops, Q seemed to predict the exact date and time of John McCain's death—literally down to the minute—one month before it happened. And Q knew this because Q knew McCain would take his own life rather than face execution for his treasonous crimes via a military tribunal.

The first was Drop #1649, from June 30, 2018, which makes a reference to the then upcoming Brett Kavanaugh confirmation vote, claiming that "no name" (Q's preferred nickname for the late Arizona senator) would be "taking action," and that "every dog has its day." The second was Drop #1706, which went up at 4:28 p.m. Pacific Time on July 25, and claimed "No name returning to headlines" with a picture of McCain speaking, with eyes closed and hands up. And sure enough, McCain died on August 25th, at 4:28 p.m., Mountain Standard Time—indeed, exactly one month (minus one hour) after Q's post of McCain with his eyes closed and hands up.

Q believers at the time viewed it as evidence that Q was right on the money regarding McCain's death, and telling us in code about what would be an earth-shaking event—if we were smart enough to get the message. As the popular Q promoter Steve Outtrim tweeted at the time,

> Q post June 2018 (about McCain, we don't say his name): "every dog has his day"
> McCain death announcement: national Dog Day.[15]

Except, of course, Q didn't predict or foretell McCain's death, only that McCain would be "returning to headlines"—which could have been for anything from his retirement to his casting a vote against Kavanaugh. Beyond that, National Dog Day was a day after McCain's death, and Pacific Time and Mountain Time are not the same time zone. The prediction is only uncanny if you factor in an extra hour here, less a day there—which is another way of saying, it is not actually accurate. On August 26, the day after McCain's death (which was publicly known to be imminent since McCain's family announced he'd be ending treatment for his brain cancer), Q made another drop hinting that they'd predicted McCain's suicide thirty days prior with the "returning to headlines" drop. But even that was wrong, since it's actually thirty-one days from July 25 to August 25. Q made a vague claim that would have inevitably come true, and, when it did, used the "future" to prove the "past."

Another "proof" QAnon believers will often rely on to backstop "Future proves past" is the use of the phrase "tip-top" by Trump. In early 2018, an anon on 8chan asked Q to "work the phrase 'tip top' into the [State of the Union] as a shout out to the board." Trump didn't—but did use the phrase three months later at the annual Easter Egg Roll to describe the White House as an "incredible house, or building—whatever you want to call it," declaring "we keep it in tip-top shape. We call it sometimes tippy-top shape."[16] Q claimed in

Drop #991 that same day that the anon's request had been granted, asking "Did you listen today?"

And anons were listening—not only did they take it as proof that Q was whispering in Trump's ear, but that "the storm" was soon going to rain down. As one anon put it on 8chan the same day, "POTUS said 'tippy top' at the Annual Easter Egg Roll. I think tippy top means WAY PAST THE LOW HANGING FRUIT. They are now taking from the very top. Sounds like big names ready to roll."[17]

If the anons really had been listening, they would have realized that Trump didn't do what was asked for in January—it took three months for Trump to use the phrase "tip top." And it was not an unusual phrase that Trump worked into his vocabulary just to please a random troll—he'd used the phrase on many other occasions, such as in 2016, when he referred to the Russian nuclear arsenal as "tippy-top," whereas American "nuclear" was "old and tired."[18]

Finally in the category of "proofs that prove nothing" are the "zero deltas" between Q drops and Trump tweets. Delta is simply a mathematical term for the difference between two numbers, but Q believers use it to denote the amount of time between two unrelated events happening—so a Q drop vaguely mentioning something, then Trump tweeting about something vaguely similar to what Q had mentioned a week later would be a "one-week delta." There are innumerable deltas, but the most important ones are "zero delta" instances, usually used by Q believers to denote any Trump tweet that came within a minute of a Q drop being posted.

Like proofs in general, there are countless deltas and markers and timestamps that "prove" Q's drops are connected to world events— so many that one anon complied them into a Google doc that runs on for twenty-five thousand entries tying each drop to various Trump tweets and world events.[19]

"This is statistical evidence that Q is not a LARP," one anon said of the "delta" theory. The Q poster was so taken with the concept of "deltas" as proof of their own greatness that deltas were often used in drops—a seventeen-minute delta between Trump tweets, a one-minute delta between Q posting a picture of the Oval Office and Trump mentioning the room in a tweet, etc. There were even deltas about deltas. In December 2019, Q linked to one anon's study of thirty-six "zero delta" instances of Trump and Q posting within a minute of each other, saying in Drop #3727 it was the "greatest statistical anomaly [ever] witnessed"—in other words, solid proof.

But as with the other proofs, two unrelated things happening around the same time doesn't suddenly mean that the two things were related. And Trump's tweeting times were fairly well established, mostly during early mornings or late at night.[20] So it would be statistically insignificant for a Trump tweet and a Q drop to land at the same time if the drop was made when Trump was known to often tweet. And if the content of the two posts didn't match up, their timing wasn't relevant in the first place.

And that study that Q linked to in December 2019? The anon who made it later admitted they'd messed up the numbers they'd used, "due to some bad data from a misunderstanding about how times were represented in the data."[21] Meaning that what looked "mathematically impossible" now looked merely mathematically improbable.

MORE FALSE CLAIMS THAN AN INSURANCE SCAM

Q clearly learned their lesson after the "No, Hillary Clinton actually means Saudi Arabia" fiasco of the first few weeks of the conspiracy theory's existence. Going forward, Q made very few concrete predictions of a specific thing happening at a specific time, preferring instead to make countless vague predictions of things that never came to pass, or specific claims that had no way of being proven. Most, like the "McCain returning to headlines" drop, could be taken countless different ways, only revealing their truth after the event had happened. And it's nearly impossible to debunk a claim like that, because it's not really a claim as much as it is a vague proclamation that something that will definitely happen at some point.

But post-2017, Q did make actual claims and predictions that were falsifiable—that is, they could be contradicted by evidence. And on this score, Q's track record is truly awful, calling into question the basic critical thinking skills of any Q believer who looks at Q's predictions as bulletproof clairvoyance.

Like the Q proofs, Q's falsifiable claims are too numerous to knock down one by one. But even a sampling of Q's predictions and conspiracy theories shows that, contrary to Q's believers, this is an Internet persona who not only has no feel for events to come, but quite the opposite. Here are some of Q's "greatest misses", starting in 2018:

- In Drop #647, Q seemed to predict a major event involving the Department of Defense for February 1st, calling it the "[D]ay [Of] [D]ays." Nothing of note happened at that agency that day.
- Q insinuated in Drop #700 that the weekend of February 10, 2018, would be a "suicide weekend" for individuals targeted by the president. There were no high-profile suicides by public figures that weekend.
- Drop #785 used quasi-military chatter to predict a possible car bombing in London around February 16th. No terrorist attack of any type happened in London at all that month.
- In Drop #854, posted in March 2018, Q hinted at a horrific video of Hillary Clinton, writing "Is the stage set for a drop of HRC +++ + +++++(raw vid 5:5). EX-rvid5774[?]" This is an allusion to the infamous "frazzledrip" video that supposedly shows the former Secretary of State Clinton killing a young girl and cutting off her face to wear as a mask. No such video exists, and the idea was quickly revealed to be a Facebook goof that went viral thanks to a fake-news story from the hoax site YourNewsWire.[22]
- Q predicted in Drop #856 that Trump would enact "a parade that

will never be forgotten" to honor the military on 11/11/18. Despite Trump having boasted several times of holding such a parade, the one he had planned was postponed, then canceled indefinitely.

- Q predicted the resignations of John McCain from the Senate, Mark Zuckerberg from Facebook, Jack Dorsey from Twitter, and Pope Francis from the papacy. None of these took place.
- In Drop #912, Q claimed that the international intelligence sharing alliance known as "Five Eyes" "won't be around much longer." It still exists.
- Q claimed in Drop #1043 that "Pics will surface of Hussein holding AK47 [sic] in tribal attire. One of many. Net shut down." No such pictures of Barack Obama holding an AK-47 have ever surfaced, and the "net" was never shut down to stop them.
- Speaking of Internet shutdowns, Q repeatedly claimed that Facebook, Google, Twitter, YouTube, and Instagram would all be turned off as part of a media blackout in advance of mass arrests. This never happened, though any time a major social media site had an outage, Q or Q believers would seize on it as proof.
- In Drop #1067, Q insinuated a major event in Asia, writing simply "China. Chongqing. Tuesday." The first Tuesday after that drop was April 10, 2018, and no newsworthy event took place on that day in that city.
- Drop #1595 saw Q claim that July would be "the month the world discovered the TRUTH." Whatever the truth was, it went undiscovered, nor did Q ever claim what it was supposed to be.
- Q predicted stunning electoral victories for the Republican Party in both 2018 and 2020, often using the term "red wave" to describe these successes. Between these two elections, the GOP lost control of both houses of Congress and the White House.
- Q predicted Brett Kavanaugh would be confirmed by a 53–47 vote. He was confirmed with a 50–48 vote, whereby Q retroactively changed the prediction to denote that they were talking about the makeup of the Senate after the 2018 election, in which the

GOP picked up two seats—a widely predicted outcomes of that election during a race where Republicans were heavily favored.

- Q wrote on several occasions of a great mass of "sealed indictments" written by various district courts and US Attorneys investigating the Democratic Party and pedophiles that would be unleashed at the right time by Donald Trump.[23] Q believers ran with the claim, positing as many as a quarter of a million, spread over the circuit courts of the country—an ever-increasing number based on a misreading of documents in the PACER court document system that counted magistrate warrants for minor offenses, and counted standard court filings that had nothing to do with arrests. No great mass of indictments was ever unsealed by Trump. In an amusing footnote, this "sealed indictment" claim was actually pooh-poohed by a child-trafficking detective interviewed in *QAnon: An Invitation to the Great Awakening*, who claimed the uptick in indictments didn't exist and seemed baffled when asked about it.
- Finally, Q teased over and over that mass arrests were coming soon, such as in Drop #2344, which rhetorically asked, "Are you ready to see arrests? Are you ready to see PAIN? Are you ready to be part of history?" And when the arrests didn't come, Q blamed "'blue checkmark' FAKE NEWS Twitter personalities" in Drop #2556 for making Q believers think arrests were coming.

At this point, it should be clear: Q had no special access and made predictions that didn't come true, and the only "proof" of any such access or clairvoyance can be found in their own constant claims of it.

LITERALLY HITLER

Finally, much of Q's story is simply ripped off or plagiarized from other sources. Q's long list of Rothschild central banks, which was copied and pasted from a right-wing blog circa 2012, has quite a bit of company in being someone else's creation.

Many of Q's core slogans and ideas are stolen from other media. The phrase "Where we go one we go all" might be a unifying rallying cry, but it wasn't originally inscribed on the bell of JFK's yacht, as Q believers claim—rather, the phrase is inscribed on the bell of the German-built sailing ship Eye of the Wind, which was used as a set for the 1996 Ridley Scott sailing movie *White Squall*. That movie, in turn, used the phrase on several occasions in its dialogue—but it has nothing to do with President Kennedy. JFK didn't even own a yacht, instead, using the same yacht that several other presidents had used in various roles.[24] Another, Q's concept of "ten days of darkness" shutting down the Internet and power grid in preparation for "the storm," first used in Drop #88, is cribbed directly from a line of dialogue in 2017's *Blade Runner 2049* describing a mass electronic outage.[25] Adrenochrome as a superdrug, of course, is stolen from *Fear and Loathing in Las Vegas*, while many of Q's other foundational concepts and plot points are grabbed from movies like *The Matrix* series and *The Godfather Part III*.

The idea of a popular uprising against the government carried out by armed patriots is copied from the seminal 1978 white supremacist novel *The Turner Diaries*, where it's given the Q-esque name "the Day of the Rope."[26] Even the very concept that kicked QAnon off, that of "the storm" washing away the evil of the world, harkens back to Nazi iconography, with the earliest Nazi paramilitaries known as the SA, or *Sturmabteilung*, literally meaning "Storm Detachment."[27] And the ideas found in "the storm" can be seen in later works highlighting violent vengeance against perceived evildoers, such as *Taxi Driver* and the inexhaustible *Death Wish* and *Taken* series of films.

Like the debunking of Q drops or proofs, a list of Q's influences and nods to other media could go on nearly forever. The point is that once you start to see Q's component parts, they become all you can see. You don't see a daring and novel form of truth-telling, you see a hokey old story dressed in the clothes of other stories and put in a shiny new box. You see a fabulist struggling to keep things fresh and exciting, as their fans demand more and more. And you see how decades and centuries of conspiracy theories and storytelling tropes could have found new audiences to pull in.

And those audiences do believe. They believe that Q is real, that Q shared some of the biggest secrets humanity had to offer, and that Q needs our help fighting a war against unimaginable evil. What we do about those people, how we help them, and indeed, if they can be helped at all, is the biggest question of all when it comes to Q.

It's the last question we're asking, and it's the one that's probably the hardest to answer.

CHAPTER 13

Where We Go One:
How to Help People Who Want to Get Out of Q

After three years of mostly ignoring or mocking Q, the media over-corrected in the wake of the election. There were dozens of Q-centered stories by major outlets picking it apart, writing explainers about it, and going into detailed examinations of its history and beliefs. Some of it was excellent reporting that opened up whole new avenues of investigation, and some of it was salacious nonsense by news sites that didn't understand the basics of what they were talking about. One question that came up over and over again in that reporting was what do we do about the people who *do* believe it—how do we help them, and can they be helped at all? Everyone seemed to suddenly know someone who believed at least some tenet of QAnon, but nobody knew what to do about it.

There was a deluge of stories about families torn apart by QAnon and the permanent damage done by fervent belief in its mythology. In one post-inauguration story, *HuffPost* spoke to nine children whose parents had been radicalized by QAnon.[1] They told harrowing stories ranging from tales of parents sucked in via the Iraqi dinar and NESARA scams to that of a woman so ensconced in Q-driven COVID-19 denial that she wore a fishnet mask full of holes to the funeral of her own mother—who had died of COVID-19. *Buzzfeed*, NPR, ABC News, *Vice*, *Newsweek*, *The Washington Post*, and countless others ran similar stories—all full of broken families, missed holidays, recriminations, and bodies and minds left decrepit thanks to sleepless nights spent "researching" the imaginary misdeeds of the "deep state."

It looked like there was nowhere to turn for distraught family members. With many other cultic movements, there's a large population of people who had already gotten out and can send the elevator back down to help more people. Unfortunately, because Q is so new and many ex-believers are too embarrassed to go on the record, there's no codified structure for how to help people get out beyond a few Reddit fora and private Facebook groups. And the United States woefully lags behind in having an organized method for deradicalizing people, leaving veterans' groups and law enforcement scrambling for help in getting former military personnel and police out of hate groups.[2] Numerous experts have spoken of the problem of how to get people out of hate groups when they've been, as former neo-Nazi Brad Galloway said of himself on WNYC's *On the Media,* "groomed" for such a life, and are held back by shame and remorse when they make the choice to walk away.[3]

That's not to say there's no hope. There are detailed guides and videos on how to leave cults. And there are vocal former members of extremist movements, fringe worldviews, and hate groups who speak without fear about what those movements provided them and how they walked away. But QAnon is so complex, so new, and has so many different facets to understand that it requires a set of skills that's virtually impossible for a single person to have.

I certainly don't have it. Since I started researching and writing about QAnon, the loved ones of believers have reached out to me for guidance and answers about what the hell was happening to the person they cared about, and what they should do. It started as a trickle of emails and Twitter direct messages. And it increased to a flood of questions in Trump's last year in office—a flood that, for a long time, I resisted answering. Why would I have an answer? I'm just someone trying to make sense of this myself, I reasoned. I'm not a trained interventionist, an expert in cultic movements, or a psychologist. I have no letters after my name earned after years of study and practice. What if I give bad advice? What if I make it worse? What if I say the wrong thing and turn a fractured relationship into a truly dangerous situation? Better to wish that person luck and protect myself, right?

Like so many aspects of QAnon, what once was a bridge too far is now a collapsing structure that we're all stuck on. Trying to stay out of it isn't an option anymore.

Fortunately, in the course of researching and writing this book, I've spoken to a number of people who are qualified to give such advice—and I've been exposed to the work of even more people who know what they're talking about. None of them have all the answers or a bulletproof formula to rescue your loved from QAnon, of course. Nobody has that, and anyone who says they do is someone to avoid at all costs. But they do have experience, and what they have to say is meaningful.

In interviews with experts in numerous fields, as well as my own experience dealing with the QAnon movement, I've developed a core set of actions to help a loved one dealing with QAnon, without any training or professional experience. They're based in principles of empathy, compassion, and love—but also a hard-won understanding that there's a decent chance they won't work, depending on how enmeshed the person is with Q, and what interest they have in leaving it behind. If they're too far gone or would rather cling to QAnon than rebuild their relationship with you, your battle might be unwinnable. But if not, you might have a chance to do some good.

WHAT TO DO

Decide if you really want to do this—Reconciliation is a two-way street, one that both you and your loved one will have to travel. It's perfectly appropriate to look at the pros and cons and decide not to, either because your loved one is still clinging to Q, or because they've made you feel unsafe at some point. "Don't bother, unless they're costing you money or doing something dangerous," *Skeptoid* host Brian Dunning said when I asked him about getting loved ones or friends out of Q. "There's not enough upside to justify the downside in creating conflict." Cultic movements and hate groups "operate similarly to an addiction, which [the believers'] lives become entirely centered around," the former white nationalist Shannon Foley Martinez, who now speaks and writes about how to help former hate-group members, told me. This leaves family and friends mostly powerless to help "until the person engaged in these behaviors is ready to enact change."

There is no requirement to get someone out of Q if they either aren't hurting themselves, or if you can't do it safely. And you simply may not be able to.

Understand the scope and difficulty of what you're attempting— Remember that humans are evolutionarily wired to see patterns, and to seek them out even when they aren't visible. QAnon and conspiratorial thought in general are as addictive and powerful as any drug or game of chance, and while you might think Q and its mythology are crazy, there's a good chance they think you're the crazy one for not wanting in on the "secret knowledge" they've collected. Keep in mind what Q provides them, and what you can replace that with. And there's a chance you simply might not be able to replace it— through no fault of your own. "People convert into worldviews and do not easily convert out of them," said Mark Juergensmeyer. "There is too much self-respect, sense of identity, and shared community that is lost by giving up a world view. These are structures of reality that are not easily abandoned." The UK cult expert Alexandra Stein echoes this, telling me that she hasn't pursued what she deems "exit counseling" because "it's very difficult, very resource intensive, very time consuming, and not always successful." Helping someone out of a cultic or coercive movement is possible, however—as we'll explore shortly.

Know you're not alone—This is the first thing I tell the loved ones and friends of QAnon believers, and it's become even more pertinent in the past year. If there truly are millions of people who believe at least some aspect of QAnon, even if they don't consider themselves to be QAnon believers, then they leave even more people in their wake. Each of these people are fighting the same battle, enduring the same loss and sleepless nights, and likely feeling like nobody can help them. There is a growing number of support groups for people left behind by QAnon, including the popular Reddit forum r/QAnonCasualties, which offers "support, resources and a place to vent" in a safe and trolling-free environment with numerous moderators. There are several other smaller Q-survival subreddits, and there are also QAnon support groups on the secure messaging app Telegram, and on Facebook.

Understand cultic groups and their appeal—People join extremist groups and conspiracy movements because those things offer them something they don't have. They offer comradeship, power to the powerless, and connection to the disconnected. They offer answers to hard questions, and explanations for events that seem to defy explanation. Understanding the appeal of a movement like QAnon is vital to being able to help someone leave it. There is a wealth of resources to help people understand coercive movements, and how to recognize them when you see them. These span books, videos, full-length docuseries, and websites that treat cults as social movements to be understood, not salacious groups of nutcases to be mocked. There are too many to name, but reading a few of the most important books can at least begin the process for you.

Robert Jay Lifton's 1961 book *Thought Reform and the Psychol-*

ogy of Totalism was one of the first books to lay out the basics of how cults change the way people think and speak, offering what he called "Eight Criteria for Thought Reform." Lifton also codified the concept of the "thought-terminating cliché," a linguistic phrase that dispenses with the doubts of believers—a concept you see illustrated by QAnon's terms like "Trust the plan" and "Where we go one we go all." There are also several books by cult expert (and former cult member) Steven Hassan, including *Combatting Cult Mind Control*, and seminal works that examine the mentality behind mass movements and cult psychology, of which Eric Hoffer's *The True Believer* and 1956's groundbreaking *When Prophecy Fails* both stand out.

The experts quoted in this book have their own books explaining the basics of thought-controlling and conspiracy-driven groups, including Rick Alan Ross's *Cults Inside Out*, Alexandra Stein's *Terror, Love and Brainwashing*, Mick West's *Escaping the Rabbit Hole*, and Mark Juergensmeyer's study of religious terrorism, *Terror in the Mind of God*. And numerous individual cultic movements have a wealth of books and series dedicated to them—everything from Scientology and Mormon fundamentalism to newer movements like NXIVM and Aum Shinrikyo.

Stay in touch, but on your terms—Overwhelmingly, experts advise that if at all possible, you should keep some line of communication open to the QAnon believer in your life, one that doesn't involve trying to litigate the conspiracy or rehash the battles you've had before. This doesn't mean you have to let them bombard you with QAnon videos and interpretations of drops, and if they try, you're well within your rights to cease communicating temporarily. But it does mean letting them know you care about them—even if they seem to have given up on caring about you.

Cultic movements like QAnon substitute the good feelings of like-minded strangers and the dopamine hits of hating the things those people hate for the ups and downs of personal relationships.

They blast away the possibility of strenuous debate or disagreement with someone you love, preferring to create a world where those who don't feel the same way as you are the enemy, meant to be either destroyed or cut off from contact. "If you get the sense that the cult wants its members to think the outside world is a scary and unsafe place, you've got to remind them 'I love you, I'm safe, I know you're interested in this stuff, I'm still here, and I'll be here whenever you're ready,'" Stein said. She suggests you tell that person that you are going to reach out just to say hi every few weeks, even if they don't respond.

"Keep talking; you might be that person's only link to reality," Mick West said. "It doesn't even matter what you talk about, just maintain communication in an effective way to establish understanding."

Shannon Foley Martinez recommends the same things—simple entreaties trying to keep in touch and talk about shared memories and experiences, examining your own relationship with that person, while listening more than speaking—but only as long as you feel safe and it's within your capacity to do these things.

Hassan advocates for discussing shared memories from the time before they were sucked into QAnon.[4] It helps you rediscover your common ground in a nonjudgmental way that has nothing to do with conspiracy theories or politics. Help the person remember that you are a safe place to turn to, help them remember their own experiences before QAnon, and maybe explore whatever might have gone wrong and pushed them down this road. But in all cases, the communication has to be gentle and nonconfrontational; otherwise it will likely do more harm than good and leave you open to attacks.

Try to unplug them—QAnon is almost an entirely digital movement, from its scriptures on 8kun to the message boards and social media sites where believers communicate. Because of that, experts are virtually unanimous that one critical aspect of helping people find a way out of Q is to get them offline.

"The key is to unplug them, give them a break, a space of time when they're not online," Rick Alan Ross said.

But because it's virtually impossible to deny someone Internet access without literally cutting off their service, this might take a significant time commitment—and might not be available at all, depending on the status of COVID-19 in your area. But if you can, "take them away on vacation," Stein said. "Get them out and give them time away where they don't have good Internet access. Go out to the beach or the woods for a few days, anything where they can't keep feeding or being fed [by fellow Q believers]. This gives them a moment where they might have some space where they can start thinking" for themselves.

If your time is more limited, even a few hours might make a difference. In deradicalizing hate-group members, Martinez suggests any sort of outdoor activity, even something as simple as a long hike or playing a game together. There's merit in helping that person take even a slight break from the constant barrage of conspiracy theories and bad news on social media, forces that disinformation researcher Brooke Binkowski said are "always keeping people outraged or fearful or otherwise negatively psychologically aroused and stimulated, [which] makes them easy to manipulate."

Likewise, if you do choose to confront a Q believer, do it in a digital-free zone. Ross, who has presided over hundreds of interventions, advocates for devices being shut down, and the Q believer sitting with their family and no other distractions. This will put the believer in an environment where "they have to think, and they have to respond and reason without going back to the subculture," he said.

If the door opens, be ready to walk through it—In time, a combination of sustained nonthreatening communication and repeated periods without Internet access might convince the QAnon believer of what you already know: that you're a safe person to talk to. It also might allow for them to begin to see the loose threads in the security blanket Q has created for them.

If they do, either because of something you've done or something they've come to on their own, you have a real opportunity to help them get out. But you have to be prepared. If they begin to question something about Q, point out some of its inconsistencies and mistakes, such as the times Q posted disinformation or made predictions that didn't come true. Or about the obvious racism and anti-Semitism of certain Q drops, such as Q's use of "Hussein" to refer to Barack Obama, or the poster's reliance on blood libel tropes. Is this something they agree with? Surely nobody just beginning to come out of the QAnon fog will double down on their own bigotry—giving you an opportunity for further discussion.

You can also talk to them about the ways Q and its mythology provide answers. Corrupt politicians and business tycoons *do* get away with things the rest of us can't—look at Jeffrey Epstein. Just because the "organized trafficking rings" posited by Q don't exist doesn't meant that we shouldn't care about children who are at risk. And while the Clintons and Barack Obama and George Soros aren't the baby-eating demons Q makes them out to be, we can all agree that they're also far from perfect people—an easy way to meet a Q believer somewhere comfortable for them, without bowing to their pet conspiracy theories. And you can agree that some of the other conspiracy touchstones Q and Q promoters talk about often, such as the CIA's mind control experiment MKUltra or the surveillance of journalists under Project Mockingbird in the 1960s, were real—though conspiracy theorists tend to vastly overinflate their importance. Talk about the difference between conspiracies and conspiracy theories, and that one can disbelieve Q while also not swallowing whole every line of propaganda the government puts out.

"Try to understand why they believe, and ask them why they believe in a gentle way," Mick West suggests of the moment when a ray of light breaks through the suffocating blackness of Q belief.

"You can say you don't believe it, that it seems unlikely to you, and that want to know more." West also believes that a potential inconsistency to be mined is Q's reliance on 8kun, a place that "doesn't make Q look good." Would a plan to "save the world," as one popular Q video puts it, really rely on a barely usable imageboard that's full of racist memes and pornography, utilizing tripcodes that could easily be broken as security? Or ask about the times Q has gone silent, such as the three months in 2019 when 8chan was down, or after Trump lost the 2020 election. Do they think that's something an intelligence operation tasked with saving children would do? How did it make them feel to be abandoned by Q for such long stretches?

This is also where it's important to understand both cults in general and QAnon in particular. What particular aspects of Q were they most wedded to? If there are parts of Q that they *didn't* believe in—such as the fantasy of JFK, Jr., still being alive or the more prophetic elements of the movement—those can be places to start with. You both agree that those things aren't real, and agreeing on something is better than agreeing about nothing.

Understand that it will not happen overnight—"Disengagement is a process, which takes time," Foley Martinez said. "Leaving the world from which one was immersed is merely a first step. If the underlying vulnerabilities [that drove the person to QAnon] aren't dealt with, the likelihood of engaging in other destructive behaviors is pretty high." Be prepared for the person emerging from QAnon to not be able to process their shame or the hurt they caused. But with a strong and genuine support system, those issues can be honestly addressed—meaning that while leaving QAnon isn't a quick or painless process, it can be done in a healthy and productive way.

WHAT NOT TO DO

Don't use outdated terms or concepts in your fight—Generally speaking, some of the traditional terms used in the past when discussing cults, such as "brainwashing" and "deprogramming" aren't universally used in the studies of movements like QAnon. Many people voluntarily choose to believe in QAnon, often finding it through other conspiracy theories, and stay with it because it provides them something they aren't getting in their real life. The stereotypical idea of "brainwashing" isn't the correct term to apply to Q, with some in the psychiatric community rejecting the concept altogether as pseudoscientific and unproven.[5] Coercive deprogramming by force is no longer used for legal and ethical reasons, and not something that should be contemplated for a Q believer.[6] Even the term "cult" has such negative and deeply embedded stereotypes that you might not want to use it at first. There are many other ways to break Q's hold on a person without venturing into territory that isn't scientifically or medically agreed on.

Don't mock or belittle—Think about every time someone called you stupid for having an opinion they disagreed with. Did it make you give up that opinion, or believe it even more fervently? This same approach applies to conspiracy theories and coercive movements. You may think QAnon is the dumbest load of crap you've ever heard, and that anyone who believes it was dropped on their head as a baby. But Q believers see themselves as soldiers on the vanguard of a war between good and evil. This is an extremely powerful belief system, one that rewards faith and action and punishes derision. It's something that a Q believer is going to cling to tightly, and mocking or scolding the belief will make them cling even harder. Q matters to them; it gives them hope and meaning. Calling it stupid doesn't insult Q—it insults the person you love for thinking it's real. They will do everything they can to avoid admitting they were misled, and attacking them or trying to pick a fight over it will only inflame the sense of grievance and specialness that Q already feeds. Understanding what Q provides them can help, but mocking it will not.

Don't attempt to debate or debunk—I don't debate conspiracy theory believers because as a skeptic and researcher, I'm beholden to the truth, while the conspiracy believer can use anything they want to in their argument. This should be your approach with QAnon. Attempting to debunk or fact-check QAnon to get someone out of QAnon will only send you down an endless path of knocking down every argument or half-baked Q proof they come up with. And you will run out of patience with their arguments long before they run out of arguments—with them declaring victory over you. When you do communicate with your Q-believing loved one, stick to common elements you can agree on, such as inconsistencies in Q's doctrine, or elements of the conspiracy they don't believe in. When you find one, that's your opening to push your conversation further. But a "fact vs. fact" battle against a Q believer will never be anything but pointless.

Don't give up if it matters to you—Deradicalizing someone is a long process that may not succeed for some time, or at all. And chances are that even if you help that person leave QAnon behind, they're still going to have the same conspiratorial way of thinking that led them to Q in the first place. Remember that virtually nobody comes to Q as their first conspiracy theory.

"In many cases the beliefs do not fundamentally change, but they take a back seat to admitting to the everyday reality that most of us see," said Mark Juergensmeyer. "The believers accommodate themselves to the reality that their worldview is not shared by everyone or likely to succeed. But they still cling to many aspects of it."

One thing that might make a difference to Q believers is the direction the movement takes as the reality of Joe Biden being president sinks in. It might be the best-case scenario that believers melt away as it becomes clear that Biden won't be magically removed from office or have his "fraud" exposed. "At present, [QAnon] is fueled by a political climate that gives credibility to its fantasies and is encouraged by political leaders," Juergensmeyer continued. "But when the situation changes, and the political climate is no longer on their side, most of the followers [of extremist movements] tend to shirk back. They continue to be in touch with one another and share their imagined worlds, but they are not, for the most part, trying to assert themselves."

There are exceptions, of course—true believers willing to risk their lives to undertake a desperate last-ditch act in the waning days of Q. But if that's the Q believer in your life, chances are you'll see at least some glimmer of it and be able to contact the relevant authorities. As we saw from the social media footprint of Capitol insurrectionists, desperate conspiracy theorists aren't especially interested in covering their tracks. Their actions present a situation that should be taken seriously and escalated to the proper authorities.

THE DANGLING THREAD

Most QAnon believers won't go down the road that ends at the wrong side of a Capitol police officer's gun. For all of the crimes and violent ideation we've seen, many believers truly want to play a role in making the world a better place. That they've chosen to do it through QAnon is a problem, of course. But it's not a problem that lacks a solution. And some Q believers do find that solution, eventually coming to it on their own with encouragement from people on the outside that they trust.

Every story of leaving QAnon behind is different, begun for a different reason and taken through a different path. Some have an ugly and public ending, such as Melissa Rein Lively, who gained national fame after a video of her destroying a rack of masks at Target while declaring she was the "QAnon spokeswoman" went viral. Lively later admitted that her public breakdown was the end result of months spent online consumed by pandemic- and QAnon-related terror.[7] In retrospect, she saw that she had immersed herself in what she now believed was a cult, and subsequently sought intensive mental health treatment.

But Lively's story is a bit of an exception. Rather than an abrupt, public breakdown, far more believers leave Q because of a "dangling thread" that unravels the entire tapestry of QAnon's mythology. One thing that no longer makes sense, one nagging inconsistency or mistake—and when they start to pull it, they find more and more threads. And they do it privately, often alone, with nobody to turn to—having alienated or pushed away those they care about most.

For the ex–Q believer Serena, whom we met in chapter 11, this was when Q began posting Bible verses in drops, something she believed a military intelligence operative would never do. She pulled on that thread, and Q fell apart for her.

For the Australian ex-believer Jitarth Jadeja, profiled in chapter 6, the beginning of that journey was the "tippy-top" Q proof. After telling himself that it was such a unique phrase that nobody could possibly have used it without coordinating with Q, he was "crushed" to find a YouTube video compiling all the other times Trump used the phrase before the White House Easter Egg Roll—none of which required any input from Q or the anons.

"That's when my world kind of came crashing down," he told *The Washington Post*, as two years of suffocating belief in Q began to unravel.[8] In our interview, he told me that with "tippy-top" already nagging at him, he started seeking out other "dangling threads" to pull, and found an article I'd written debunking the "sealed indictments" aspect of the conspiracy. That was it for him. Realizing how far he'd fallen, Jadeja began a public process not only of speaking out against QAnon, but of making amends—going so far as to apologize on the air to CNN host Anderson Cooper for accusing him of "eating babies."

But even in the process of turning against QAnon, there's peril. Jadeja told me that once he started speaking out against Q, he "almost fell back into the trap of getting sucked in." Curious about what was going on in the Q community now that he was on the outside, he again lost himself. When he surfaced, he realized he'd spent four days looking at Q posts, only this time to debunk them, rather than seek truth in them. "Q has a sucking in effect on anyone who looks at it, positive or negative," he told me, shaking his head. "It attracts your mental energy because it's so dense."

BEA'S STORY

Ultimately, every Q believer's journey out of Q is personal and unique. There are ways to help them out of it, but they have to want to accept that help, and realize that the problem isn't QAnon, but an extant predilection for conspiratorial thinking.

This the core of QAnon survivor Bea's story. Bea (a pseudonym) has never publicly spoken about her journey through QAnon, the damage that it did to her, or how she escaped from it. But she opened up to me over email—not over the phone, because she was embarrassed to even say the words out loud.

Bea came across QAnon in October 2019 through one of the New Age Facebook groups that she belonged to. She joined her first Q-specific Facebook group in December 2019, and got deeply into the NESARA scam through that group. Between QAnon, NESARA, and general New Age beliefs, Bea was seeing more and more of her time sucked up through research, "intel updates," and conspiracy theories.

"I was in three different groups with the NESARA thing on Telegram: the main New Age group; a group that received daily updates on the status of NESARA; and then another one that was more focused on New Age beliefs and aliens," she told me. Even before the pandemic, she was taking part in Zoom meetings about NESARA and the logistics of what to do when the "prosperity packets" were released—the same windfall that Dove of Oneness had been pushing twenty years earlier, only it was going out to a whole new generation.

Bea's doubts crept in, particularly about NESARA—but they were quickly banished. "One of the things that did catch me off guard was the fact that if the funds ever went into effect, we would need to use an offshore account," she said. "This was a tad alarming to me, but I went along with it." The big payoff was worth any lingering doubt or trepidation.

Her radicalization continued over the next few months. Like Jitarth Jadeja, Bea was dealing with a recent mental health diagnosis—in this case, clinical depression and anxiety. And like everyone else during the early days of the COVID-19 pandemic, those extant illnesses were being inflamed by the constant churn of doom. And the hope and community provided by those beliefs—New Age, NESARA, and QAnon—became more and more crucial to her overall health and well-being.

"The thing that appealed to me about Q the most was the mystery in it," Bea said. "It filled the hole of spirituality, and given the New Age groups that I was [already] involved in, it fit in well." She also watched popular QAnon channels on YouTube, went to QAnon aggregator sites like QMap, read blogs for updates on NESARA, and joined more and more Facebook groups and Telegram channels. As she told me, she believed everything, only struggling to understand how it fit together.

Unfortunately, as these conspiracy theories began to play a bigger role in managing her mental health, they weren't helping her make sense of anything or find any answers. They were actually making her conditions worse, contributing to anxiety attacks, increased insomnia, and worst of all, her pulling away from her family—including her children.

"I started noticing increased heart palpitations due to my increased anxiety," she wrote. "I was weepy and cried almost every day starting in April 2020. I think a lot of the crying had to do with me being scared because of the pandemic and also being very confused because of being into Q. I felt like I started to pull away from my family."

It was in April that Bea started to realize something was wrong. Aspects of QAnon and NESARA started to make less sense, even as the effect they had on her increased. And finally, the dangling thread presented itself in the form of one of the many COVID-19 conspiracy theories that the Q community had embrace: that the lockdown was a ploy to rescue trafficked children from "Deep Underground Military Bases"—also called "DUMBs."

"The main thing that became too absurd for me was when [QAnon promoters began claiming] DUMBs were being blown up as a ploy to rescue children in tunnels. That part did not sit right with me at all." Once that single doubt started to take hold, Bea began to realize what her rapid radicalization from inoffensive New Age beliefs to QAnon had done to her—and how much worse it could all get.

So she pulled on the thread. While close friends had begun to take notice of "the insane shit" she said she was posting on Facebook, her husband hadn't noticed a change. But with doubt creeping in, and her groups offering nothing in the way of answers, she reached out to him for help. Crucially, he reacted with empathy and understanding, rather than mockery and derision. It helped her begin to question everything she was hearing from all of the social media groups she'd been in—and to start the process of walking away. The endless conspiracies and intel updates and prophecies no longer made sense to her. And she no longer wanted them in her life.

"I would say the pulling away started in April, but I fully pulled out of all of it by May," Bea wrote. "I was tired of the same old drivel coming out of the NESARA groups and the Q posts. I just decided one day that I didn't want to be involved in Q, NESARA, or anything New Age anymore. Mentally, I was struggling with a whole lot of it."

Finally, Bea left all the QAnon and NESARA groups she was in and blocked all of their members on Facebook. And while she continues to do the work she needs to do to manage her depression and anxiety, she doesn't lean on QAnon or other conspiracy theories to do that work for her. She's out, and she's not looking back.

Having approached the precipice of losing her family and her sanity to QAnon and its related conspiracy theories, Bea now sees what she was involved in. To the QAnon believers still haunting those Telegram channels, Facebook groups, and all over the world, Bea has a message.

"This right-wing 'conspiracy theory' is literally ripping families, friends, and loved ones apart," she said. "This has got to stop before others get hurt, or worse yet, killed."

Friends and Happy Memories

"My Q cousin thinks [the Capitol insurrection] was a false flag carried out by antifa. My aunt, her mother, was a COVID-19 denier who stopped paying her mortgage last year because she thought Trump or JFK (Jr.) was going to abolish the Federal Reserve. She's dead from COVID-19 now."

—*Anonymous, via Twitter DM*

On January 20, 2021, less than an hour after Joe Biden took the oath of office and dashed the dark clouds of "the storm" forever, Ron Watkins, the ringleader of the Stop the Steal movement and one of the figures believed to be directly linked to the posts of QAnon, appeared to quit the "stolen election" movement he'd helped create.

"We need to keep our chins up and go back to our lives as best we are able," Watkins wrote on Telegram, where he'd piled up over 120,000 subscribers. "We have a new president sworn in and it is our responsibility as citizens to respect the Constitution regardless of whether or not we agree with the specifics. As we enter into the next administration please remember all the friends and happy memories we made together over the past few years." He alluded to "a new project" he'd unveil in "a few days," but in the next month, he never spoke of it, and it would be months before he posted on Telegram again.[1]

With both Q silent and the movement's champion, Donald Trump, thrown out of office by voters, whatever the Q movement had been would have to change. No philosophy based around a prophecy of Donald Trump triumphantly destroying his enemies in the final battle between good and evil could survive a failure as grand as Trump no longer being in office without some kind of shift.

Indeed, QAnon believers and gurus did not just move the goalposts that would denote the prophecy's fulfillment, but changed the nature of the game itself. The new prophecy was now Biden's impending removal from office and the reinstatement of Trump—the one true president of the United States who had won the election in a landslide. Early in Biden's administration, it emerged that Q believers were saying that March 4, 2021, would be the "real" date that the "real" US president would be inaugurated (which they arrived at by misreading a 1871 law and the Twentieth Amendment).[2] News reports all over the world warned of Q followers and militia members converging on Washington to enact a repeat of the January 6 insurrection, with the National Guard on alert and Congress closed down for two days. But absolutely nothing happened. This wasn't an attempted coup in the making, merely another QAnon-prophecy can being kicked down an old road.

Q might continue this way as a prophetic movement devoted to waiting for Trump to return to office. Or an entirely new conspiracy might take Q's component parts and merge them with other theories to make something even worse. Either option will likely take years to develop, and we won't know which it is until it presents itself. Hopefully, social media companies will move faster and more seriously in dealing with whatever that next iteration will be.

But the damage from this iteration is done. Q's legacy wasn't "the friends and happy memories" made since October 2017, but broken families, shattered minds, and a country teetering on the brink. Millions of people wake up each morning and go to bed each night believing in the mythology of QAnon, while millions more of their loved ones struggle to understand it. The arrests continue to mount—more than a dozen Capitol rioters indicted in the weeks following Biden's inauguration were QAnon believers.[3] And the far-right neo-Nazi and other hate groups that stormed the Capitol alongside them now see a golden opportunity to recruit disaffected Q believers in the wake of the social media crackdowns after the insurrection.

Nobody dealing with a Q believer in their life has any "happy memories" of the time, either. While a few lucky people have gotten out of Q and are doing their best to help others make the same journey, far more people continue to deal with its fallout in their own lives. These are pieces that it will take years to pick up—if they can be picked up at all.

"Rick," the man who told me the story of his long friendship with "Garth" collapsing into stalking and death threats driven by QAnon, followed up to tell me what happened after Garth had a hearing to determine his competency to stand trial.

"He broke his bond by screaming at me outside the courthouse, calling me a murderer, a traitor, and yelling that I need to die," Rick said. After four outbursts in court against the judge, against Rick, and against his other family members, Garth was dragged out of the courtroom in handcuffs, and soon found incompetent to stand trial. He was remanded to a psychiatric facility pending extensive treatment. "He also got two felony bail-jumping charges and two disorderly conduct charges. He will not step foot out of a state institution until he has completed his forthcoming prison sentence," Rick continued. "We can finally breathe for a little while."

Other Q survivors told me of friendships forever lost, relationships broken, and at least in one case, a separation and potential custody battle between a Q-pilled woman and her spouse. After several go-rounds of her leaving and coming back to Q, it finally all fell apart and they split up.

"I feel better after being away from her for about two months now," he told me. "I am bummed when I don't have my son, but it's nice to be away from that weird negative energy she gave off when she was on a Q kick. I don't know if she will snap out of it this time. On the bright side, she doesn't seem to want to keep my son away from me. We split custody and so far, it's been pretty civil. I get worried when these big events happen that she will snap and do something crazy, but it hasn't happened yet."

QAnon's impact on the Republican Party is just as real. After the Capitol insurrection, it was clear that Q and conservatism would be enmeshed for the foreseeable future, though the form of that enmeshment likely won't be known for several election cycles. After his loss, Trump spoke of forming a "Patriot Party" that would compete with the GOP to fly the banner of true MAGAism. Such a third party, based on populist rhetoric and grievance, would be a twenty-first-century version of the rabidly nativist Know Nothing Party of the 1850s, which used street violence and anti-Catholic conspiracy theories to win dozens of seats around the country, only to collapse in the run-up to the Civil War.[4]

But such a drastic (and likely doomed) gesture probably won't be necessary for Q to persist in today's GOP—the movement's wild conspiracy theories about trafficking rings and the deep state stealing the 2020 election are becoming just as entrenched in conservative orthodoxy as the fake controversies over Benghazi and Hillary Clinton's email server. Democrats even began running ads explicitly tying QAnon to the GOP, though they used unfair and inaccurate stereotypes of Q believers in particular and MAGA devotees in general as uneducated yokels to do it.[5]

But as QAnon envelops the GOP, the Q poster has receded into the background. After the last drop, made on December 6, 2020—a now-dead link to a Trump propaganda video—Q went silent. Maybe forever—or maybe not. Q might never make another drop, or Q might suddenly return and make hundreds of drops, opening up vast new tranches of leads and clues for decoders and promoters to decode and promote. Nobody knows, other than whoever makes the drops.

And we might never know who that is, either.

To be clear, most of the experts I spoke to for this book, and most journalists who cover the disinformation beat in general, feel like we have a pretty good idea of who made the first Q posts—likely Paul Furber, with Coleman Rogers, or Tracy "Beanz" Diaz as possible accomplices. It was Furber's board that Q started to posted on once Q jumped to 8chan, while Rogers livestreamed himself accidentally logging in as Q, and Diaz made the first videos about QAnon that truly went viral. As guesses go, they're the best ones we've got—though all three continue to deny having started making the Q drops.

We also have a good idea of who appears likely to have made the bulk of the drops on 8chan/8kun—someone directly connected to the Watkins family, and more than likely Ron himself. After all, there was no reason for Q to wait around for 8chan to come back in 2019 without some link to the Watkins family, and Q went almost completely silent the moment Ron announced he'd left 8kun on Election Day 2020, with Ron spewing a slew of Q-esque tweets, only to vanish as well. The Ron-Q connection wasn't new, but revelations in HBO's docuseries *Q: Into the Storm* all but sealed Ron as the most likely suspect. For one, Ron and Q shared a number of hobbies, including a love of expensive watches and pens, both of which were featured in numerous Q drops. Ron also had a habit of using the same phrases Q did, had total control over the tripcodes used on the 8chan boards where Q posted, and seemed to ensure that Q could post on the nascent 8kun when nobody else could—which Ron chalked up to Q having "tried really hard."[6]

Finally, Ron all but admitted his involvement with Q to *Into the Storm* director Cullen Hoback late in the last episode when he seemed to slip up during an interview and claim his deluge of baseless voter fraud claims and invented expertise with voting machines were legit because he had "three years of intelligence training, teaching normies how to do intelligence work. It was basically what I was doing anonymously before, but never as Q."[7] Naturally, he immediately claimed he wasn't Q, and has continued to do so on Telegram.

But we don't know for sure. It also likely doesn't matter to the people enmeshed in the movement. No serious Q researcher or journalist covering disinformation believes that the naming of Q would have any impact whatsoever on the trajectory of the movement, especially after Q left when new drops were needed the most. As one believer put it to me when I asked if Q's identity matters, "God, no! Who cares?" Many former believers also told me they never spent any time thinking about it, and if they had found out, it wouldn't have changed anything for them.

But the truth of Q's identity is also a natural question—and one that matters for the historical record. After all, *someone* made the posts. And even if they weren't a military intelligence agent at the president's elbow, they were a person who quite clearly had at least some talent for storytelling and keeping an audience hooked. *Someone* built Q out of spare parts and extant conspiracy theories and 4chan trolling, and someone else kept it going for years, building a huge audience and getting national attention for their work. *Someone* did this, and they're out there somewhere. Can they be held accountable for what they've done?

Very quickly, though, a serious dive into who made those first posts becomes a journey into a mystery that offers no solution other than guesses and conspiracies. It introduces a raft of unstable personalities known to be serial liars and provocateurs who have either claimed they came up with the idea for QAnon, or have been claimed by others to have created QAnon. None have any credible proof behind their claims, leaving one to wonder why any of them should be taken any more or less seriously than others.

Various theories as to who "really" created QAnon have emerged pointing to everyone from members of the online puzzle collective Cicada 3301 to a former CIA officer turned conspiracy theorist named Robert David Steele to an alt-right troll who goes by the handle Microchip to Q champion Michael Flynn himself to Roger Stone to Q guru David "Praying Medic" Hayes to former Trump administration intelligence staffer Ezra Cohen-Watnick to an Italian anarchist collective known as "Luther Blissett" to a self-proclaimed Defense Intelligence Agency operative named Austin Steinbart to New Age guru Lisa Clapier to Alex Jones and Jerome Corsi. All of them either deny having made the posts, or have no compelling evidence to support their claims that they did, A few haven't even publicly supported QAnon. Some people think Donald Trump was its origin point; others believe Vladimir Putin is behind it. Conservative media figures have called it a liberal psyop, while liberal media figures have called it a conservative psyop.

Searching for Q's "real" identity ignores the very real psychological and social forces that made it such a successful movement, in favor of conspiracy theories that offer up vast plots to explain Q—but don't offer any insight to explain it. Instead, such theories become blizzards of claims and social media finger-pointing that are both hopelessly complex to decipher and not especially rewarding for those who attempt to do so.

In fact, it's overwhelmingly likely that Q is exactly what this book posited at the beginning—an undistinguished 4chan LARP that caught on because it told a story about bad people being punished and good people doing the punishing. Its believers wanted it to be true. And that's the most important aspect of Q, not who typed text into a window on 8kun and hit "post." When you've accepted that whoever makes the posts isn't special or a party to secret knowledge, then who they are matters only for the sake of closing the circle. It could be any of the abovementioned figures. Or someone nobody has ever heard of. And even with HBO's *Q: Into the Storm* having provided the most conclusive evidence that Ron Watkins has made at least some of the Q drops, we still don't know who made the first Q drops. Even the first Q poster on 4chan might not know who made the subsequent posts, and the reverse – rendering authorship arguments for Q drops as moot as debating who wrote the Old and New Testaments. It may simply be impossible to have the entire chronology of who did what and when.

"Who started QAnon?" is also a question with no useful answer for when QAnon rebrands or is pulled in by another conspiracy theory. Just as Q repurposed parts of countless older scams and tropes, it's inevitable that Q itself will be repurposed by something else. At that point, figuring out who made the drops will become altogether irrelevant. The real questions to be asked as the next version of QAnon rears its ugly head will be much simpler.

Why this conspiracy? Why now? What need does this fill in the lives of its believers? What about it matters? How does it fit with past conspiracy theories and cultic movements, and how is it different? How dangerous is it? How can it be de-platformed without giving the appearance of censorship? And how do we help the people who have chosen to believe it?

The "storm" prophesized by QAnon in those 4,953 drops might have passed. But we know there will be another. What it looks like and how to deal with it will be unknown—but it's coming.

At least this time, we might be able to recognize it when we see it.

Acknowledgments

Writing a book about a subject that rapidly evolves during the writing process is like flying a kite in a hurricane. Doing so while a global pandemic changes everything about how we live and work and parent is like flying a kite in a hurricane while another hurricane envelops the first hurricane. It's a lot. And it never would have been possible without the help, expertise, and encouragement of a huge number of people—some of whom I'm sure I've forgotten to mention.

I want to thank my manager Seth Nagel, and my book agent, Kristen Moeller at Waterside. Seth has consistently seen the value of what I was doing and helped me work through the constant discouragement and failure that is the life of a writer to find a unique and sustainable career path. And Kristen understood the desperate need for a book on QAnon long before the movement was everywhere in the mainstream media, becoming a champion and advocate for a project that virtually nobody else wanted to touch.

In that advocacy, we found a great partnership in Melville House. I'm especially grateful to my editor, Athena Bryan, who understood right away why Q mattered so much and joined me in an ongoing conversation about how to tell its story. She helped me shape the book's tone and pacing, keeping me out of the weeds of endless detail, and staying focused on turning a hugely complicated conspiracy theory into a relatable story about why people believe unbelievable things. I'm also grateful for the ridiculously sharp copyediting of Amanda Gersten, who found errors I couldn't believe I made, and for which I entirely blame pandemic fatigue. I also want to thank Ethan Whang for crucial last-minute assistance, and the publicity and marketing team at Melville, including Stephanie DeLuca, Gregory Henry, Amelia Stymacks, and Tim McCall. Your enthusiasm to get this book in the hands of readers was boundless. And thanks as well to my UK publisher, Jake Lingwood at Octopus Books, for seeing how an explanation of a uniquely American conspiracy movement like Q would appeal to people in the rest of the world.

My editor at the Daily Dot, David Covucci, was the first to give me the opportunity to write about pretty much any aspect of QAnon that I felt was worth digging into—work that formed the basis of my understanding of this movement.

QAnon is a hugely complicated subject that no one person could ever hope to fully grasp. Fortunately, I didn't have to try. Thank you to all the journalists and researchers who have been digging into this rabbit hole alongside me. Will Sommer, Ben Collins, Brandy Zadrozny, Alex Kaplan, Jared Holt, Dale Beran, E. J. Dickson, Anna Merlan, Kevin Roose, Joe Ondrak and Nick Backovick at Logically. ai, PJ Vogt, Adrienne LaFrance, Rachel Greenspan, David Gilbert, Kelly Weill, Amarnath Amarasingam, and so many others all broke incredible stories about the world of QAnon that I relied on again and again in putting this book together.

My thanks also to the experts and sleuths who have done so much to put the pieces together in public on social media, often using pseudonyms to protect themselves from the wrath of Q followers. Travis View (who reviewed an early draft of the first chapters), Julian Feeld, and Jake Rockatansky of the QAnon Anonymous podcast have done incredible work on this beat and their show is a vital resource for understanding all of this nonsense. Marc-André Argentino's Twitter threads on the growth and spread of QAnon were invaluable, as were the discoveries of researchers like the Q Origins Project account, Mike Rains, Dappergander, Shayan Sardarizadeh, and Sara Aniano. I especially want to single out Fredrick Brennan for walking me through the technical aspects of 8chan for previous stories and never making me feel stupid, and Sarah Hightower for connecting me with experts in cults and extremism, and for her empathy and understanding toward the people caught up in Q.

Thanks to everyone I spoke to in the process of researching and writing the book, and in particular, the QAnon survivors and loved ones who trusted me with their stories. A book without original interviewing is just content curation, and I appreciate all of the hard-won expertise and history you brought to the project. I couldn't use all of the stories I got from the loved ones and family members of Q believers, but every one of them matters and deserves the ear of a listener. Special thanks to Brian Dunning, whose podcast *Skeptoid* was my first real inkling that someone could make a career out of debunking hoaxes and conspiracy theories, and who gave me my first shot at writing about this stuff.

The biggest thanks of all go to my long-suffering friends and family, who have put up with me rambling about all of this stuff for too long. My parents, Jan and Ed; my in-laws, Carolyn, Michael, and Gerti; and my immediate family have never discouraged me from doing a lot of work for free when I was getting started in the conspiracy theory beat, and have been huge advocates of everything I've done. They've watched and read pretty much every interview I've done, sent me articles and books as resources, and even let me use their homes for writing and interviewing during the worst of pandemic lockdown when all I needed was an hour of quiet. My two boys have showered me with love and support even though they think what daddy does is really boring.

And most of all, my patient and ever-encouraging wife Caryn helped me with this project in every way possible that didn't involve actual writing, and this book simply wouldn't exist without her support and positivity.

Glossary of QAnon Terms

Any look into QAnon brings up a dizzying array of jargon, slang, codes, keywords, and catchphrases. Some of them are more important than others, but all work together to create a language that Q believers use as a shorthand to communicate with and encourage each other, and to exclude and frustrate outsiders. Some important terms that are frequently used in the QAnon movement include:

17: Q is the 17th letter of the alphabet, meaning that Q believers see special connotations in the number 17, and will often point out its appearance in relatively anodyne situations.

4chan: An anonymous, lightly moderated image board started by 15-year-old Christopher Poole in 2003 as an American version of the popular Japanese imageboard 2chan. Known for its links to both internet memes and harassment, 4chan was the home of Q drops from October through December 2017.

8chan: Started in 2013 by Fredrick Brennan as "a "free-speech" alternative to 4chan, 8chan allowed users to create and run their own boards without restrictions on content. It was purchased by Jim Watkins and run by his son Ron, with Brennan leaving Watkins's company soon after. 8chan was Q's home until the site was brought down in 2019.

8kun: The reconstituted version of 8chan, still owned and run by Jim Watkins, and administered by Ron until November 2020. 8kun was Q's home from the board's launch in November 2019 until the last Trump-era drop in December 2020.

Adrenochrome: An oxidized form of adrenaline thought by Q believers to be a super-powerful drug extracted from children that extends life and imbues its user with almost godlike powers.

Anons: the anonymous followers of Q who dissect drops for clues to their meaning. Some anons are more well known, going by names like FBIAnon, White House Insider Anon, and of course, QAnon.

Autists: Anons who specialize at obsessively digging into Q drops to find obscure connections and events. It's a compliment, believe it or not.

Bakers/Breads: Anons who put together threads on chan boards or social media to decode Q posts are called "bakers," and those threads are called "breads."

Cabal: Q's concept of the group of wealthy string-pullers and globalists who secretly run the world, much as the New World Order was in the 1990s, and the Illuminati continue to be. The bad guys in the Q mythology.

Comms: Common abbreviation for "communications." Q believers will often say "no outside comms" to claim that anyone posting as Q outside 8kun is fake.

Deep state: Originally the name given to the coordinated "state within a state" run by the government and military in Turkey, the term is now applied to any governmental body that opposes Trump or Q through official channels.

Delta: A mathematical term denoting the difference between two numbers, the term is also applied to the amount of time that passes between a Q drop and a Trump tweet or world event.

Digital Soldier: A term used by former National Security Adviser Michael Flynn in a speech praising Trump's online followers after the 2016 election, and later adopted by QAnon believers to mean digital researchers and meme-makers. Flynn later was one of a number of QAnon believers to take a "digital soldier oath" over 4th of July weekend, 2020.

Drops: The posts Q makes on 4chan, 8chan, or 8kun; which are reposted on social media and aggregator sites.

False flag: A method of warfare where one party pretends to be friendly to lure another in to attack them. Used by conspiracy theorists to refer to incidents they believe were staged or faked to advance the aims of the deep state—e.g., a false flag school shooting.

Future proves past: A Q catchphrase denoting that future events will prove past Q drops as the truth.

Guru/Promoter: The social media personalities most responsible for decoding Q drops, making Q videos, writing Q books, and evangelizing Q to the wider world. Prominent Q gurus discussed in this book include David "Praying Medic" Hayes, Robert "Neon Revolt" Cornero, Jr., Jeff "InTheMatrixxx" Pederson, Jordan Sather, and Joe M.

Hussein: Q's codename for Barack Obama, based on the former president's middle name, Hussein.

LARP: Abbreviation for "Live Action Roleplaying Game." Some speculate that QAnon is simply an internet roleplaying game, which Q often mocks by posting links to articles about the conspiracy theory, and rhetorically asking "all for a LARP?"

The map: Also known as the "Deep State Mapping Project," this is a document that links hundreds of world events and personalities throughout recorded history, as well as concepts in conspiracy theories and the occult. Q often would say that news events would "unlock the map."

MSM: Mainstream media, the liberal collective working overtime to undermine the Q team and Trump.

Patriot's Soapbox: An all-Q all-the-time livestream running 24/7 on YouTube, and later on its own site. Started by Coleman "PamphletAnon" Rogers and his wife Christina "Radix" Urso, two of the original Q promoters.

Pedogate: The catch-all term given to what Q believers think is high-level sex trafficking of children going on in the Democratic Party, Hollywood, big business, and banking.

Pilled: Someone who has been turned on to conspiracy theories.

Pizzagate: Forerunner conspiracy theory to QAnon that claimed Hillary Clinton and other prominent Democrats were running a child sex trafficking ring out of a Washington DC pizza restaurant.

Pol: Also written out as /pol/, this is the "Politically Incorrect" forum on 4chan that spawned numerous anon accounts, including QAnon in October 2017.

Proofs: Memes or graphics that present evidence that Q is real, or that Q drops have revealed information on future events which were proven to have come true.

Q: The self-applied codename of the image board poster claiming to leak cryptic and coded classified intelligence online for their followers. Believers in the Q mythology think Q is a team of "less than ten" people of whom "three are non-military." The identity or identities of the Q poster remains unknown.

QAnon: The movement based around the interpretation of Q's posts. Q believers are fond of saying that there is no actual "QAnon," only "Q" and "anons," while claiming that the term was made up by the media. It was not, as "QAnon" was used by Q adherents shortly after the first drops were made.

Q+: The codename Donald Trump supposedly uses when he personally makes Q drops. Note that Trump is computer illiterate and doesn't use email or the Internet.

Q Clearance: A Department of Energy security level related to working with nuclear weapons. Q's first drops were made by a character calling themselves "Q Clearance Patriot."

QMap: Formerly the most popular aggregator of Q drops, until its creator was revealed to be a Citibank executive, and the site went down.

QResearch: The board on 8chan where Q made most of their drops from 2018 until 2019.

R/CBTS_Stream: the first major Reddit forum dedicated to QAnon, started by Paul "Baruch The Scribe" Furber and Coleman Rogers shortly after the first Q drops. The forum was banned in May 2018, replaced by r/GreatAwakening, which was closed in September when Q content was banned from the site.

Red pill: The act of exposing "normies" (non-believers) to Q drops. Originated in the movie *The Matrix* and used by a variety of fringe and conspiracy groups seeking to turn non-believers into followers.

Sealed indictments: QAnon believers tout that there are hundreds of thousands of sealed indictments in the federal district court system as proof that the mass arrests promised in "The Storm" were about to happen. The large number stems from a misunderstanding in how sealed court documents work.

Shill: Originally meaning a member of a con who enthusiastically supported a rigged game in order to get others to play, in conspiracy theory terms this is usually applied to media members who report favorably on the government or cabal interests.

Silent war: Q's concept of the secret war between good and evil going on in the shadows, unknown to the slumbering public, which will only be revealed when "the storm" is unleashed.

The Storm: The long-awaited purge of the deep state that formed the core of Q's mythology, based on a cryptic remark from President Trump on October 7, 2017 hinting that a gathering of military officers was "the calm before the storm." Also known as "the Great Awakening."

Tripcode: The unique sequence of letters used on 4chan and its successor boards that allows a user's identity to be recognized by displaying a scrambled version of the user's password. Tripcodes are notoriously easy to crack.

Trust the plan: Another Q catchphrase, imploring believers to have faith that all will be well. Phrases like this are also known as "thought-terminating cliches." More such cliches used by Q include "God wins," "nothing can stop what's coming," "enjoy the show," and "dark to light."

White hat: A government official or military officer who supports Trump and Q. Opposed by "black hats" in the cabal.

WWG1WGA: An abbreviation for "where we go one we go all," and used by both Q and conspiracy believers. Q incorrectly attributed the quote to John F. Kennedy, which Q believers took as evidence that Kennedy was the last non–deep–state president before Trump.

Notes

INTRODUCTION The Plan to Save the World

1 Phillip Bump, "Trump's Actions That Led to the Violence at the Capitol Began Months Ago," *The Washington Post*, January 13, 2021, https://www.washingtonpost.com/politics/2021/01/13/trumps-actions-which-led-violence-capitol-began-months-ago/.

2 Peter Baker, Maggie Haberman, and Annie Karni, "Pence Reached His Limit with Trump. It Wasn't Pretty," *The New York Times*, January 12, 2021, https://www.nytimes.com/2021/01/12/us/politics/mike-pence-trump.html.

3 Julia Carrie Wong, "'We're the News Now': Pro-Trump Mob Targeted Journalists at US Capitol," *The Guardian*, January 7, 2021, https://www.theguardian.com/us-news/2021/jan/07/capitol-attack-trump-targeted-journalists.

4 "Trump Praises QAnon Supporters: 'I Understand They Like Me Very Much,'" *Axios*, August 20, 2020, https://www.axios.com/trump-praises-qanon-supporters-i-understand-they-like-me-very-much-42146fb3-bd69-4943-8e80-2f0bcf4b0b17.html.

5 Martin Pengelly, "'Hang Mike Pence': Twitter Stops Phrase Trending After Capitol Riot," *The Guardian*, January 10, 2021, https://www.theguardian.com/us-news/2021/jan/10/hang-mike-pence-twitter-stops-phrase-trending-capitol-breach.

6 Mack Lamoureux, "People Tell Us How QAnon Destroyed Their Relationships," *Vice*, July 11, 2019, https://www.vice.com/en_us/article/xwnjx4/people-tell-us-how-qanon-destroyed-their-relationships.

7 Meira Gebel, "Baby Boomers Share Nearly 7 Times as Many 'Fake News' Articles on Facebook as adults under 30, Study Finds," *Insider*,

January 13, 2019, https://www.businessinsider.com/baby-boomers-more-likely-to-share-fake-news-on-facebook-study-2019-1.

PART I: ORIGINS

CHAPTER 1 Learn to Read the Map: The Basics of QAnon

1 "Departmental Personnel Security FAQs," Office of Environment, Health, Safety & Security, accessed March 5, 2021, https://www.energy.gov/ehss/security-policy-guidance-reports/departmental-personnel-security-faqs.

2 Joshua Keating, "How QAnon Went Global," *Slate*, September 8, 2020, https://slate.com/technology/2020/09/qanon-europe-germany-lock-down-protests.html.

3 Nick Backovic and Joe Ondrak, "NESARA and the Business of False Hope: Why Times of Austerity and Pandemic Create Fertile Ground for Die-Hard Scams," *Logically*, September 3, 2020, https://www.logic-ally.ai/articles/nesara-and-the-business-of-false-hope.

4 Eric Hoffer, *The True Believer* (New York: Harper Perennial, 2010), 101.

5 December 5, 2018, qposts.online, https://qposts.online/?q=255v9&s=postnum. All Q drops are available and searchable at qposts.online.

6 Joe M (stormisuponus), "The Plan to Save the World," first published July 1, 2018, BitChute video, https://www.bitchute.com/video/gBXHNIkqYdBG/.

7 Rayne, "Michael Flynn's 'Revolution,'" *Empty Wheel* (blog), March 30, 2018, https://www.emptywheel.net/2018/03/30/michael-flynns-revolution/.

8 Marshall Cohen, "Michael Flynn Posts Video Featuring QAnon Slogans," *CNN*, July 7, 2020, https://www.cnn.com/2020/07/07/politics/michael-flynn-qanon-video/index.html.

9 Roland Betancourt, "What the QAnon of the 6th Century Teaches Us About Conspiracies," *Time*, February 3, 2021, https://time.com/5935586/qanon-6th-century-conspiracies/.

CHAPTER 2 The Calm Before the Storm: How QAnon Started

1 NBC News, "President Trump: 'It's the Calm Before the Storm,'" filmed October 6, 2017, YouTube video, https://www.youtube.com/watch?v=BREos5woyXc&ab_channel=NBCNews.

2 NBC News, "'Calm Before the Storm': Donald Trump Makes Cryptic Remark At Military Dinner," filmed October 6, 2017, YouTube video, https://www.youtube.com/watch?v=VrF7alkwdHw&ab_channel=NBCNews.

3 John Bowden, "Pence Directs Press to WH on Trump's 'Calm Before

the Storm' Remark," *The Hill*, October 6, 2017, https://thehill.com/homenews/administration/354338-pence-dodges-on-trumps-calm-before-the-storm-remark.

4 Louis Nelson, "White House Won't Clarify What Trump Meant by 'the Calm Before the Storm," *Politico*, October 6, 2017, https://www.politico.com/story/2017/10/06/trump-calm-before-the-storm-military-response-243544.

5 Andrew Prokop, "Trump's Odd and Ominous 'Calm Before the Storm' Comment, Not Really Explained," *Vox*, October 7, 2017, https://www.vox.com/2017/10/7/16441232/trump-calm-before-storm; Tom Toles, "Opinion: 'Calm Before the Storm' Really Means 'Chaos Before the Bedlam,'" *The Washington Post*, October 6, 2017, https://www.washingtonpost.com/news/opinions/wp/2017/10/06/calm-before-the-storm-really-means-chaos-before-the-bedlam/; Mark Landler, "What Did President Trump Mean by 'Calm Before the Storm?'," *The New York Times*, October 6, 2017, https://www.nytimes.com/2017/10/06/us/politics/trump-calls-meeting-with-military-leaders-the-calm-before-the-storm.html.

6 Dale Beran and Julian Feeld, "Episode 128: From Anonymous to QAnon feat Dale Beran, Matt Alt, Fredrick Brennan & Fuxnet," February 4, 2021, *QAnon Anonymous*, podcast, Soundcloud, https://soundcloud.com/qanonanonymous/episode-128-from-anonymous-to-qanon-feat-dale-beran-matt-alt-fredrick-brennan-fuxnet.

7 "The Making of QAnon: A Crowdsourced Conspiracy," *Bellingcat* (blog), January 7, 2021, https://www.bellingcat.com/news/americas/2021/01/07/the-making-of-qanon-a-crowdsourced-conspiracy/.

8 "High Level Insider," High Level Insider, accessed March 3, 2021, http://hli.anoninfo.net/.

9 "The Making of QAnon: A Crowdsourced Conspiracy," *Bellingcat*.

10 Feminist Proper Gander (@dappergander), "I have potentially upsetting news for @_MAArgentino / The very first 4chan user to say "QAnon" was Canadian / I'm so sorry," Twitter, February 3, 2021, 4:08 p.m., https://twitter.com/dappergander/status/1357073466546130950?s=20.

11 Feminist Proper Gander (@dappergander), "To be fair he needed a new name DESPERATELY / 'LARPer Guy' and 'Info Dump Anon' just weren't cutting it," Twitter, February 3, 2021, 4:38 p.m., https://twitter.com/dappergander/status/1357081059926638593?s=20.

12 Reply no. 147448067 to "Bread Crumbs - Q Clearance Patriot Q," /pol/ - Politically Incorrect, 4chan, November 1, 2017, archived at 4plebs, https://archive.4plebs.org/pol/thread/147433975/#q147448067.

13 Reply no. 147590776 to "Calm before the Storm," /pol/ - Politically

Incorrect, 4chan, Nov 1, 2017, archived at 4plebs, https://archive.4plebs. org/pol/thread/147547939/#q147590776.

14 Brandy Zadrozny and Ben Collins, "How Three Conspiracy Theorists Took 'Q' and Sparked Qanon," *NBC News*, August 14, 2018, https:// www.nbcnews.com/tech/tech-news/how-three-conspiracy- theorists-took-q-sparked-qanon-n900531.

15 Ben Collins (@oneunderscore__), "People like to call Qanon 'Piz- zagate on steroids,' but it's really both emotionally and socioeconom- ically Pizzagate on bath salts," Twitter, July 31, 2018, 7:33 p.m., https:// twitter.com/oneunderscore__/status/1024437843563831301.

16 Kim LaCapria, "Is Comet Ping Pong Pizzeria Home to a Child Abuse Ring Led by Hillary Clinton?," Snopes, November 21, 2016, https:// www.snopes.com/fact-check/pizzagate-conspiracy/.

17 Craig Silverman, "How the Bizarre Conspiracy Theory Behind "Piz- zagate" Was Spread," *Buzzfeed News*, December 5, 2016, https://www. buzzfeed.com/craigsilverman/fever-swamp-election.

18 Mark Tuters, Emilija Jokubauskaitė, and Daniel Bach, "Post-Truth Protest: How 4chan Cooked Up the Pizzagate Bullshit," *M/C Jour- nal* 21, no. 3 (2018), https://journal.media-culture.org.au/index.php/ mcjournal/article/view/1422.

19 Erik Ortiz, "'Pizzagate' Gunman Edgar Maddison Welch Sentenced to Four Years in Prison," *NBC News*, June 22, 2017, https://nbcnews.com/ news/us-news/pizzagate-gunman-edgar-maddison-welch-sentenced- four-years-prison-n775621.

20 Tracybeanz, "She Stood in the Storm," steemit, May 17, 2018, https:// steemit.com/drama/@tracybeanz/she-stood-in-the-storm.

21 Marc-André Argentino (@_MAArgentino), "3/ Prior to being shut down CBTS_stream had 23,000 members and greatawakening had 68,000. Of those, we can see that each subreddit has a unique active user rate," Twitter, March 3, 2020, 5:28 p.m., https://twitter.com/_MA Argentino/status/1234969027350495233.

22 David D. Kirkpatrick, "Saudi Arabia Arrests 11 Princes, Including Bil- lionaire Alwaleed bin Talal," *The New York Times*, November 4, 2017, https://www.nytimes.com/2017/11/04/world/middleeast/saudi-ara- bia-waleed-bin-talal.html.

23 Sorcha Faal, "Daughter of Adolph Hitler Vows to Complete European Union," WhatDoesItMean.com, January 7, 2007, http://www.whatdoes itmean.com/index973.htm.

CHAPTER 3 You Have More Than You Know: QAnon Hits the Big Time

1 Adrian Hon, "What Alternate Reality Games Teach Us about the Dangerous Appeal of QAnon," *Vice*, August 5, 2020, https://www.vice.com/en/article/qj4xbm/what-alternate-reality-games-teach-us-about-the-dangerous-appeal-of-qanon.

2 "What is a 'secure tripcode'?," "FAQ," 4chan, last modified March 3, 2021, https://www.4channel.org/faq#trip.

3 Paul Furber, email to Brandy Zadrozny on August 14, 2018, PaulFurber.net, https://paulfurber.net/nbc/gmail-nbcnews.pdf.

4 Cristina López, "Infowars' Attempt to Hijack and Exploit the Wild Conspiracy Theory That Is QAnon Is Backfiring," *MediaMatters*, May 5, 2018, https://www.mediamatters.org/alex-jones/infowars-attempt-hijack-and-exploit-wild-conspiracy-theory-qanon-backfiring.

5 Meira Gebel, "Baby Boomers Share Nearly 7 Times as Many 'Fake News' Articles on Facebook as Adults Under 30, Study Finds," *Insider*, January 13, 2019, https://www.businessinsider.com/baby-boomers-more-likely-to-share-fake-news-on-facebook-study-2019-1.

6 8chan (8ch.net) (@infinitechan), "We joked about it for years, but #QAnon is making it a reality: Boomers! On your imageboard," Twitter, January 7, 2018, 4:34 p.m., https://twitter.com/infinitechan/status/950118385517408256.

7 Nick Backovic, "EXCLUSIVE: Failed Screenwriter from New Jersey Behind One of QAnon's Most Influential Personas," *Logically*, January 11, 2021, https://www.logically.ai/articles/exclusive-failed-screenwriter-from-new-jersey-behind-one-of-qanons-most-influential-personas.

8 Chris Francescani, "The Men Behind QAnon," *ABC News*, September 22, 2020, https://abcnews.go.com/Politics/men-qanon/story?id=73046374.

9 Drew Harwell and Timothy McLaughlin, "From Helicopter Repairman to Leader of the Internet's 'Darkest Reaches': The Life and Times of 8chan Owner Jim Watkins," *The Washington Post*, September 12, 2019, https://www.washingtonpost.com/technology/2019/09/12/helicopter-repairman-leader-internets-darkest-reaches-life-times-chan-owner-jim-watkins/.

10 Ethan Chiel, "Meet the Man Keeping 8chan, the World's Most Vile Website, Alive," *Splinter*, April 19, 2016, https://splinternews.com/meet-the-man-keeping-8chan-the-worlds-most-vile-websit-1793856249.

11 Timothy McLaughlin, "The Weird, Dark History of 8chan," *Wired*, August 6, 2019, https://www.wired.com/story/the-weird-dark-history-8chan/.

12 Furber, email to Brandy Zadrozny on August 14, 2018.

13 P. J. Vogt and Alex Goldman, "#166 Country of Liars," September 16, 2020, *Reply All*, podcast, Gimlet Media, https://gimletmedia.com/shows/reply-all/llhe5nm.

14 Vogt and Goldman, "#166 Country of Liars."

15 Furber, email to Brandy Zadrozny on August 14, 2018.

16 Jerome Corsi, "QAnon Post #151134," Scribd, December 27, 2017, https://www.scribd.com/document/368027592/QAnon-Post-151134-Dec-27-2017-DECIPHER-Vers-21-0-Dec-27-2017.

17 "Alex Jones: 'The White House Directly Asked [Jerome] Corsi to Be on the 8chan Beat,' Cover 'QAnon' Conspiracy Theory," *MediaMatters*, January 29, 2018, https://www.mediamatters.org/alex-jones/alex-jones-white-house-directly-asked-jerome-corsi-be-8chan-beat-cover-qanon-conspiracy.

18 Rebecca Speare-Cole, "Alex Jones' QAnon Rant Watched Over 2 Million Times: 'I'm Sick of It!,'" *Newsweek*, January 11, 2021, https://www.newsweek.com/alex-jones-qanon-rant-viral-infowars-1560394.

19 Jason Le Miere, "Hillary Clinton, Pedophilia and Ankle Bracelets; New Trump-Supporter Conspiracy Theory Is Pizzagate on Steroids," *Newsweek*, November 20, 2017, https://www.newsweek.com/hillary-clinton-conspiracy-theory-trump-717398.

20 Paris Martineau, "The Storm Is the New Pizzagate—Only Worse," *New York Magazine*, December 19, 2017, https://nymag.com/intelligencer/2017/12/qanon-4chan-the-storm-conspiracy-explained.html.

21 Kelly Weill, "Roseanne Keeps Promoting QAnon, the Pro-Trump Conspiracy Theory That Makes Pizzagate Look Tame," *Daily Beast*, last updated June 19, 2018, https://www.thedailybeast.com/roseanne-keeps-promoting-qanon-the-pro-trump-conspiracy-theory-that-makes-pizzagate-look-tame.

22 John Bowden, "Roseanne Barr Faces Backlash over Trump Conspiracy Theory Tweet," *The Hill*, March 31, 2018, https://thehill.com/homenews/media/381123-roseanne-barr-faces-social-media-backlash-over-trump-conspiracy-theory-tweet.

23 Will Sommer, "QAnon, the Crazy Pro-Trump Conspiracy, Melts Down Over OIG Report," *Daily Beast*, June 19, 2018, https://www.thedailybeast.com/qanon-the-crazy-pro-trump-conspiracy-melts-down-over-oig-report.

24 Henry Brean and Katelyn Newberg, "Henderson Man in Armored Truck on Hoover Dam Bypass Bridge Arrested," *Las Vegas Review Journal*, June 15, 2018, https://www.reviewjournal.com/crime/henderson-man-in-armored-truck-on-hoover-dam-bypass-bridge-arrested/.

25 Sommer, "QAnon, the Crazy Pro-Trump Conspiracy."

26 Richard Ruelas, "Plea Deal Rejected for Qanon Follower Who Drove Armored Vehicle Onto Bridge Near Hoover Dam," *The Arizona Republic*, June 1, 2020, https://www.azcentral.com/story/news/local/arizona/2020/06/01/plea-deal-rejected-matthew-wright-qanon-bridge/5274943002/.

27 Reply no. 1765986 to "Q Research General #2223: Ready the .223 Edi 'QAnon' Conspiracy at His Tampa Rally. Here's What You Need to Know," *Tampa Bay Times*, August 1, 2018, https://www.tampabay.com/florida-politics/buzz/2018/08/01/dozens-of-trump-supporters-championed-the-qanon-conspiracy-at-his-tampa-rally-heres-what-you-need-to-know/

28 See https://nebula.wsimg.com/7f571caa06ec819e7dd16f7a75e7d683?AccessKeyId=A46309A05E2048F24273&disposition=0&alloworigin=1.

29 Mike Rothschild, "George H. W. Bush Death Conspiracy Theories," TheMikeRothschild.com (blog), accessed March 5, 2021, https://themikerothschild.com/2018/12/03/george-h-w-bush-death-conspiracy-theories/.

30 Comment no. 2363457 titled "ARTICLES ABOUT Q," /qresearch/ - Q Research Board, 8chan, July 30, 2018, archived at 8kun, https://8kun.top/qresearch/res/2363217.html#q2363457.

31 Kirby Wilson, "Dozens of Trump Supporters Championed the 'QAnon' Conspiracy at His Tampa Rally. Here's What You Need to Know," *Tampa Bay Times*, August 1, 2018, https://www.tampabay.com/florida-politics/buzz/2018/08/01/dozens-of-trump-supporters-championed-the-qanon-conspiracy-at-his-tampa-rally-heres-what-you-need-to-know/.

32 Glenna Milberg (@GlennaWPLG), "'Military intelligence . . . letting us know what's going on behind the scenes.' That's the headline of #QAnon, a web-based driving force for many Trump supporters," Twitter, August 1, 2018, 1:10 p.m., https://twitter.com/GlennaWPLG/status/1024703813603737600.

33 Jake Cutter (@JakeCutter99), "Had a great time tonight at the Trump rally! Thank you patriots! God bless President Trump! #TampaTrumpRally #TampaTrump #TrumpTampa #Qanon," Twitter, July 31, 2018, 9:39 p.m., https://twitter.com/JakeCutter99/status/1024469702150684672?s=20.

34 Isaac Stanley-Becker, "'We Are Q': A Deranged Conspiracy Cult Leaps from the Internet to the Crowd at Trump's 'MAGA' Tour," *The Washington Post*, August 1, 2018, https://www.washingtonpost.com/news/

morning-mix/wp/2018/08/01/we-are-q-a-deranged-conspiracy-cult-leaps-from-the-internet-to-the-crowd-at-trumps-maga-tour.

35 "Sarah Huckabee Sanders on 'QAnon' Conspiracy Theory," *CBS News*, August 2, 2018, https://www.cbsnews.com/video/sarah-huckabee-sanders-on-qanon-conspiracy-theory/.

36 Kaitlin Tiffany, "Reddit Squashed QAnon by Accident," *The Atlantic*, September 23, 2020, https://www.theatlantic.com/technology/archive/2020/09/reddit-qanon-ban-evasion-policy-moderation-facebook/616442/.

37 Brandy Zadrozny and Ben Collins, "Reddit Bans Qanon Subreddits After Months of Violent Threats," *NBC News*, September 12, 2018, https://www.nbcnews.com/tech/tech-news/reddit-bans-qanon-subreddits-after-months-violent-threats-n909061.

38 Marc-André Argentino (@_MAArgentino), "8/ at the bottom of the 2018 charts we see amazon trending, which correlates with the release of 'An invitation to the Great Awakening," Twitter, February 10, 2020, 4:26 p.m., https://twitter.com/_MAArgentino/status/1226980759514296325/photo/1.

39 Thomas Burr, "US Attorney for Utah John Huber Won't Testify Before House Panel on Clinton Probe," *The Salt Lake Tribune*, December 12, 2018, https://www.sltrib.com/news/politics/2018/12/12/us-attorney-utah-john/.

40 Natasha Bertrand, "Rosenstein Submits Resignation from Justice Department," *Politico*, April 29, 2019, https://www.politico.com/story/2019/04/29/rod-rosenstein-resigns-1292500.

CHAPTER 4 Boom Week Coming:
The Scams and Conspiracy Theories That Begat QAnon

1 Emily Tamkin, "Five Myths About George Soros," *The Washington Post*, August 6, 2020, https://www.washingtonpost.com/outlook/five-myths/five-myths-about-george-soros/2020/08/06/ad195582-d1e9-11ea-8d32-1ebf4e9d8e0d_story.html.

2 Brian Dunning, "Deconstructing the Rothschild Conspiracy," May 22, 2012, *Skeptoid*, podcast, Skeptoid Media, https://skeptoid.com/episodes/4311.

3 "Hatechan: The Hate and Violence-Filled Legacy of 8chan," ADL, August 7, 2019, https://www.adl.org/blog/hatechan-the-hate-and-violence-filled-legacy-of-8chan.

4 Reply no. 10333879 to "Q Research General #13223: Potus Rally/ Briefing Edition," /qresearch/ - Q Research, 8kun, August 18, 2020, https://8kun.top/qresearch/res/10333299.html#10333879.

5 Talia Lavin, "QAnon, Blood Libel, and the Satanic Panic," *The New Republic*, September 29, 2020, https://newrepublic.com/article/159529/qanon-blood-libel-satanic-panic.

6 Abram Hoffer, Humphrey [*sic*] Osmond, and John Smythies, "Schizophrenia: A New Approach. II. Result of a Year's Research," in *Psychopathology: A Source Book*, eds. Charles F. Reed, Irving E. Alexander, and Silver S. Tomkins (Cambridge, MA: Harvard University Press, 1958), 651.

7 Aldous Huxley, *The Doors of Perception* (New York: HarperPerennial, 2009), 11.

8 Hunter S. Thompson, *Fear and Loathing in Las Vegas and Other American Stories* (New York: Modern Library), 131.

9 Thompson, 132.

10 The Q Origins Project (@Qorigins), "Two. Exactly two. Really, he vanished. So what's the moral of the story? Partly this: in HWP's downfall, there are lessons for Q," Twitter, November 16, 2020, 5:49 a.m., https://twitter.com/QOrigins/status/1328289112931987456.

11 Ben Sixsmith, "Fear and Adrenochrome," *The Spectator*, May 4, 2020, https://spectator.us/fear-adrenochrome-conspiracy-theory-drug/.

12 Kyle Mantyla, "Liz Crokin Claims Celebrities Are Getting Coronavirus from Tainted 'Adrenochrome Supply,'" *Right Wing Watch*, March 18, 2020, https://www.rightwingwatch.org/post/liz-crokin-claims-celebrities-are-getting-coronavirus-from-tainted-adrenochrome-supply/.

13 Sam Westreich, "Why is QAnon Obsessed with Adrenochrome?," Medium, October 19, 2020, https://medium.com/@westwise/why-is-qanon-obsessed-with-adrenochrome-b300d7f4ba32.

14 "Woman Claims Missing Daughter Was 'Tortured for the Drug Adrenochrome," Dr. Phil (website), September 8, 2020, https://www.drphil.com/videos/woman-claims-missing-daughter-was-tortured-for-the-drug-adrenochrome/.

15 Tarpley Hitt, "How QAnon Became Obsessed With 'Adrenochrome,' an Imaginary Drug Hollywood Is 'Harvesting' from Kids," *Daily Beast*, August 14, 2020, https://www.thedailybeast.com/how-qanon-became-obsessed-with-adrenochrome-an-imaginary-drug-hollywood-is-harvesting-from-kids.

16 Pam Belluck with Jo Thomas, "Wads of Cash, Gossip, Then Fraud Charges," *The New York Times*, September 2, 2000, https://www.nytimes.com/2000/09/02/us/wads-of-cash-gossip-then-fraud-charges.html.

17 "That Old-Time Religion," *Forbes*, June 9, 2002, https://www.forbes.com/forbes/2002/0610/212.html?sh=2ea164c17d40.

18 Sean Robinson, "Snared by a Cybercult Queen," *The News Tribune*,

July 18, 2004, https://www.thenewstribune.com/news/special-reports/article25855081.html.

19 Robinson, "Snared by a Cybercult Queen."

20 "The Omega Chronicles," Quatloos, accessed March 3, 2021, https://www.quatloos.com/cm-omega/omega-chronicals.htm.

21 "Exhibit: Omega Trust and Trading Ltd.," Quatloos, accessed March 3, 2021, https://www.quatloos.com/cm-omega/cm-omega.htm.

22 Rob Stroud, "Man Convicted with Creating Omega Scam Dies," *JG-TC*, last modified July 28, 2012, https://jg-tc.com/news/man-convicted-of-creating-omega-scam-dies/article_83df49c0-d831-11e1-bc18-001a4b-cf887a.html.

23 Robinson, "Snared by a Cybercult Queen."

24 "The Basic Components of an Online Course That Helps People Learn Actively," Nesara, accessed March 3, 2021, http://nesara.org/bill/executive_summary.htm.

25 "Crisis in America #3: More Startling Revelations Coming Out," EarthRainbowNetwork.com, last modified September 13, 2001, http://www.earthrainbownetwork.com/CrisisAmerica3.htm.

26 Sean Robinson, "Dove Battles the 'Dark Agenda,'" Cult Education Institute, July 19, 2004, https://culteducation.com/group/897-dove-of-oneness-nesara/5760-dove-battles-the-dark-agenda.html.

27 Sean Robinson, "Some Lucrative 'New Age Hooey,'" Cult Education Institute, June 19, 2006, https://culteducation.com/group/897-dove-of-oneness-nesara/5762-some-lucrative-new-age-hooey.html.

28 Deep Knight, "Dove of Oneness Sacrifices Life," Quatloos! forums, June 11, 2010, http://www.quatloos.com/Q-Forum/viewtopic.php?t=5963.

29 Deep Knight, "Dove of Oneness Sacrifices Life."

30 Tom Lane, "Betting Millions on Iraqi Money," *ABC News*, September 19, 2006, https://abcnews.go.com/US/story?id=2448772.

31 John F. Wasick, "The Curse of Saddam: Iraqi Dinar Deals," *Forbes*, January 19, 2012, https://www.forbes.com/sites/johnwasik/2012/01/19/the-curse-of-saddam-iraqi-dinar-deals.

32 "Forum Facts," *Dinar Douchebags* (blog), accessed March 3, 2021, http://dinardouchebags.blogspot.com/p/fact-fiction.html.

33 *Dinar Recaps* email newsletter, September 24, 2013, https://myemail.constantcontact.com/Dinar-Recaps-9-24-6pm-Newsletter-.html?soid=1105984884317&aid=aAt9fat2B1k.

34 *My Big, Fat, Wonderfully, Wealthy Life*, Internet Archive, last modified February 19, 2014, https://archive.org/stream/pdfy-I0f4oyt-d69xoT1Uz/My+Big+Fat++Wonderfully+Wealthy+Life_djvu.txt.

35 John F. Wasick, "The Dinar's Dismal Future: Sell Now," *Forbes*,

July 28, 2014, https://www.forbes.com/sites/johnwasik/2014/07/28/the-dinars-dismal-future-sell-now.

36 Mitchell Hartman, "Here's How Much Money There Is in the World—and Why You've Never Heard the Exact Number," *Insider*, November 17, 2017, https://www.businessinsider.com/heres-how-much-money-there-is-in-the-world-2017-10.

37 Jesselyn Cook, "'I Miss My Mom': Children of QAnon Believers Are Desperately Trying to Deradicalize Their Own Parents," *HuffPost*, February 11, 2021, https://www.huffpost.com/entry/children-of-qanon-believers_n_601078e9c5b6c5586aa49077.

38 Department of Justice, US Attorney's Office, Northern District of Georgia, "Owners of Currency Exchange Business That Made $600 Million Convicted of Fraud," Justice.gov, October 10, 2018, https://www.justice.gov/usao-ndga/pr/owners-currency-exchange-business-made-600-million-convicted-fraud; Andrea Day, "Inside a $24 Million Investment Scam: Buy the Iraqi Dinar," *CNBC*, January 15, 2015, https://www.cnbc.com/2015/01/15/inside-a-24-million-investment-scam-buy-the-iraqi-dinar.html; Department of Justice, US Attorney's Office: Southern District of New York, "Virginia Man Pleads Guilty to Defrauding Investors of $2 Million in Iraqi Dinar Fraud Scheme," Justice.gov, March 27, 2019, https://www.justice.gov/usao-sdny/pr/virginia-man-pleads-guilty-defrauding-investors-2-million-iraqi-dinar-fraud-scheme; Department of Justice, US Attorney's Office, District of Kansas, "California Man Pleads Guilty to Operating $1.6 Million Internet Fraud," Justice.gov, May 21, 2015, https://www.justice.gov/usao-ks/pr/california-man-pleads-guilty-operating-16-million-internet-fraud.

CHAPTER 5 We Are the News Now: QAnon Has a Big 2019

1 Ben Mathis-Lilley, "Trump Endorses Publication That Has Reported That the Pope Uses Magic to Control World Events," *Slate*, November 27, 2017, https://slate.com/news-and-politics/2017/11/trump-endorses-magapill-conspiracy-site.html.

2 "Reshaping the White House," *The New York Times*, last modified October 15, 2019, https://www.nytimes.com/interactive/2019/11/02/us/politics/trump-twitter-presidency.html.

3 Jane Coaston, "The Mueller Investigation Is Over. QAnon, the Conspiracy Theory That Grew Around It, Is Not," *Vox*, March 29, 2019, https://www.vox.com/policy-and-politics/2019/3/29/18286890/qanon-mueller-report-barr-trump-conspiracy-theories.

4 Ben Collins (@oneunderscore__), "I've been covering Qanon for a year, and the amount of pro-Q people in this video from yesterday's

Trump rally line in Grand Rapids is absolutely shocking," Twitter, March 29, 2019, 12:43 p.m., https://twitter.com/oneunderscore__/status/1111489128644968448.

5 Will Sommer, "QAnoners Say Their QAnon Merch Is Being Banned by Secret Service at Trump Rallies," *Daily Beast*, October 2, 2018, https://www.thedailybeast.com/qanoners-say-their-qanon-merch-is-being-banned-by-secret-service-at-trump-rallies.

6 Quirky ☆☆☆ (@QuirkyFollowsQ), Twitter, March 28, 2019 (account suspended); quoted in Mike Rothschild, "Trump's Michigan Rally Breathed New Life into the QAnon Conspiracy," *Daily Dot*, March 29, 2019, https://www.dailydot.com/debug/qanon-trump-michigan-rally/.

7 Mike Rothschild (@rothschildmd), "Looks like some QAnon acolytes are going to crash Trump's rally in Grand Rapids. Q already shouted one out, and I'd imagine more head-pats are coming," Twitter, March 28, 2019, 2:47 p.m., https://twitter.com/rothschildmd/status/1111339147694751744?s=20.

8 Mike Rothschild, "Trump's Michigan Rally Breathed New Life into the QAnon Conspiracy."

9 https://twitter.com/realDonaldTrump/status/1111374017418559493. Trump's tweets are archived at TTA - Search (thetrumparchive.com).

10 Brandy Zadrozny and Ben Collins, "Like the Fringe Conspiracy Theory QAnon? There's Plenty of Merch for Sale on Amazon," *NBC News*, July 18, 2018, https://www.nbcnews.com/business/business-news/fringe-conspiracy-theory-qanon-there-s-plenty-merch-sale-amazon-n892561.

11 Rachel Greenspan, "Americans Are Trying to Cash In on 'QAnon' in a Race to Trademark the Conspiracy Theory's Slogans," *Insider*, October 8, 2020, https://www.insider.com/qanon-americans-trying-to-cash-in-conspiracy-theory-trademark-2020-10.

12 Jeffrey Dastin, Sheila Dang, and Anna Irrera, "Online Merchants Linked to QAnon Down, but Not Out, Following Platform Bans," Reuters, January 25, 2021, https://www.reuters.com/article/us-usa-trump-qanon-financing/online-merchants-linked-to-qanon-down-but-not-out-following-platform-bans-idUSKBN29U193.

13 Josh Gerstein, "Flynn Had $4.6M Unpaid Legal Tab, Records Show," *Politico*, July 18, 2019, https://www.politico.com/story/2019/07/18/michael-flynn-unpaid-legal-tab-1420304.

14 WWG1WGA, *QAnon: An Invitation to the Great Awakening* (Dallas: Relentlessly Creative Books, 2019), 2.

15 Will Sommer, "The Co-Authors of a Bestselling QAnon Book Are at War with Each Other," *The Daily Beast*, June 17, 2019, https://www.

thedailybeast.com/the-co-authors-of-a-bestselling-qanon-book-are-at-war-with-each-other.

16 Ben Collins, "On Amazon, a QAnon Conspiracy Book Climbs the Charts—with an Algorithmic Push," *NBC News*, March 4, 2019, https://www.nbcnews.com/tech/tech-news/amazon-qanon-conspiracy-book-climbs-charts-algorithmic-push-n979181.

17 Dave Chamberlain, "Hope everyone, not just Q followers will take a look at this book. Take the Red Pill," customer review, Amazon, March 1, 2019, https://www.amazon.com/gp/customer-reviews/R36C5ZDNL9LM9L/ref=cm_cr_getr_d_rvw_ttl?ie=UTF8&ASIN=1942790139.

18 Will Sommer, "The Co-Authors of a Bestselling QAnon Book Are at War with Each Other."

19 "QAnon" search data, United States, March 1, 2019 to March 30, 2019, Google Trends, accessed March 3, 2021, https://trends.google.com/trends/explore?date=2019-03-01%202019-03-30&geo=US&q=qanon.

20 "QAnon Conspiracy Theory on James Comey Shuts School Festival," *BBC News*, May 10, 2019, https://www.bbc.com/news/world-us-canada-48231708.

21 Top Blog Sites (@TopInfoBlogs), Twitter, April 28, 2019, 11:59 p.m., https://twitter.com/TopInfoBlogs/status/1122712096066560000?s=20.

22 Joe M (@StormIsUponUs), Twitter, April 29, 2019 (account suspended); quoted in Mike Rothschild, "Brain Worms All the Way Down," *TheMikeRothschild.com* (blog), April 29, 2019, https://themikerothschild.com/2019/04/29/grass-valley-qanon/.

23 Mike Rothschild, "The Inside Story of How QAnon Derailed a Charter School's Annual Fundraiser," *Daily Dot*, first published May 10, 2019, updated January 26, 2021, https://www.dailydot.com/debug/qanon-grass-valley-charter-school-foundation/. All quotes from Willoughby and Kathy Dotson are drawn from this interview.

24 Joe M (@StormIsUponUs), Twitter, May 3, 2019, 12:44 p.m. (account suspended); quoted by Travis View (@travis_view), "Even after a QAnon conspiracy theory causes a school to cancel a fundraiser, a QAnon follower comments 'Thank you Anons for decoding these,'" Twitter, May 3, 2019, 5:00 p.m., https://twitter.com/travis_view/status/1124418405581242368/photo/3.

25 Liz Kellar, "Report of Pipe Bombs Leads to Woman's Arrest in Grass Valley," *The Union*, May 19, 2019, https://www.theunion.com/news/crime/report-of-pipe-bombs-leads-to-womans-arrest-in-grass-valley/.

26 Reply no. 6554812 to "Q Research General #8381: New Baker 2nd Bake - Carb Loading Edition," /qresearch/ - Q Research Board, 8chan, May 21, 2019, archived at 8kun, https://8kun.top/qresearch/res/6554411.

html#6554812; Mary C (@electricalmama), Twitter, May 21, 2019 (account suspended), quoted in Mike Rothschild, "QAnon Believers Link Small-Town Arrest to Deep State Conspiracy Without Evidence," *Daily Dot*, January 26, 2021, https://www.dailydot.com/debug/qanon-pipe-bomb-grass-valley-charter-school/.

27 Farid Hafez, "The Manifesto of the El Paso Terrorist," *Bridge*, August 26, 2019, https://bridge.georgetown.edu/research/the-manifesto-of-the-el-paso-terrorist/; Brian Barrett, "The Wrong Way to Talk About a Shooter's Manifesto," *Wired*, August 4, 2019, https://www.wired.com/story/wrong-way-talk-about-shooter-manifesto/.

28 Abby Olheiser, *Washington Post*, March 15, 2019. https://www.washingtonpost.com/technology/2019/03/15/christchurch-mosque-shooter-steeped-online-culture-knew-how-make-his-massacre-go-viral/

29 Matthew Prince, "Terminating Service for 8chan," Cloudfare, August 4, 2019, https://blog.cloudflare.com/terminating-service-for-8chan/.

30 Kevin Poulsen, "8Chan Refugees Blow Their Anonymity," *Daily Beast*, August 9, 2019, https://www.thedailybeast.com/8chan-users-migrating-to-zeronet-are-accidentally-revealing-their-locations; Kelly Weill, "8chan Refugees Worried They're Downloading Child Porn," *Daily Beast*, August 8, 2019, https://www.thedailybeast.com/8chan-refugees-worried-theyre-downloading-child-porn-on-peer-to-peer-site-zeronet.

31 Sarah Ruth Ashcraft (@SaRaAshcraft), "We are the news now. Expect Q team to be 'officially' silent until 8chan is back online, which will only be AFTER congressional hearings on 9/5," Twitter, August 28, 2019, 9:38 p.m., https://twitter.com/SaRaAshcraft/status/11668878349 19288834?s=20; "Thompson and Rogers Announce Subpoena of 8chan Owner Watkins," Committee on Homeland Security, August 14, 2019, https://homeland.house.gov/news/press-releases/thompson-and-rogers-announce-subpoena-of-8chan-owner-watkins.

32 Makena Kelly, "8chan Could Be Back Online as Soon as Next Week, Lawyer Says," *The Verge*, September 5, 2019, https://www.theverge.com/2019/9/5/20851949/8chan-jim-watkins-benjamin-barr-congress-deposition-testimony-el-paso-shooting.

33 Rebecca Aydin, "The Controversial Company Now Protecting 8chan from Online Attacks Also Services an Infamous Neo-Nazi Site," *Insider*, August 5, 2019, https://www.businessinsider.com/bitmitigate-web-protection-service-hosting-8chan-explained-2019-8.

34 William Turton and Joshua Brustein, "QAnon High Priest Was Just Trolling Away as a Citigroup Tech Executive," *Bloomberg Businessweek*, October 7, 2020, https://www.bloomberg.com/news/fea-

tures/2020-10-07/who-is-qanon-evangelist-qmap-creator-and-former
-citigroup-exec-jason-gelinas.

35 Quinn Norton, Micah Loewinger, and Molly Webster, "Band-Aid on
a Bulletwound," November 1, 2019, *On the Media*, podcast, WNYC
Studios, https://www.wnycstudios.org/podcasts/otm/episodes/on-the-
media-2019-11-01.

36 Dale Beran and Julian Feeld, "Episode 54: Autopsy of 8chan with
Founder Fredrick Brennan," August 25, 2019, *QAnon Anonymous*, podcast, Soundcloud, https://soundcloud.com/qanonanonymous/episode-
54-autopsy-of-8chan-w-founder-fredrick-brennan.

37 Norton, Loewinger, and Webster, "Band-Aid on a Bulletwound."

38 Nick Lim (@LimTheNick), "History has shown that when these three
things are aligned; community, liberty, and ambition - failure is impossible. 8kun will be back, and stronger than ever," Twitter, October 28,
2019, 2:07 p.m., https://twitter.com/LimTheNick/status/11888800488
13555712?s=20.

39 Brian Krebs, "Meet the World's Biggest 'Bulletproof' Hoster," *Krebs
on Security* (blog), July 16, 2019, https://krebsonsecurity.com/2019/07/
meet-the-worlds-biggest-bulletproof-hoster/.

40 Anthony Macuk, "8chan Back Online Under The Name 8kun," *The
Columbian*, November 7, 2019, https://www.columbian.com/news/
2019/nov/07/8chan-back-online-under-the-name-8kun/; Fredrick Brennan (@fr_brennan), "Again: Vanwatech has essentially three custom-
ers. * Vanwatech itself * Jim Watkins * Daily Stormer I've been able
to prove every other domain is somehow related," Twitter, August 24,
2020, 7:11 a.m., https://twitter.com/fr_brennan/ status/1297853986
905579520. William Turton and Joshua Brustein, *Bloomberg News*,
April 14, 2021. https://www.bloomberg.com/news/features/2021-04-14/
qanon-daily-stormer-far-right-have-been-kept-online-by-nick-lim-s-
vanwatech.

CHAPTER 6 God Wins: Why People Believe in QAnon

1 Will Sommer, "Trump Fans Sink Savings into 'Iraqi Dinar' Scam," *Daily
Beast*, November 20, 2018, https://www.thedailybeast.com/trump-
fans-sink-savings-into-iraqi-dinar-scam.

2 Nick Backovic and Joe Ondrak, "NESARA and the Business of False
Hope: Why Times of Austerity and Pandemic Create Fertile Ground
for Die-Hard Scams," *Logically*, September 3, 2020, https://www.logic-
ally.ai/articles/nesara-and-the-business-of-false-hope.

3 Rob Brotherton, *Suspicious Minds: Why We Believe Conspiracy Theories* (New York: Bloomsbury Sigma, 2015), 21.

4 Joseph E. Uscinski, ed., *Conspiracy Theories and the People Who Believe Them* (New York: Oxford University Press, 2018), 299.

5 Antonia Noori Farzan, "Chuck E. Cheese's Oddly Shaped Pizza Ignites a Bizarre Conspiracy Theory Viewed by Millions on YouTube," *The Washington Post*, February 13, 2019, https://www.washingtonpost.com/nation/2019/02/13/chuck-e-cheeses-oddly-shaped-pizza-ignites-bizarre-conspiracy-theory-viewed-by-millions-youtube/.

6 Brian Dunning, "Conspiracy Theorists Aren't Crazy," June 28, 2011, *Skeptoid*, podcast, Skeptoid Media, https://skeptoid.com/episodes/4264.

7 Philip Edwards, "6 Myths About the Ides of March and Killing Caesar," *Vox*, March 15, 2017, https://www.vox.com/2015/3/15/8214921/ides-of-march-caesar-assassination.

8 Brian Dunning, "5 Conspiracy Theories That Turned Out to be True . . . Maybe?," May 27, 2014, *Skeptoid*, podcast, Skeptoid Media, https://skeptoid.com/episodes/4416.

9 "CIA Report on Project Mockingbird," *The Washington Post*, accessed March 4, 2021, https://apps.washingtonpost.com/g/documents/local/cia-report-on-project-mockingbird/295/.

10 Kat Eschner, "What We Know About the CIA's Midcentury Mind-Control Project," *Smithsonian Magazine*, April 13, 2017, https://www.smithsonianmag.com/smart-news/what-we-know-about-cias-midcentury-mind-control-project-180962836/.

11 EJ Dickson, "Former QAnon Followers Explain What Drew Them In—And Got Them Out," *Rolling Stone*, September 23, 2020, https://www.rollingstone.com/culture/culture-features/ex-qanon-followers-cult-conspiracy-theory-pizzagate-1064076/.

12 Miles Klee, "The Rise of 'Weaponized Autism,'" *Mel Magazine*, October 2, 2017, https://melmagazine.com/en-us/story/the-rise-of-weaponized-autism-2.

13 Jan-Willem van Prooijen, "The Psychology of Qanon: Why Do Seemingly Sane People Believe Bizarre Conspiracy Theories?," *NBC News*, August 13, 2018, https://www.nbcnews.com/think/opinion/psychology-qanon-why-do-seemingly-sane-people-believe-bizarre-conspiracy-ncna900171.

14 Randall Colburn, "There's New, Insane Conspiracy Theory Tearing Up 4chan," *AV Club*, December 19, 2017, https://www.avclub.com/theres-a-new-insane-conspiracy-theory-tearing-up-4chan-1821432397; Drusilla Moorhouse and Emerson Malone, "Here's Why BuzzFeed News Is Calling QAnon a 'Collective Delusion' From Now On," *Buzzfeed News*, September 4, 2020, https://www.buzzfeednews.com/article/

drumoorhouse/qanon-mass-collective-delusion-buzzfeed-news-copy-desk.

15 Philip Bump, "How to Talk—and Ask—About QAnon," *The Washington Post*, August 20, 2020, https://www.washingtonpost.com/politics/2020/08/20/how-talk-ask-about-qanon/.

16 Mick West (@MickWest), "What Makes People Fall for QAnon? How can you help someone after they end up down one of the most insidious rabbit holes in recent times?," Twitter, September 15, 2020, 11:03 a.m., https://twitter.com/MickWest/status/1305885011279667200.

17 Nick Backovic, "EXCLUSIVE: Failed Screenwriter from New Jersey Behind One of QAnon's Most Influential Personas," *Logically*, January 11, 2021, https://www.logically.ai/articles/exclusive-failed-screenwriter-from-new-jersey-behind-one-of-qanons-most-influential-personas.

18 Robert Cornero (@RobertCornero), "Twitter Archive," Twitter, accessed March 4, 2021, https://archive.is/FuzvL.

19 Mike Rothschild (@rothschildmd), "Here's something interesting: @RobertCornero, Neon Revolt's Twitter account under his real name, is long gone. And Wayback has almost nothing," January 12, 2021, 1:03 a.m., https://twitter.com/rothschildmd/status/1348873315885072384.

20 Kyle Mantyla, "Stick a Fork in QAnon: Alex Jones and Jerome Corsi Claim That QAnon Has Been 'Completely Compromised,'" *Right Wing Watch*, May 11, 2018, https://www.rightwingwatch.org/post/stick-a-fork-in-qanon-alex-jones-and-jerome-corsi-claim-that-qanon-has-been-completely-compromised/.

21 "Urgent: QAnon Followers," MAGApill News, September 8, 2018, archived at https://web.archive.org/web/20180912205137/http:/www.magapill.com/o/urgent-qanon-followers.html.

PART II: ESCALATION

CHAPTER 7 This Is Not a Game: The Many Crimes of QAnon Followers

1 Caroline Enos, "Dorchester Man Leads Police on 25 Mile Chase in Two States with His 5 Children in Vehicle," *The Boston Globe*, June 12, 2020, https://www.bostonglobe.com/2020/06/12/metro/dorchester-man-leads-police-25-mile-chase-two-states-with-his-5-children-vehicle/.

2 Will Sommer, "QAnon Promotes Pedo-Ring Conspiracy Theories. Now They're Stealing Kids," *Daily Beast*, August 15, 2020, https://www.thedailybeast.com/qanon-promotes-pedo-ring-conspiracy-theories-now-theyre-stealing-kids.

3 Nathan Schneider, "Cosmic War on a Global Scale: An Interview with

Mark Juergensmeyer," *The Immanent Frame*, July 23, 2010, The Social Science Research Council, https://tif.ssrc.org/2010/07/23/cosmic-war/.

4 Marc-André Argentino (@_MAArgentino), "1/ Going to Start a Thread on Alpalus Slyman the QAnon follower from Massachusetts who was arrested after livestreaming himself leading police on a car chase," Twitter, June 13, 2020, 11:55 p.m., https://twitter.com/_MAArgentino/status/1272014864924409856.

5 Jason Schreiber, "'We Don't Want to Die': Father Livestreams Multi-Town Police Chase with 5 Kids in Van," *New Hampshire Union Leader*, June 11, 2020, https://www.unionleader.com/news/crime/we-dont-want-to-die-father-livestreams-multi-town-police-chase-with-5-kids-in/article_b4663e11-e42c-51ca-8067-c10803777ef8.html.

6 Michael Wilson and Benjamin Weiser, "Frank Cali, the Slain Gambino Boss, Was a 'Ghost' Who Avoided the Limelight," *The New York Times*, March 14, 2019, https://www.nytimes.com/2019/03/14/nyregion/frank-cali-dead-gambino.html.

7 Tim Stelloh, "Suspect in Killing of Mafia Boss Was Influenced by Right-Wing Hate Speech, Lawyer Says," *NBC News*, March 25, 2019, https://www.nbcnews.com/news/us-news/suspect-killing-mafia-boss-was-influenced-right-wing-hate-speech-n987231.

8 Sara Jean Green, "'God Told Me He Was a Lizard': Seattle Man Accused of Killing His Brother with a Sword," *The Seattle Times*, January 8, 2019, https://www.seattletimes.com/seattle-news/crime/god-told-me-he-was-a-lizard-seattle-man-accused-of-killing-his-brother-with-a-sword/.

9 Will Sommer, "Qanon-Believing Proud Boy Accused of Murdering 'Lizard' Brother with Sword," *Daily Beast*, January 9, 2019, https://www.thedailybeast.com/proud-boy-member-accused-of-murdering-his-brother-with-a-sword-4.

10 Emily G (@EmilyGorcenski), "So I think I'm the first one to notice that Buckey Wolfe, the alleged Proud Boy who killed his brother with a sword, was acquitted by reason of insanity," Twitter, March 27, 2020, 7:33 p.m., https://twitter.com/EmilyGorcenski/status/1243682567456534528.

11 Andrew Denney and Lorena Mongelly, "Conspiracist Accused in Gambino Boss Killing Goes on Bizarre Courtroom Rant," *New York Post*, February 7, 2020, https://nypost.com/2020/02/07/conspiracist-accused-in-gambino-boss-killing-goes-on-bizarre-courtroom-rant/.

12 "The People of the State of New York Against Anthony Comello Defense Motion," Supreme Court of the State of New York, last modified July 19, 2019, https://www.documentcloud.org/docu-

ments/6209320-The-PEOPLE-of-the-STATE-of-NEW-YORK-Against.html.

13 Bobby Allyn, "Lawyer: Shooter Wasn't Trying to Kill a Mob Boss. He Was Under 'QAnon' Delusion," *NPR*, July 22, 2019, https://www.npr.org/2019/07/22/744244166/shooters-lawyer-he-wasn-t-trying-to-kill-a-mob-boss-he-was-under-qanon-delusion.

14 Court documents, page 19. https://www.documentcloud.org/documents/6209320-The-PEOPLE-of-the-STATE-of-NEW-YORK-Against.html.

15 Frank Donnelly, "Alleged Mob-Boss Killer Found Mentally Unfit to Stand Trial," *Staten Island Advance*, June 3, 2020, https://www.silive.com/news/2020/06/alleged-mob-boss-killer-found-mentally-unfit-to-stand-trial.html.

16 Brittany Shammas, "A Mother Teamed Up with Qanon Followers to Kidnap Her Son from Protective Custody, Police Say," *The Washington Post*, January 8, 2020, https://www.washingtonpost.com/crime-law/2020/01/08/mother-teamed-up-with-qanon-followers-kidnap-her-son-protective-custody-police-say/.

17 Will Sommer, "QAnon Incited Her to Kidnap Her Son and Then Hid Her from the Law," *Daily Beast*, August 16, 2020, https://www.thedailybeast.com/qanon-incited-her-to-kidnap-her-son-and-then-hid-her-from-the-law.

18 Travis View (@travis_view), "Notice the blue QAnon-themed bracelets piled on the table at the Finnish QAnon follower meetup. Those bracelets are being distributed by a Chicago woman," Twitter, September 22, 2019, 10:26 p.m., https://twitter.com/travis_view/status/1175959705048322048.

19 Will Sommer, "QAnon Believer Teamed Up with Conspiracy Theorists to Plot Kidnapping, Police Say," *Daily Beast*, January 4, 2020, https://www.thedailybeast.com/cynthia-abcug-qanon-conspiracy-theorist-charged-in-kidnapping-plot.

20 Will Sommer, "Another QAnon Mom Has Allegedly Kidnapped Her Kid," *Daily Beast*, October 1, 2020, https://www.thedailybeast.com/another-qanon-mom-has-allegedly-kidnapped-her-kid.

21 Scott D. Pierce, "Utah Woman Who Fled State with Her 6-Year-Old Son Is Facing Felony Charge," *The Salt Lake Tribune*, October 6, 2020, https://www.sltrib.com/news/2020/10/06/utah-woman-who-fled-state/.

22 Will Sommer, "QAnon Mom Charged with Kidnapping Her Kids," *Daily Beast*, March 28, 2020, https://www.thedailybeast.com/qanon-mom-charged-with-kidnapping-her-kids.

23 Max Winitz, "Twins Found Unharmed, Mother Taken into Cus-

tody," *WNKY 40 News*, March 26, 2020, https://www.wnky.com/twins-found-unharmed-mother-taken-into-custody/.

24 Simone Boyce, "QAnon Beliefs, Promise of Child Custody Help Hang Over Deadly Shooting," *NBC News*, December 1, 2020, https://www.nbcnews.com/news/us-news/qanon-beliefs-promise-child-custody-help-hang-over-deadly-shooting-n1249602.

25 Austin L. Miller, "More Details Emerge in Marion Oaks Fatal Shooting," *Ocala StarBanner*, November 17, 2020, https://www.ocala.com/story/news/2020/11/17/more-details-emerge-marion-oaks-fatal-shooting/6330403002/.

26 Curt Anderson, "Police: Florida Man Who Questioned Government Powers Slain," *AP News*, November 17, 2020, https://apnews.com/article/georgia-ocala-florida-arrests-shootings-66b87bf526619674e3fcf-5d40123d6cd.

27 Melissa Yeager, "Vandalism at Sedona's Chapel of the Holy Cross Linked to QAnon Supporter," *The Arizona Republic*, October 1, 2019, https://www.azcentral.com/story/travel/arizona/2019/10/01/sedona-chapel-of-the-holy-cross-vandalism-qanon-supporter-arrested/3826336002/.

28 Kelly Weill, "QAnon Fan Arrested for Threatening Massacre at YouTube Headquarters," *Daily Beast*, September 27, 2018, https://www.thedailybeast.com/qanon-fan-arrested-for-threatening-massacre-at-youtube-headquarters.

29 Margot Harris, "A Woman Inspired by Qanon Conspiracy Videos Was Arrested After Live-Streaming Her Trip to 'Take Out' Joe Biden," *Insider*, May 1, 2020, https://www.insider.com/biden-qanon-supporter-arrested-attemp-live-streaming-trip-to-take-2020-5.

30 Julian Feeld, "Texas QAnon Supporter Used Car to Attack Strangers She Believed Were 'Pedophiles,'" *Right Wing Watch*, August 20, 2020, https://www.rightwingwatch.org/post/texas-qanon-car-attack-cecilia-fulbright/.

31 Ryan Briggs and Max Marin, "Armed Qanon Follower Arrested in Alleged Philly Convention Center Threat Linked to Far-Right Va. Senator," *WHYY*, November 6, 2020, https://whyy.org/articles/armed-qanon-follower-arrested-in-alleged-philly-convention-center-threat-linked-to-far-right-va-senator/; Kelly Weill, "Sword Attacking MAGA Fanatics Busted in Philly Vote Scheme Joined Capitol Riot, Prosecutors Say," *Daily Beast*, January 14, 2021, https://www.thedailybeast.com/maga-fanatics-antonio-lamotta-and-joshua-macias-busted-in-philly-scheme-joined-capitol-riot-prosecutors-say.

32 Virginia Barreda, "Man Arrested at Capitol Protest in Salem Now

Charged with Shooting at Federal Courthouse in Portland," *States-man Journal*, January 11, 2021, https://www.statesmanjournal.com/story/news/crime/2021/01/11/oregon-man-charged-shooting-federal-courthouse-portland-election-protest/6628090002/.

33 FBI Phoenix Field Office, "Anti-Government, Identity Based, and Fringe Political Conspiracy Theories Very Likely Motivate Some Domestic Extremists to Commit Criminal, Sometimes Violent Activity," JustSecurity.com, May 30, 2019, https://www.justsecurity.org/wp-content/uploads/2019/08/420379775-fbi-conspiracy-theories-domestic-extremism.pdf.

34 "QAnon and the Press—Anatomy of a Smear Campaign," *Praying Medic* (blog), August 10, 2020, https://prayingmedic.com/2020/08/10/qanon-and-the-press-the-anatomy-of-a-smear-campaign/; Reply no. 11149530 to "Q Research General #14258: Comfy Company Reporting-Inn Edition," /qresearch/ - Q Research, 8kun, October 19, 2020, https://8kun.top/qresearch/res/11149092.html#11149530; Reply no. 7712899 to "Q Research General #9870: Dems propose Bill to Defend Iran Edition," /qresearch/ - Q Research, 8kun, January 4, 2020, https://8kun.top/qresearch/res/7712301.html#7712899.

35 "QAnon and the Press," *Praying Medic*.

CHAPTER 8 Save the Children:
QAnon Transforms in 2020 with the Pandemic

1 All quotes in this paragraph are drawn from Antonia Noori Farzan,- "NOT TRUE': Oprah Winfrey Debunks Bizarre Qanon Conspiracy Theory Spreading Across the Internet," *The Washington Post*, March 18, 2020, https://www.washingtonpost.com/nation/2020/03/18/oprah-winfrey-qanon-conspiracy/.

2 Michelle L. Holshue et al., "First Case of 2019 Novel Coronavirus in the United States," *New England Journal of Medicine*, last updated March 5, 2020, https://www.nejm.org/doi/full/10.1056/NEJMoa2001191.

3 Meagan Vazquez and Betsy Klein, "Trump Again Defends Use of the Term 'China Virus,'" *CNN*, March 19, 2020, https://www.cnn.com/2020/03/17/politics/trump-china-coronavirus/index.html; u/hogancheveipp off, "Maximum secuity biolab opened a few years ago in . . . ahem . . . Wuhan, China . . . ," /r/conspiracy, Reddit, January 22, 2020, https://www.reddit.com/r/conspiracy/comments/eslg29/maximum_security_biolab_opened_a_few_years_ago/.

4 Matt Stieb, "QAnon Influencers Are Encouraging Their Followers to Drink Bleach to Stave Off Coronavirus," *New York Magazine*, January 28, 2020, https://nymag.com/intelligencer/2020/01/qanon-supporters-

are-drinking-bleach-to-fend-off-coronavirus.html.

5 Will Sommer, "QAnon-ers' Magic Cure for Coronavirus: Just Drink Bleach!," *Daily Beast*, January 28, 2020, https://www.thedailybeast. com/qanon-conspiracy-theorists-magic-cure-for-coronavirus-is-drinking-lethal-bleach.

6 Matt Stieb, "QAnon Influencers Are Encouraging Their Followers to Drink Bleach to Stave Off Coronavirus"; EJ Dickson, "QAnon You-Tubers Are Telling People to Drink Bleach to Ward Off Corona-virus," *Rolling Stone*, January 29, 2020, https://www.rollingstone. com/culture/culture-news/qanon-conspiracy-theorists-coronavirus-mms-bleach-youtube-twitter-944878/.

7 Tom Porter, "Taking Toxic Bleach MMS Has Killed 7 People in the US, Colombian Prosecutors Say—Far More Than Previously Known," *In-sider*, August 12, 2020, https://www.businessinsider.com/mms-bleach-killed-7-americans-new-from-colombia-arrest-2020-8.

8 Will Sommer, "Trump Fans Gobble Up His Favorite, Unproven COVID Drug—Some Are Even Trying to Cook it Themselves," *Daily Beast*, May 20, 2020, https://www.thedailybeast.com/trump-fans-gob-ble-up-his-favorite-unproven-covid-drugsome-are-even-trying-to-cook-it-themselves.

9 "'What Do You Have to Lose?' How Trump Has Promoted Malaria Drug," *The New York Times*, April 22, 2020, https://www.nytimes. com/video/us/politics/100000007101599/trump-coronavirus-hy-droxychloroquine.html.

10 Julia Carrie Wong, "Hydroxychloroquine: How an Unproven Drug Became Trump's Coronavirus 'Miracle Cure,'" *The Guardian*, April 7, 2020, https://www.theguardian.com/world/2020/apr/06/hydroxy-chloroquine-trump-coronavirus-drug.

11 Jessica Grose, "Misinformation Is 'Its Own Pandemic' Among Par-ents," *The New York Times*, September 16, 2020, https://www.nytimes. com/2020/09/16/parenting/qanon-moms-misinformation.html.

12 Brittany Martin, "Why Are Wellness Influencers Pushing the 'Pland-emic' Conspiracy Video?," *LA Magazine*, May 14, 2020, https://www. lamag.com/citythinkblog/influencers-plandemic-conspiracy/

13 Stephanie McNeal, "The Conspiracy Theory About Wayfair Is Spread-ing Fast Among Lifestyle Influencers on Instagram," *Buzzfeed News*, July 13, 2020, https://www.buzzfeednews.com/article/stephaniemc-neal/wayfair-qanon-influencers-instagram.

14 Eden Gillespie, "'Pastel QAnon': The Female Lifestyle Bloggers and Influ-encers Spreading Conspiracy Theories Through Instagram," *The Feed*, Special Broadcasting Services, September 30, 2020, https://www.sbs.

com.au/news/the-feed/pastel-qanon-the-female-lifestyle-bloggers-and-influencers-spreading-conspiracy-theories-through-instagram.

15 Kaitlin Tiffany, "The Women Making Conspiracy Theories Beautiful," *The Atlantic*, August 18, 2020, https://www.theatlantic.com/technology/archive/2020/08/how-instagram-aesthetics-repackage-qanon/615364/.

16 Lili Loofbourow, "It Makes Perfect Sense That QAnon Took Off with Women This Summer," *Slate*, September 18, 2020, https://slate.com/news-and-politics/2020/09/qanon-women-why.html.

17 Kevin Roose, "QAnon Followers Are Hijacking the #SaveTheChildren Movement," *The New York Times*, August 12, 2020, https://www.nytimes.com/2020/08/12/technology/qanon-save-the-children-trafficking.html.

18 Amanda Seitz, "QAnon's 'Save the Children' Morphs into Popular Slogan," *AP News*, October 28, 2020, https://apnews.com/article/election-2020-donald-trump-child-trafficking-illinois-morris-aab978bb7e9b-89cd2cea151ca13421a0.

19 Joshua Potash (@JoshuaPotash), "There's a QAnon/Pizzagate protest in Hollywood right now. The signs are absolutely wild. And no masks. Something is deeply wrong with this country," Twitter, July 31, 2020, 4:24 p.m., https://twitter.com/JoshuaPotash/status/1289295787197739014.

20 Joshua Potash (@JoshuaPotash), "A few QAnon people are having a rally to 'Save the children' in Chicago. But they're chanting 'ICE loves our children' You can't make this stuff up," Twitter, August 7, 2020, 6:51 p.m., https://twitter.com/JoshuaPotash/status/1291869514364313600.

21 Voices 4 Victims (@VoicesVictims), "Part of the save the children rally 2020 Sandusky ohio," Twitter, September 12, 2020, 9:41 p.m., https://twitter.com/VoicesVictims/status/1304958302607101952.

22 jordan (@JordanUhl), "@hasanthehun is on the ground covering a "save the children" rally in la where they don't believe trump actually has coronavirus," Twitter, October 10, 2020, 3:14 p.m., https://twitter.com/JordanUhl/status/1315007877740929026.

23 Roose, "QAnon Followers Are Hijacking the #SaveTheChildren Movement."

24 "Polaris Statement on Wayfair Sex Trafficking Claims," Polaris, July 20, 2020, https://polarisproject.org/press-releases/polaris-statement-on-wayfair-sex-trafficking-claims/.

25 Brandy Zadrozny, "QAnon Looms Behind Nationwide Rallies and Viral #SaveTheChildren Hashtags," *NBC News*, August 21, 2020, https://www.nbcnews.com/tech/tech-news/qanon-looms-behind-nationwide-rallies-viral-hashtags-n1237722.

26 Mike Rothschild (@rothschildmd), "Example: a 28 tweet thread from

Jordan Sather on how Save The Children marchers are deep state infiltrators and plants," Twitter, August 22, 2020, 4:50 p.m., https://twitter.com/rothschildmd/status/1297275077281505280.

27 Judy Thomas, "Kansas City Protest Is Billed as a Save Our Children Event, but Will QAnon Show Up?," *The Kansas City Star*, August 28, 2020, https://www.kansascity.com/news/politics-government/article245299775.html.

28 Justin Vallejo, "A Third of Republicans Believe QAnon Theory of Deep State Paedophile Cannibals Is 'Mostly True', Poll Finds," *The Independent*, September 30, 2020, https://www.independent.co.uk/news/world/americas/us-election/qanon-conspiracy-mostly-true-republicans-trump-daily-kos-civiqs-poll-a9702261.html.

29 Marc-André Argentino (@_MAArgentino), "1/ Lets talk about QAnon Worldwide, after compiling data from Facebook, Twitter, Telegram and Instagram I have found evidence of a QAnon presence in 71 countries," Twitter, August 8, 2020, 7:45 p.m., https://twitter.com/_MAArgentino/status/1292245485403635712.

30 Emily Rauhala and Loveday Morris, "In the United States, QAnon Is Struggling. The Conspiracy Theory Is Thriving Abroad," *The Washington Post*, November 13, 2020, https://www.washingtonpost.com/world/qanon-conspiracy-global-reach/2020/11/12/ca312138-13a5-11eb-a258-614acf2b906d_story.html.

31 Taisa Sgenzerla, "New Age Communities Are Driving QAnon Conspiracies in Brazil," *GlobalVoices*, September 13, 2020, https://globalvoices.org/2020/09/13/new-age-communities-are-driving-qanon-conspiracies-in-brazil/.

32 Michael McGowan, "How Australia Became Fertile Ground for Misinformation and QAnon," *The Guardian*, February 15, 2021, https://www.theguardian.com/australia-news/2021/feb/16/how-australia-became-fertile-ground-for-misinformation-and-qanon.

33 Sam Williamson, "The QAnon Threat to Australia's Vaccine Rollout," *The Strategist*, Australian Strategist Policy Institute, February 2, 2021, https://www.aspistrategist.org.au/the-qanon-threat-to-australias-vaccine-rollout/.

34 Travis Andrews, "She Fell into Qanon and Went Viral for Destroying a Target Mask Display. Now She's Rebuilding Her Life," *Washington Post*, November 11, 2020, https://www.washingtonpost.com/technology/2020/11/11/masks-qanon-target-melissa-rein-lively/.

35 Ben Collins, "How Qanon Rode the Pandemic to New Heights—and Fueled the Viral Anti-Mask Phenomenon," *NBC News*, August 14, 2020, https://www.nbcnews.com/tech/tech-news/how-qanon-rode-pandemic-new-heights-fueled-viral-anti-mask-n1236695.

Chapter 9 Memes at the Ready:
The War Between QAnon and Social Media

1 Jed Oelbaum, "Ong's Hat: The Early Internet Conspiracy Game That Got Too Real," *Gizmodo*, February 21, 2019, https://gizmodo.com/ongs-hat-the-early-internet-conspiracy-game-that-got-t-1832229488; Tom Dowe, "News You Can Abuse," *Wired*, January 1, 1997, https://www.wired.com/1997/01/netizen-6/.

2 "Persecuted by the Security Service," MI5, last updated October 11, 2018, archived at https://web.archive.org/web/20140731000057/http:/mi5.com/.

3 Dowe, "News You Can Abuse."

4 "Fact Check: Explaining 'Fake Texas Snow' Posts and 'Scorched Snow' Videos," Reuters, February 23, 2021, https://www.reuters.com/article/uk-factcheck-not-fake-snow/fact-check-explaining-fake-texas-snow-posts-and-scorched-snow-videos-idUSKBN2AN1R8.

5 "QAnon" search data, United States, Google Trends, accessed March 29, 2021, https://trends.google.com/trends/explore?date=2019-03-01%20 2019-03-30&geo=US&q=qanon.

6 Aoife Gallagher, Jacob Davey, and Mackenzie Hart, *The Genesis of a Conspiracy Theory: Key Trends in QAnon Activity Since 2017*, ISD, 2020, https://www.isdglobal.org/wp-content/uploads/2020/07/The-Genesis-of-a-Conspiracy-Theory.pdf.

7 Marc-André Argentino (@_MAArgentino), "1/ Continuing from my last thread i've been able to pull some more data based on the top twenty five "influencers" and the top forty domains," Twitter, February 10, 2020, 4:26 p.m., https://twitter.com/_MAArgentino/status/1226980740635725824?s=20.

8 Andrew Wyrich, "Reddit Bans Popular Deep State Conspiracy Forum for 'Inciting Violence,'" *Daily Dot*, March 15, 2018, https://www.daily-dot.com/debug/reddit-bans-r-cbts_stream/.

9 Brandy Zadrozny and Ben Collins, "How Three Conspiracy Theorists Took 'Q' and Sparked Qanon," *NBC News*, August 14, 2018, https://www.nbcnews.com/tech/tech-news/how-three-conspiracy-theorists-took-q-sparked-qanon-n900531.

10 Zadrozny and Collins, "How Three Conspiracy Theorists Took 'Q' and Sparked Qanon."

11 Paris Martineau, "When Conspiracy Theories Become Weaponized," *The Outline*, April 6, 2018, https://theoutline.com/post/4063/when-conspiracy-theories-become-weaponized.

12 Taylor Lorenz, "Instagram Is the Internet's New Home for Hate," *The Atlantic*, March 21, 2019, https://www.theatlantic.com/technology/archive/2019/03/instagram-is-the-internets-new-home-for-hate/585382/.

13 Ari Sen and Brandy Zadrozny, "QAnon Groups Have Millions of Members on Facebook, documents show," *NBC News*, August 10, 2020, https://www.nbcnews.com/tech/tech-news/qanon-groups-have-millions-members-facebook-documents-show-n1236317.

14 Aoife Gallagher, Jacob Davey, and Mackenzie Hart, *The Genesis of a Conspiracy Theory*.

15 Lennlee Keep, "From Kilroy to Pepe: A Brief History of Memes," *Independent Lens*, PBS, October 8, 2020, https://www.pbs.org/independentlens/blog/from-kilroy-to-pepe-a-brief-history-of-memes/.

16 Caitlin Dewey, "Absolutely Everything You Need to Know to Understand 4chan, the Internet's Own Bogeyman," *The Washington Post*, September 25, 2014, https://www.washingtonpost.com/news/the-intersect/wp/2014/09/25/absolutely-everything-you-need-to-know-to-understand-4chan-the-internets-own-bogeyman/.

17 Reply no. 51592 to "Q Research #61: I've Got A Q For You Edition," /qresearch/ - Q Research, 8chan, January 14, 2018, archived at 8kun, https://8kun.top/qresearch/res/51117.html#51592.

18 Reply no. 43700 to "Q Research General #51: WE LISTENED [40/60] Edition," /qresearch/ - Q Research, 8chan, January 14, 2018, archived at 8kun, https://8kun.top/qresearch/res/42982.html#43700.

19 Alex Kaplan, "Mapping the Meme: How a Viral Image Went from 4chan and QAnon Supporters to Trump's Twitter," *Media Matters*, November 28, 2018, https://www.mediamatters.org/maga-trolls/mapping-meme-how-viral-image-went-4chan-and-qanon-supporters-trumps-twitter.

20 Ryan Broderick, "The Radicalization of Giggle Palooza," *Garbage Day* (newsletter), January 15, 2020, https://www.garbageday.email/p/the-radicalization-of-giggle-palooza.

21 Timothy Bella, "Trump Tweets a Meme of Himself Fiddling, Drawing a Comparison to Roman Emperor Nero," *The Washington Post*, March 9, 2020, https://www.washingtonpost.com/nation/2020/03/09/trump-coronavirus-nero-qanon/.

22 Louis Matsakis, "QAnon Is Trying to Trick Facebook's Meme-Reading AI," *Wired*, September 18, 2018, https://www.wired.com/story/qanon-conspiracy-facebook-meme-ai/.

23 "Fact Check: Patton Oswalt Tweet Has Been Manipulated," Reuters, July 17, 2020, https://www.reuters.com/article/uk-factcheck-patton-oswalt-tweet-fake/factcheckpatton-oswalttweet-has-beenmanipulated-idUSKCN24I1V9.

24 Jack Brewster, "QAnon Accounts Ambush Chrissy Teigen Following Death of Baby," *Forbes*, October 1, 2020, https://www.forbes.com/sites/

jackbrewster/2020/10/01/qanon-accounts-ambush-chrissy-teigen-following-death-of-newborn/.

25 Emma Grey Ellis, "Crying 'Pedophile' Is the Oldest Propaganda Trick in the Book," *Wired*, August 1, 2018, https://www.wired.com/story/crying-pedophile-is-the-oldest-propaganda-trick-in-the-book/.

26 Benjamin Schneider, "The Doxxing of Senator Wiener," *SF Weekly*, September 9, 2020, https://www.sfweekly.com/news/the-doxxing-of-senator-wiener/.

27 Senator Shannon Grove (@ShannonGroveCA), "There are times as a Senator when I take great pride in my votes & actions," Twitter, September 1, 2020, 8:42 p.m., https://twitter.com/ShannonGroveCA/status/1300957194335039493?s=20.

28 Julia Carrie Wong, "'The Difference Is QAnon': How a Conspiratorial Hate Campaign Upended California Politics," *The Guardian*, September 16, 2020, theguardian.com/us-news/2020/sep/16/qanon-republicans-conspiracy-theory-politics-save-the-children.

29 Craig Timberg, "As QAnon Grew, Facebook and Twitter Missed Years of Warning Signs About the Conspiracy Theory's Violent Nature," *The Washington Post*, October 3, 2020, https://www.washingtonpost.com/technology/2020/10/01/facebook-qanon-conspiracies-trump/.

30 Julia Carrie Wong, "Revealed: QAnon Facebook Groups are Growing at a Rapid Pace Around the World," *The Guardian*, August 11, 2020, https://www.theguardian.com/us-news/2020/aug/11/qanon-facebook-groups-growing-conspiracy-theory.

31 Ryan Mac and Craig Silverman, "'Mark Changed the Rules': How Facebook Went Easy on Alex Jones and Other Right-Wing Figures," *Buzzfeed News*, February 22, 2021, https://www.buzzfeednews.com/article/ryanmac/mark-zuckerberg-joel-kaplan-facebook-alex-jones.

32 Sam Levin, "'They Don't Care': Facebook Factchecking in Disarray as Journalists Push to Cut Ties," *The Guardian*, December 13, 2018, https://www.theguardian.com/technology/2018/dec/13/they-dont-care-facebook-fact-checking-in-disarray-as-journalists-push-to-cut-ties.

33 Olivia Solon, "Facebook Struggling to End Hate Speech in Myanmar, Investigation Finds," *The Guardian*, August 15, 2018, https://www.theguardian.com/technology/2018/aug/15/facebook-myanmar-rohingya-hate-speech-investigation.

34 Brooke Binkowski, "I Was a Facebook Fact-Checker. It Was Like Playing a Doomed Game of Whack-A-Mole," *Buzzfeed News*, February 8, 2019, https://www.buzzfeednews.com/article/brookebinkowski/fact-checking-facebook-doomed.

35 Gene Park, "'Y'all Are Seriously Some Bad Researchers': Conspiracy

Theorists Misidentify Reddit User as Madden Shooter," *The Washington Post*, August 28, 2018, https://www.washingtonpost.com/news/the-intersect/wp/2018/08/28/yall-are-seriously-some-bad-researchers-conspiracy-theorists-misidentify-reddit-user-as-madden-shooter/.

36 Kaitlyn Tiffany, "Reddit Squashed QAnon by Accident," *The Atlantic*, September 23, 2020, https://www.theatlantic.com/technology/archive/2020/09/reddit-qanon-ban-evasion-policy-moderation-facebook/616442/.

37 Joe Ondrak and Nick Backovic, "QAnon Key Figure Revealed as Financial Information Security Analyst from New Jersey," *Logically*, September 10, 2020, https://www.logically.ai/articles/qanon-key-figure-man-from-new-jersey.

38 Marc-André Argentino, "How QAnon Will Fight Back Against Twitter's Ban and What Happens Next," *Observer*, July 22, 2020, https://observer.com/2020/07/how-qanon-will-fight-back-against-twitters-ban-and-what-happens-next/.

39 Rachel Greenspan, "QAnon Spread Like Wildfire on Social Media. Here's How 16 Tech Companies Have Reacted to the Conspiracy Theory," *Insider*, January 13, 2021, https://www.businessinsider.com/how-every-tech-company-social-media-platform-handling-qanon-2020-10.

40 Ben Collins, "QAnon Leaders Look to Rebrand After Tech Crack Downs," *NBC News*, September 25, 2020, https://www.nbcnews.com/tech/tech-news/qanon-leaders-look-rebrand-after-tech-crack-downs-n1241125.

41 Roger McNamee, "Platforms Must Pay for Their Role in the Insurrection," *Wired*, January 7, 2021, https://www.wired.com/story/opinion-platforms-must-pay-for-their-role-in-the-insurrection/.

42 Kim Lyons, "Social Media and Telco Companies Urged to Preserve Evidence from Capitol Attack," *The Verge*, January 9, 2021, https://www.theverge.com/2021/1/9/22222200/social-media-telco-urged-preserve-evidence-capitol-attack-twitter-facebook-google-verizon-apple.

43 Donie O'Sullivan (@donie), "Facebook has new QAnon numbers out tonight that highlights how vast the conspiracy theory is. Since August Facebook says it has removed: -3,300 Pages," Twitter, January 19, 2021, 11:35 p.m., https://twitter.com/donie/status/1351750277347602434?s=20.

44 Cameron Peters, "Every Online Platform That Has Cracked Down on Trump," *Vox*, January 10, 2021, https://www.vox.com/2021/1/10/22223356/every-platform-that-banned-trump-twitter-facebook-snapchat-twitch.

CHAPTER 10 Change of Batter Coming?: QAnon and the 2020 Election

1 Peter Jamison et al., "'The Storm Is Here': Ashli Babbitt's Journey from Capital 'Guardian' to Invader," *The Washington Post*, January 10, 2021, https://www.washingtonpost.com/dc-md-va/2021/01/09/ashli-babbitt-capitol-shooting-trump-qanon/.

2 Garrison Davis, "The Journey of Ashli Babbitt," *Bellingcat* (blog), January 8, 2021, https://www.bellingcat.com/news/2021/01/08/the-journey-of-ashli-babbitt/.

3 Eric Hananoki, "Nevada GOP-backed Congressional Candidate Promotes QAnon Video," *Media Matters*, October 30, 2018, https://www.mediamatters.org/qanon-conspiracy-theory/nevada-gop-backed-congressional-candidate-promotes-qanon-video.

4 "Joyce Bentley," Ballotpedia, accessed March 5, 2021, https://ballotpedia.org/Joyce_Bentley.

5 Matthew Chapman, "QAnon's True Believers Are Devastated as the Conspiracy Theory Goes Down in Flames," *Salon*, November 15, 2018, https://www.salon.com/2018/11/15/qanons-true-believers-are-devastated-as-the-conspiracy-theory-goes-down-in-flames/.

6 April Glaser, "QAnon Conspiracy Theorists Warned That Antifa Would Ruin the Election. Mockery Ensued," *Slate*, November 6, 2018, https://slate.com/technology/2018/11/qanon-conspiracy-theorists-warned-antifa-ruin-election.html.

7 Kelly Weill, "Homeland Security Fell For YouTube Videos About 'Antifa Civil War,'" *Daily Beast*, November 2, 2018, https://www.thedailybeast.com/homeland-security-fell-for-youtube-videos-about-antifa-civil-war.

8 Jared Holt, "This GOP Challenger to Ilhan Omar '100%' Stands With QAnon," *Right Wing Watch*, July 23, 2019, https://www.rightwingwatch.org/post/this-gop-challenger-to-ilhan-omar-100-stands-with-qanon/.

9 Reuters fact check, February 27, 2020. https://www.reuters.com/article/uk-factcheck-stella-twitter/partly-false-claim-twitter-suspends-account-of-ilhan-omars-challenger-for-no-reason-idUSKCN20L33A.

10 Alex Kaplan, "Here Are the Qanon Supporters Running for Congress in 2020," *Media Matters*, January 7, 2020, https://www.mediamatters.org/qanon-conspiracy-theory/here-are-qanon-supporters-running-congress-2020.

11 Alex Kaplan, "Here Are the QAnon Supporters Running For Congress," *Media Matters*, January 7, 2020. https://www.mediamatters.org/qanon-conspiracy-theory/here-are-qanon-supporters-running-congress-2020.

12 James Walker, "The QAnon Super PAC Was a Flop," *Washington*

Monthly, November 18, 2020, https://washingtonmonthly.com/2020/11/18/the-qanon-super-pac-was-a-flop/.

13 Madeleine Marr, "'Beyoncé, You Are On Notice!' Florida Politician Calls Out Superstar in a Bizarre Rant," *Miami Herald*, July 6, 2020, https://www.miamiherald.com/entertainment/celebrities/article244021727.html.

14 Eric Hananoki, "A Guide to Rep. Marjorie Taylor Greene's Conspiracy Theories and Toxic Rhetoric," *Media Matters*, February 2, 2021, https://www.mediamatters.org/congress/guide-rep-marjorie-taylor-greenes-conspiracy-theories-and-toxic-rhetoric.

15 Danielle Kurtzleben, "GOP Candidates Open to QAnon Conspiracy Theory Advance in Congressional Races," *NPR*, July 1, 2020, https://www.npr.org/2020/07/01/885991730/gop-candidates-open-to-qanon-conspiracy-theory-advance-in-congressional-races.

16 Kenneth Vogel and Iuliia Mendel, "Biden Faces Conflict of Interest Questions That Are Being Promoted by Trump and Allies," *The New York Times*, May 1, 2019, https://www.nytimes.com/2019/05/01/us/politics/biden-son-ukraine.html; Lukas Mikelionis, "Biden Faces Scrutiny for Demanding Ouster of Ukraine Official Probing Firm That Employed His Son," *Fox News*, April 2, 2019, https://www.foxnews.com/politics/bidens-scrutiny-demanding-ouster-ukraine-official.

17 Douglas MacKinnon, "A Hillary Clinton-Barack Obama Ticket to Replace Joe Biden? Is It Even Possible?," *The Hill*, May 2, 2020, https://thehill.com/opinion/white-house/495580-a-hillary-clinton-barack-obama-ticket-to-replace-joe-biden; The Redfield & Wilton Strategies Research Team, "Michelle Obama Would Be Likely Biden Voters' Top Choice to Replace Biden as Candidate, If Biden Stood Down," Redfield & Wilton Strategies, July 17, 2020, https://redfieldandwiltonstrategies.com/michelle-obama-would-be-likely-biden-voters-top-choice-to-replace-biden-as-candidate-if-biden-stood-down/.

18 Grace Segers, Kathryn Watson, and Stefan Becket, "First Debate Descends into Chaos as Trump and Biden Exchange Attacks," *CBS News*, September 30, 2020, https://www.cbsnews.com/live-updates/first-presidential-debate-trump-biden-wrap-up-moments/.

19 Vishal Tiwari, "Trump Gives Joe Biden a New Nickname as US Election Campaigning Intensifies," *Republic World*, September 5, 2020, https://www.republicworld.com/world-news/us-news/trump-gives-joe-biden-a-new-nickname-as-us-election-campaigning-intens.html.

20 Nicholas Riccardi, "Here's the Reality Behind Trump's Claims About Mail Voting," *AP News*, September 30, 2020, https://apnews.com/article/virus-outbreak-joe-biden-election-2020-donald-trump-elections-3e8170c3348ce3719d4bc7182146b582.

21 Glenn Kessler, "Trump Campaign Ad Manipulates Three Images to Put Biden in a 'Basement,'" *The Washington Post*, August 7, 2020, https://www.washingtonpost.com/politics/2020/08/07/trump-campaign-ad-manipulates-three-images-put-biden-basement/; Zach Nayer, "Community Outbreaks of Covid-19 Often Emerge After Trump's Campaign Rallies," *STAT*, October 16, 2020, https://www.statnews.com/2020/10/16/trump-campaign-rallies-leave-a-trail-of-community-outbreaks/; Eric Garcia, "Trump's Attack on Hunter Biden Will Only Increase the Stigma of Addiction," *The Washington Post*, September 30, 2020, https://www.washingtonpost.com/outlook/2020/09/30/trump-hunter-biden-stigma/.

22 Jessica Guynn, "Save the Children? Extremist Conspiracy Movement QAnon Fabricates Pedophile Claims Against Joe Biden as Election Looms," *USA Today*, September 28, 2020, https://www.usatoday.com/story/tech/2020/09/28/qanon-pedophile-claims-biden-trump-save-the-children-facebook-instagram/3522626001/.

23 Charlotte Alter, "How Conspiracy Theories Are Shaping the 2020 Election—and Shaking the Foundation of American Democracy," *Time*, September 10, 2020, https://time.com/5887437/conspiracy-theories-2020-election/; Kevin Roose, "The Long History of 'Hidden Earpiece' Conspiracy Theories," *The New York Times*, September 29, 2020, https://www.nytimes.com/2020/09/29/technology/the-long-history-of-hidden-earpiece-conspiracy-theories.html; Ben Collins and Brandy Zadrozny, "Inside the Campaign to 'Pizzagate' Hunter Biden," *NBC News*, October 22, 2020, https://www.nbcnews.com/tech/tech-news/inside-campaign-pizzagate-hunter-biden-n1244331.

24 Kevin Breuninger, "Trump Says He Appreciates Support from Followers of Unfounded QAnon Conspiracy," *CNBC*, August 19, 2020, https://www.cnbc.com/2020/08/19/trump-says-he-appreciates-qanon-support.html.

25 Colby Itkowitz et al., "Trump Praises Baseless QAnon Conspiracy Theory, Says He Appreciates Support of Its Followers," *The Washington Post*, August 19, 2020, https://www.washingtonpost.com/politics/trump-praises-baseless-qanon-conspiracy-theory-says-he-appreciates-support-of-its-followers/2020/08/19/e50f8d46-e25e-11ea-8181-606e603bb1c4_story.html.

26 Mike Rothschild (@rothschildmd), "The president publicly validated the violent conspiracy cult QAnon, while dodging all personal knowledge of it. And its biggest promoters are delighted," Twitter, August 19, 2020, 6:23 p.m., https://twitter.com/rothschildmd/status/1296211328860745728?s=20.

27 Russell Berman, "Trump Fails the QAnon Test," *The Atlantic*, Octo-

ber 15, 2020, https://www.theatlantic.com/politics/archive/2020/10/trump-qanon-denounce/616751/.

28 Jack Brewster, "Trump Promotes Baseless, QAnon-Endorsed Conspiracy Theory Alleging Obama Staged Bin Laden's Killing," *Forbes*, October 14, 2020, https://www.forbes.com/sites/jackbrewster/2020/10/14/trump-promotes-baseless-qanon-endorsed-conspiracy-theory-alleging-obama-staged-bin-ladens-killing/?sh=6adcbb025b16; Alex Kaplan, "Trump Has Repeatedly Amplified QAnon Twitter Accounts. The FBI Has Linked the Conspiracy Theory to Domestic Terror," *Media Matters*, August 1, 2019, https://www.mediamatters.org/twitter/fbi-calls-qanon-domestic-terror-threat-trump-has-amplified-qanon-supporters-twitter-more-20.

29 Ben Collins, "QAnon's Dominion Voter Fraud Conspiracy Theory Reaches the President," *NBC News*, November 13, 2020, https://www.nbcnews.com/tech/tech-news/q-fades-qanon-s-dominion-voter-fraud-conspiracy-theory-reaches-n1247780.

30 Mike Rothschild (@rothschildmd), "Another day of 'Trump actually won a landslide and is only pretending he lost to expose the deep state' dawns from the Q community," Twitter, November 8, 2020, 1:37 p.m., https://twitter.com/rothschildmd/status/1325507756476882944.

31 Mike Rothschild (@rothschildmd), "Joe M, one of the most destructive and delusional people in the QAnon influencer hierarchy, is absolutely spinning out on Parler. He thinks Trump won," Twitter, November 7, 2020, 2:43 p.m., https://twitter.com/rothschildmd/status/1325161865182236673?s=20.

32 David Gilbert, "QAnon Lies Are Taking Over Election Conversations Online," *Vice*, November 23, 2020, https://www.vice.com/en/article/wg5bv54/qanon-lies-are-taking-over-election-conversations-online.

33 David Gilbert, "Meet the Dangerous QAnon Figure Doing Whatever It Takes to Win Trump's Approval," *Vice*, December 15, 2020, https://www.vice.com/en/article/93wqm7/ron-watkins-meet-the-dangerous-qanon-figure-doing-whatever-it-takes-to-win-trumps-approval.

34 Collins, "QAnon's Dominion Voter Fraud Conspiracy Theory Reaches the President."

35 Camilla Caldera, "Fact Check: Dominion Voting Machines Didn't Delete Votes from Trump, Switch Them to Biden," *USA Today*, November 14, 2020, https://www.usatoday.com/story/news/factcheck/2020/11/14/fact-check-dominion-voting-machines-didnt-delete-switch-votes/6282157002/.

36 Dan Friedman and Pema Levy, "Giuliani Alleges a Vast International Conspiracy to Steal the Election from Trump," *Mother Jones*, Novem-

ber 19, 2020, https://www.motherjones.com/politics/2020/11/giuliani-alleges-a-vast-international-conspiracy-to-steal-the-election-from-trump/.

37 David Gilbert, "QAnon Left a Noose Outside a 20-Year-Old Election Worker's Home," *Vice*, December 2, 2020, https://www.vice.com/en/article/xgzgqa/qanon-left-a-noose-outside-a-20-year-old-election-workers-home.

38 Aaron Blake, "The Trump Campaign's Much-Hyped Affidavit Features a Big, Glaring Error," *The Washington Post*, November 21, 2020, https://www.washingtonpost.com/politics/2020/11/20/trump-campaigns-much-hyped-affidavit-features-big-glaring-error/.

39 Cameron Joseph, "Trump's 'Elite Strike Force' Has Now Lost More Than 50 Election Challenges," *Vice*, December 9, 2020, https://www.vice.com/en/article/k7a74w/trumps-elite-strike-force-has-now-lost-more-than-50-election-challenges; Kyle Cheney, "Trump Campaign Cuts Sidney Powell from President's Legal Team," *Politico*, November 11, 2020, https://www.politico.com/news/2020/11/22/trump-campaign-sidney-powell-legal-439357.

40 Keith Kloor, "The #MAGA Lawyer Behind Michael Flynn's Scorched-Earth Legal Strategy," *Politico Magazine*, January 17, 2020, https://www.politico.com/news/magazine/2020/01/17/maga-lawyer-behind-michael-flynn-legal-strategy-098712; Rachel E. Greenspan, "The Attorney for Kenosha Shooter Kyle Rittenhouse Appears to Be a QAnon Believer," *Insider*, November 23, 2020, https://www.insider.com/attorney-kenosha-shooter-kyle-rittenhouse-tweets-qanon-conspiracy-2020-11.

41 Ryan Mac, "Trump-Supporting Lawyer Lin Wood Has Been Permanently Banned From Twitter," *Buzzfeed News*, January 7, 2021, https://www.buzzfeednews.com/article/ryanmac/twitter-bans-lin-wood; Ron (@CodeMonkeyZ), Twitter profile, last modified February 24, 2021, archived at https://web.archive.org/web/20210107023201/https:/twitter.com/CodeMonkeyZ.

42 Mike Rothschild, "With Q Silent, Who Will Become the New Leader of the QAnon Movement?," *Daily Dot*, December 30, 2020, https://www.dailydot.com/debug/qanon-new-leader/.

43 Ben Collins, "As Trump Meets with Qanon Influencers, the Conspiracy's Adherents Beg for Dictatorship," *NBC News*, December 22, 2020, https://www.nbcnews.com/tech/internet/trump-meets-qanon-influencers-conspiracy-theory-s-adherents-beg-dictatorship-n1252144.

44 Shayan Sardarizadeh and Jessica Lussenhop, "Trump Riots: 65 Days That Led to Chaos at the Capitol," BBC, January 10, 2021, https://www.

bbc.com/news/world-us-canada-55592332.

45 Tom Winter, Ben Collins, Daniel Arkin, and Brandy Zadrozny, "2 Men Arrested Near Philadelphia Vote Center Had QAnon Paraphernalia, AR-15 in Car," *NBC News*, November 6, 2020, https://www.nbcnews.com/news/us-news/2-men-detained-after-police-learn-possible-threat-philadelphia-vote-n1246774.

46 "Prosecutors Cite US Capitol Riots in Attempt to Revoke Bail for Heavily-Armed Man Arrested Near Philadelphia Vote Counting Center," *CBS Philadelphia*, January 8, 2021, https://philadelphia.cbslocal.com/2021/01/08/joshua-macias-philadelphia-bail-capitol-qanon-vets-for-trump/.

47 Colby Itkowitz and Josh Dawsey, "Pence Under Pressure as the Final Step Nears in Formalizing Biden's Win," *The Washington Post*, December 24, 2020, https://www.washingtonpost.com/politics/pence-biden-congress-electoral/2020/12/24/48f48da8-4604-11eb-a277-49a6d1f9dff1_story.html.

48 Rob Kuznia et al., "Extremists Intensify Calls for Violence Ahead of Inauguration Day," *CNN*, January 8, 2021, https://www.cnn.com/2021/01/08/us/online-extremism-inauguration-capitol-invs/index.html.

49 Dan Barry and Sheera Frenkel, "'Be There. Will Be Wild!': Trump All but Circled the Date," *The New York Times*, January 6, 2021, https://www.nytimes.com/2021/01/06/us/politics/capitol-mob-trump-supporters.html.

50 Jack Butler, "Trump as God Emperor," *Yahoo!*, January 24, 2021, https://www.yahoo.com/lifestyle/trump-god-emperor-113053135.html.

51 Sudhin Thanawala, Stefanie Dazio, and Jeff Martin, "Family: Trump Supporter Who Died Followed QAnon Conspiracy," *AP News*, January 9, 2021, https://apnews.com/article/election-2020-joe-biden-donald-trump-police-elections-7051411972c58cfbbf079876ce527ab4.

PART III: FALLOUT

CHAPTER 11 The Only Cult That Teaches You to Think for Yourself: What Experts Think QAnon Is (and Is Not)

1 Travis View, "The Cult of QAnon," *Richard Heffner's Open Mind*, PBS, accessed March 5, 2021, https://www.wgbh.org/program/the-open-mind/the-cult-of-qanon; Steven Hassan, "Trump's Qanon Followers Are a Dangerous Cult. How to Save Someone Who's Been Brainwashed," *NBC News*, September 11, 2020, https://www.nbcnews.com/

think/opinion/trump-s-qanon-followers-are-dangerous-cult-how-save-someone-ncna1239828.

2 Daryl Johnson, "Holy Hate: The Far Right's Radicalization of Religion," *Intelligence Report* (Southern Poverty Law Center), 2018 Spring Issue, February 10, 2018, https://www.splcenter.org/fighting-hate/intelligence-report/2018/holy-hate-far-right%E2%80%99s-radicalization-religion.

3 Candida Moss, "How a New Religion Could Rise from the Ashes of QAnon," *Daily Beast*, January 21, 2021, https://www.thedailybeast.com/how-a-new-religion-could-rise-from-the-ashes-of-qanon.

4 Julie Beck, "The Christmas the Aliens Didn't Come," *The Atlantic*, December 18, 2015, https://www.theatlantic.com/health/archive/2015/12/the-christmas-the-aliens-didnt-come/421122/.

5 David L. Rowe, *God's Strange Work: William Miller and the End of the World* (Grand Rapids, MI: Eerdmans, 2008), 201.

6 Jack Jenkins, "QAnon Conspiracies Sway Faith Groups, Including 1 in 4 White Evangelicals," *Christianity Today*, February 11, 2021, https://www.christianitytoday.com/news/2021/february/white-evangelicals-qanon-election-conspiracy-trump-aei.html.

7 Joseph Menn, "QAnon Received Earlier Boost from Russian Accounts on Twitter, Archives Show," *Reuters*, November 2, 2020, https://www.reuters.com/article/us-usa-election-qanon-cyber/qanon-received-earlier-boost-from-russian-accounts-on-twitter-archives-show-idUSKBN27I18I.

8 Steven Inskeep, interview with Michael Isikoff, "The Origins of the Seth Rich Conspiracy Theory," July 11, 2019, *Morning Edition*, podcast, NPR, https://www.npr.org/2019/07/11/740608323/the-origins-of-the-seth-rich-conspiracy-theory; Salvador Hernandez, "Russian Trolls Spread Baseless Conspiracy Theories Like Pizzagate and QAnon After the Election," *Buzzfeed News*, August 15, 2018, https://www.buzzfeednews.com/article/salvadorhernandez/russian-trolls-spread-baseless-conspiracy-theories-like.

9 Eric Tucker, Colleen Long, and Michael Balsamo, "FBI Documents Reveal That Roger Stone Was in Direct Communication with Wikileaks Founder Julian Assange," *Insider*, April 29, 2020, https://www.businessinsider.com/fbi-reveals-roger-stone-was-directly-communicating-with-julian-assange-2020-4.

10 Eugene Kiely, "Michael Flynn's Russia Timeline," *FactCheck.org*, December 1, 2017, https://www.factcheck.org/2017/12/michael-flynns-russia-timeline/.

11 Brian Krebs, "Meet the World's Biggest 'Bulletproof' Hoster," *Krebs*

on Security (blog), July 16, 2019, https://krebsonsecurity.com/2019/07/meet-the-worlds-biggest-bulletproof-hoster/.

12 Julia Davis, "Russian Media Turns to QAnon Conspiracies to Help Re-Elect Trump," *Daily Beast*, August 24, 2020, https://www.thedaily beast.com/russian-media-turns-to-qanon-conspiracies-to-help-re-elect-trump.

13 Greg Myre and Shannon Bond, "'Russia Doesn't Have to Make Fake News': Biggest Election Threat Is Closer to Home," *NPR*, September 29, 2020, https://www.npr.org/2020/09/29/917725209/russia-doesn't-have-to-make-fake-news-biggest-election-threat-is-closer-to-home.

14 Gabe Cohn, "How Slender Man Became a Legend," *The New York Times*, August 15, 2018, https://www.nytimes.com/2018/08/15/movies/slender-man-timeline.html.

15 Alex Nichols, "Slender Man for Boomers," *The Outline*, June 26, 2019, https://theoutline.com/post/7621/slender-man-for-boomers-andreno chrome-qanon.

16 Darren Linvill and Patrick Warren, "That Uplifting Tweet You Just Shared? A Russian Troll Sent It," *Rolling Stone*, November 25, 2019, https://www.rollingstone.com/politics/politics-features/russia-troll-2020-election-interference-twitter-916482/.

17 Conspirador Norteño (@conspirator0), "#FollowTheWhiteRabbit," Twitter, November 18, 2017, 3:29 p.m., https://twitter.com/conspirator0/status/931983301597913088?s=20; Ben Collins, "Russian Troll Accounts Purged by Twitter Pushed Qanon and Other Conspiracy Theories," *NBC News*, February 2, 2019, https://www.nbcnews.com/tech/social-media/russian-troll-accounts-purged-twitter-pushed-qanon-other-conspiracy-theories-n966091.

18 Thomas Rid, *Active Measures: The Secret History of Disinformation and Political Warfare* (New York: Farrar, Straus, and Giroux, 2020), 409.

19 Claire Goforth, "Here's Why Prominent Conservatives Now Are Calling QAnon a 'Psyop'," *Daily Dot*, January 28, 2021, https://www.daily-dot.com/debug/conservatives-claim-qanon-psyop/.

20 Emily Bicks, "Is Thomas Schoenberger the Mastermind Behind QAnon?," *Heavy*, January 26, 2021, https://heavy.com/news/thomas-schoenberger-qanon/.

21 Adrian Hon, "What ARGs Can Tell Us About QAnon," *MSSV* (blog), August 2, 2020, https://mssv.net/2020/08/02/what-args-can-teach-us-about-qanon/; Reed Berkowitz, "A Game Designer's Analysis of QAnon," *curiouserinstitute*, Medium, September 30, 2020, https://medium.com/curiouserinstitute/a-game-designers-analysis-of-qanon-580972548be5.

CHAPTER 12 Mathematically Impossible: Debunking QAnon and Its Prophecies

1 Ewan Palmer, "QAnon Beliefs Plummet Among Republicans After Capitol Riots: Poll," *Newsweek*, February 2, 2021, https://www.news-week.com/qanon-conspiracy-theory-poll-2021-1.

2 "More Than 1 in 3 Americans Believe a 'Deep State' Is Working to Undermine Trump," Ipsos, December 30, 2020, https://www.ipsos.com/en-us/news-polls/npr-misinformation-123020.

3 Charles Davis, "30% of Republicans Have 'Favorable' View of QAnon Conspiracy Theory, Yougov Poll Finds," *Insider*, January 13, 2021, https://www.businessinsider.com/30-of-republicans-have-favorable-view-of-qanon-conspiracy-theory-poll-2021-1.

4 Ben Quinn, "One in Four Britons Believe in Qanon-Linked Theories— Survey," *The Guardian*, October 21, 2020, https://www.theguardian.com/us-news/2020/oct/22/one-in-four-britons-believe-in-qanon-linked-theories-survey.

5 Cade Metz, "Study Considers a Link Between QAnon and Polling Errors," *The New York Times*, November 6, 2020, https://www.nytimes.com/2020/11/06/technology/study-considers-a-link-between-qanon-and-polling-errors.html.

6 James Beverley, *The QAnon Deception* (independently published, 2018), 31.

7 Angela Wang and Sawyer Click, "We Analyzed Every Message Ever Posted by 'Q,' the Enigmatic Persona That Started the QAnon Conspiracy Theory," *Insider*, November 3, 2020, https://www.businessinsider.com/every-qanon-message-q-drop-analyzed-2020-10.

8 OrphAnalytics, "QAnon is Two Different People, Shows Machine Learning Analysis from OrphAnalytics," Cision PR Newswire, December 15, 2020, https://www.prnewswire.com/news-releases/qanon-is-two-different-people-shows-machine-learning-analysis-from-orphanalytics-301192981.html.

9 Mark Burnett (@m8urnett), "I was looking at some QAnon posts and saw this one with "codes" which I find pretty interesting," Twitter, August 13, 2018, 5:36 p.m.,https://twitter.com/m8urnett/status/1029119453345198080

10 Mike Rothschild, "All the Times the Secret 'Military Intelligence' Poster Behind QAnon Fell For Pranks," *Daily Dot*, October 21, 2020, https://www.dailydot.com/debug/qanon-hoaxes-duped/.

11 Heather Schwedel, "Two Years into His Presidency and Donald Trump Still Doesn't Use Computers," *Slate*, August 28, 2018, https://slate.com/technology/2018/08/trump-still-doesnt-use-computers-and-calls-an-ipad-the-flat-one.html.

12 Ed Kilgore, "Heads We Win, Tails You Lose: For Trump, All Democratic Election Wins Are 'Rigged,'" *New York Magazine*, May 12, 2020, https://nymag.com/intelligencer/2020/05/for-trump-all-democratic-election-wins-are-rigged.html.

13 Qproofs, last modified March 6, 2021, https://www.qproofs.com/home.html; also at https://web.archive.org/web/20210124214454/https://www.qproofs.com/military.html.

14 Department of Defense (@DeptofDefense), Twitter, April 15, 2018, 10:19 a.m., https://twitter.com/DeptofDefense/status/985523235113627648.

15 Mike Rothschild, "QAnon Did Not Predict John McCain's Death," *TheMikeRothschild.com* (blog), October 2, 2018, https://themikeroths-child.com/2018/10/02/qanon-predict-mccain-death/.

16 Ed Mazza, "Donald Trump Mocked After He Can't Quite Describe the White House," *HuffPost*, April 2, 2018, https://www.huffpost.com/entry/donald-trump-white-house-tippy-top_n_5ac2ddeae4b04646b645698e.

17 Reply no. 869716 to "Q Research General #1080: Autistic AND Awesome Edition," /qresearch/ - Q Research, 8chan, April 2, 2018, archived at 8kun, https://8kun.top/qresearch/res/869635.html#869716.

18 Ed Rogers, "Opinion: Trump Called Russia's Nukes 'Tippy-Top.' Here's Why It Matters," *The Washington Post*, June 16, 2016, https://www.washingtonpost.com/blogs/post-partisan/wp/2016/06/16/trump-called-russias-nukes-tippy-top-heres-why-it-matters/.

19 "Q & POTUS Timestamps," Google Docs, accessed March 5, 2021, https://docs.google.com/spreadsheets/d/1OqTR0hPipmL9NE4u_JAzBiWXov3YYOIZIw6nPe3t4wo/edit#gid=1919753853.

20 Philip Bump, "How Much of Trump's Presidency Has He Spent Tweeting?," *The Washington Post*, May 12, 2020, https://www.washingtonpost.com/politics/2020/05/12/how-much-trumps-presidency-has-he-spent-tweeting/.

21 André van Delft, "Sorry Q, This Graph Is Wrong," Medium, December 26, 2019, https://medium.com/@AndreVanDelft/sorry-q-this-graph-is-wrong-cea30166b7ca.

22 David Emery, "Is a Hillary Clinton 'Snuff Film' Circulating on the Dark Web?," Snopes, April 16, 2018, https://www.snopes.com/fact-check/hillary-clinton-snuff-film/.

23 Mike Rothschild, "Inside the 25,000 Sealed Indictments Fueling the QAnon Conspiracy," *Daily Dot*, January 27, 2021, https://www.daily-dot.com/debug/sealed-indictments-qanon-conspiracy/.

24 Adrienne LaFrance, "The Prophecies of Q," *The Atlantic*, May 14, 2020, https://www.theatlantic.com/magazine/archive/2020/06/qanon-nothing-can-stop-what-is-coming/610567/.

25 Dennis Villeneuve, *Blade Runner 2049* (Burbank, CA: Warner Bros. Pictures, 2017).

26 "Day of the Rope," ADL, accessed March 5, 2021, https://www.adl.org/ education/references/hate-symbols/day-of-the-rope.

27 "SA: Nazi organization," *Britannica*, accessed March 5, 2021, https:// www.britannica.com/topic/SA-Nazi-organization.

CHAPTER 13 Where We Go One:
How to Help People Who Want to Get Out of Q

1 Jesselyn Cook, "'I Miss My Mom': Children of QAnon Believers Are Desperately Trying to Deradicalize Their Own Parents," *HuffPost*, February 11, 2021, https://www.huffpost.com/entry/children-of-qanon-believers_n_601078e9c5b6c5586aa49077.

2 Steve Walsh, "Following Capitol Siege, Veterans Hope for More Deradicalization Programs," January 20, 2021, *Morning Edition*, podcast, NPR, https://www.npr.org/2021/01/20/958689584/following-capitol-siege-veterans-hope-for-more-deradicalization-programs.

3 Bob Garfield and Brad Galloway, "An Ex-Neo-Nazi on De-radicalization," February 19, 2021, *On the Media*, podcast, WNYC Studios, https:// www.wnycstudios.org/podcasts/otm/segments/ex-neo-nazi-de-radicalization-on-the-media.

4 Sara Li, "How to Help a Friend Who Believes in QAnon Conspiracy Theories," *Cosmopolitan*, October 28, 2020, https://www.cosmopolitan .com/politics/a34416177/how-to-help-friend-qanon-conspiracy-theories/.

5 Rebecca Moore, "The Brainwashing Myth," *The Conversation*, July 18, 2018, https://theconversation.com/the-brainwashing-myth-99272.

6 James T. Richardson, "A Social Psychological Critique About 'Brainwashing' Claims About Recruitment to New Religions," in J. Hadden and D. Bromley, eds., *The Handbook of Cults and Sects in America* (Greenwich, CT: JAI Press, Inc., 1993), 75–97; available at CESNUR, last modified December 10, 1999, https://www.cesnur.org/testi/Socpsy. htm.

7 Rafi Schwartz, "Ex-QAnon Believer Pleads for People Not to Make Fun of QAnon Believers," *Mic*, February 8, 2021, https://www.mic.com/p/ ex-qanon-believer-pleads-for-people-not-to-make-fun-of-qanon-believers-61193386.

8 Travis M. Andrews, "He's a Former QAnon Believer. He Doesn't Want to Tell His Story, but Thinks It Might Help," *The Washington Post*, October 24, 2020, https://www.washingtonpost.com/technology/2020/10/ 24/qanon-believer-conspiracy-theory/.

EPILOGUE Friends and Happy Memories

1 Anna Merlan, "Major Q Figure Urges Followers to Go Back to Their Real Lives," *Vice*, January 20, 2021, https://www.vice.com/en/article/akdy7e/major-q-figure-urges-followers-to-go-back-to-their-real-lives.

2 Nicholas Reimann, "QAnon Pushed March 4 as Trump's 'True Inauguration Day'—but Officials Don't Expect Violence," *Forbes*, March 2, 2021, https://www.forbes.com/sites/nicholasreimann/2021/03/02/qanon-pushed-march-4-as-trumps-true-inauguration-day-but-officials-dont-expect-violence/.

3 Jennifer Valentino-DeVries et al., "Arrested in Capitol Riot: Organized Militants and a Horde of Radicals," *The New York Times*, February 4, 2021, https://www.nytimes.com/interactive/2021/02/04/us/capitol-arrests.html.

4 Lorraine Boissoneault, "How the 19th-Century Know-Nothing Party Reshaped American Politics," *Smithsonian Magazine*, January 26, 2017, https://www.smithsonianmag.com/history/immigrants-conspiracies-and-secret-society-launched-american-nativism-180961915/.

5 Reid J. Epstein, "New Democratic Ad Campaign Ties G.O.P. to QAnon," *The New York Times*, February 2, 2021, https://www.nytimes.com/2021/02/02/us/politics/democrats-republicans-greene-qanon.html.

6 Samantha Putterman, "Q Into the Storm," PolitiFact, April 9, 2021, https://www.politifact.com/article/2021/apr/09/what-hbo-qanon-documentary-series-revealed-about-i/

7 Drew Harwell and Craig Timburg, "Q's Identity Was Right There All Along," *Washington Post*, April 5, 2021, https://www.washingtonpost.com/technology/2021/04/05/ron-watkins-qanon-hbo/

Index

ABOUT THE AUTHOR

Mike Rothschild is a journalist who explores the intersections between Internet culture and politics through the lens of conspiracy theories and the author of the book *The World's Worst Conspiracies*, along with hundreds of articles in different outlets. As a subject matter expert in the field of fringe beliefs, he has been interviewed by *The New York Times*, *The Washington Post*, CNN, the BBC, NPR, Yahoo!, *Daily Beast*, CBS, *San Francisco Chronicle*, *Rolling Stone*, Snopes, NBC News, *Vice*, *Slate*, and *Politico*, among many others. Mike has also made frequent TV, radio, and podcast appearances in the United States and internationally, including CNN, *The Mehdi Hasan Show* on Peacock, the *Reply All* podcast, and many others.